THE GREATEST
SEARCH AND RESCUE STORIES
EVER TOLD

EDITED BY TOM MCCARTHY

LYONS
PRESS

Guilford, Connecticut

An imprint of The Rowman & Littlefield Publishing Group, Inc.
4501 Forbes Blvd., Ste. 200
Lanham, MD 20706
www.rowman.com

Distributed by NATIONAL BOOK NETWORK

British Library Cataloguing in Publication Information available

Library of Congress Cataloging-in-Publication Data available

ISBN 978-1-4930-3965-4 (paperback)
ISBN 978-1-4930-3966-1 (e-book)

♾™ The paper used in this publication meets the minimum requirements of American National Standard for Information Sciences—Permanence of Paper for Printed Library Materials, ANSI/NISO Z39.48-1992.

CONTENTS

Introduction

No one sets out to become lost.

For the incautious, ill prepared, overconfident, or unlucky, being lost is a hell unto itself. It's frightening; peace—physical, mental, spiritual—is elusive if not impossible. Fear rules everything, which of course makes the situation worse. Supreme among the invading fears is that one might not make it back to safety—that just around the corner is a chance to meet one's Maker.

Getting lost is rarely painless either. There is hunger and discomfort to go with the overpowering anxiety. Throw in a twisted ankle or a broken leg and the whole trip begins to head south quickly.

The survivors of the Donner Party waiting on the very edge of starvation for a rescue could do nothing more than hope. The remnants of what had months before been a hopeful group heading for the promise of California could only pray that William Lewis Manly would find a way out of Death Valley and return. For a man trapped under a Maine waterfall watching the water around him rise, there was nothing to do but contemplate his imminent demise. Climbers and hikers and part-time adventurers are not immune to the vicissitudes of fate—of being lost and powerless—perhaps hanging from a precipice in Yosemite, or hiking a canyon in Zion, or living near Mount St. Helens, knowing an entire mountain was about to erupt.

Being lost is terrible, of course, and this collection is ripe with people who faced the loneliness and terror with grace and grit and stunning strength—though we will not know how some of the unfortunates recounted here faced their final hours, because they did not survive. That is the ultimate and unfortunate final act in the narrative that began as a day hike or a simple climb or a mild adventure.

On the other side of the coin, there are plenty of heroes here. This collection is a joyous and reaffirming tribute to the rescuers—the men and women who at great sacrifice put themselves on the knife edge between life and death to bring people back to safety. The stories here are a tribute to these unselfish people—the brave and skilled rescuers who take care of the unlucky souls who are lost—for whatever reason.

The stories you are about to dig into, more than anything else, will entertain you, pulling you so completely into the action and the people and the excitement you will forget where you are and what you had planned to do. And the beauty of it is that you can read it in your favorite chair, in your living room, knowing exactly where you are.

The entire point of reading is to get so caught up in something that an afternoon flashes by, or an entire evening you had thought would be painfully boring before you picked up the book. The most interesting thing about survival stories is that a good one will make you wonder if you could do the same thing. Would you have the smarts and the strength and the coolness to get out of a tough situation?

Here you will find the aforementioned William Lewis Manly, who found his way out of Death Valley, collected food and water and hope for the dying members of his party, then returned. At one point he saw a single blade of green grass near a rock and ate it "to obtain the little moisture it contained."

The rescuers of the Donner Party put themselves at death's door to bring to safety the unfortunate survivors. Their rescue expedition was bleak and trying, but they went ahead. One observer said of them: "Words cannot picture, nor mind conceive, more torturing hardships and privations than were endured by that little band."

You will learn here about Lieutenant William Diebold, a World War II jungle rescue expert whose job was to bail out over the impenetrable and rugged Burmese jungle to aid a downed and injured airman, plucking off leeches, ignoring inhuman temperatures and an almost overpowering jungle with a devil-may-care insouciance thousands of miles from home.

This calls to mind two truisms that the stories here evoke. There is never a good time to have an emergency. And, as you will read about, "There are old climbers and there are bold climbers, but there are no old bold climbers." You'll read about Mount Rainier rescue teams taking great risks, despite knowing even as they set out in frightening conditions that they are likely to be bringing back a body.

That same bravery and coolness runs through each story here, whether it is in Yosemite or Zion or on Maine's Mount Katahdin. Rescuers do what they have always done; they save people—never judging or questioning. Then they go home and wait for the next call.

Read and enjoy. That's the point of reading. Anything you might learn along the way is just the gravy.

One

Bringing Out the Donner Party

Eliza P. Donner Houghton

ALTHOUGH WE WERE SO MEAGRELY INFORMED, IT IS WELL THAT MY readers should, at this point, become familiar with the experiences of the expedition known as the Forlorn Hope, and also the various measures taken for our relief when our precarious condition was made known to the good people of California. It will be remembered that the Forlorn Hope was the party of fifteen which, as John Baptiste reported to us, made the last unaided attempt to cross the mountains.

Words cannot picture, nor mind conceive, more torturing hardships and privations than were endured by that little band on its way to the settlement. It left the camp on the sixteenth of December, with scant rations for six days, hoping in that time to force its way to Bear Valley and there find game. But the storms which had been so pitiless at the mountain camps followed the unprotected refugees with seemingly fiendish fury. After the first day from camp, its members could no longer keep together on their marches. The stronger broke the trail, and the rest followed to night-camp as best they could.

On the third day, Stanton's sight failed, and he begged piteously to be led; but, soon realizing the heart-rending plight of his companions, he uncomplainingly submitted to his fate. Three successive nights, he staggered into camp long after the others had finished their stinted meal. Always he was shivering from cold, sometimes wet with sleet and rain.

It is recorded that at no time had the party allowed more than an ounce of food per meal to the individual, yet the rations gave out on the night of the twenty-second, while they were still in a wilderness of snow-peaks. Mr. Eddy only was better provided. In looking over his pack that morning for the purpose of throwing away any useless article, he unexpectedly found a small bag containing about a half-pound of dried bear-meat. Fastened to the meat was a pencilled note from his wife, begging him to save the hidden treasure until his hour of direst need, since it might then be the means of saving his life. The note was signed, "Your own dear Elinor." With tenderest emotion, he slipped the food back, resolving to do the dear one's bidding, trusting that she and their children might live until he should return for them.

The following morning, while the others were preparing to leave camp, Stanton sat beside the smouldering fire smoking his pipe. When ready to go forth, they asked him if he was coming, and he replied, "Yes, I am coming soon." Those were his parting words to his friends, and his greeting to the Angel of Death. He never left that fireside, and his companions were too feeble to return for him when they found he did not come into camp.

Twenty-four hours later, the members of that hapless little band threw themselves upon the desolate waste of snow to ponder the problems of life and death; to search each the other's face for answer to the question their lips durst not frame. Fathers who had left their families, and mothers who had left their babes, wanted to go back and die with them, if die they must; but Mr. Eddy and the Indians—those who had crossed the range with Stanton—declared that they would push on to the settlement. Then Mary Graves, in whose young heart were still whisperings of hope, courageously said:

"I, too, will go on, for to go back and hear the cries of hunger from my little brothers and sisters is more than I can stand. I shall go as far as I can, let the consequences be what they may."

W. F. Graves, her father, would not let his daughter proceed alone, and finally all decided to make a final, supreme effort. Yet—think of it— they were without one morsel of food! Even the wind seemed to hold its breath as the suggestion was made that, "were one to die, the rest might live." Then the suggestion was made that lots be cast, and whoever drew the longest slip should be the sacrifice. Mr. Eddy endorsed the plan.

Despite opposition from Mr. Foster and others, the slips of paper were prepared, and great-hearted Patrick Dolan drew the fatal slip. Patrick Dolan, who had come away from camp that his famishing friends might prolong their lives by means of the small stock of food which he had to leave! Harm a hair of that good man's head? Not a soul of that starving band would do it.

Mr. Eddy then proposed that they resume their journey as best they could until death should claim a victim. All acquiesced. Slowly rising to their feet, they managed to stagger and to crawl forward about three miles to a tree which furnished fuel for their Christmas fire. It was kindled with great difficulty, for in cutting the boughs, the hatchet blade flew off the handle and for a time was lost in deep snow.

Meanwhile, every puff of wind was laden with killing frost, and in sight of that glowing fire, Antonio froze to death. Mr. Graves, who was also breathing heavily, when told by Mr. Eddy that he was dying, replied that he did not care. He, however, called his daughters, Mrs. Fosdick and Mary Graves, to him, and by his parting injunctions, showed that he was still able to realize keenly the dangers that beset them. Remembering how their faces had paled at the suggestion of using human flesh for food, he admonished them to put aside the natural repugnance which stood between them and the possibility of life. He commanded them to banish sentiment and instinctive loathing, and think only of their starving mother, brothers, and sisters whom they had left in camp, and avail themselves of every means in their power to rescue them. He begged that his body be used to sustain the famishing, and bidding each farewell, his spirit left its bruised and worn tenement before half the troubles of the night were passed.

About ten o'clock, pelting hail, followed by snow on the wings of a tornado, swept every spark of fire from those shivering mortals, whose voices now mingled with the shrieking wind, calling to heaven for relief. Mr. Eddy, knowing that all would freeze to death in the darkness if allowed to remain exposed, succeeded after many efforts in getting them close together between their blankets where the snow covered them.

With the early morning, Patrick Dolan became delirious and left camp. He was brought back with difficulty and forcibly kept under cover until late in the day, when he sank into a stupor, whence he passed quietly into that sleep which knows no waking.

The crucial hour had come. Food lay before the starving, yet every eye turned from it and every hand dropped irresolute.

Another night of agony passed, during which Lemuel Murphy became delirious and called long and loud for food; but the cold was so intense that it kept all under their blankets until four o'clock in the afternoon, when Mr. Eddy succeeded in getting a fire in the trunk of a large pine tree. Whereupon, his companions, instead of seeking food, crept forth and broke off low branches, put them down before the fire and laid their attenuated forms upon them. The flames leaped up the trunk, and burned off dead boughs so that they dropped on the snow about them, but the unfortunates were too weak and too indifferent to fear the burning brands.

Mr. Eddy now fed his waning strength on shreds of his concealed bear meat, hoping that he might survive to save the giver. The rest in camp could scarcely walk, by the twenty-eighth, and their sensations of hunger were deminishing. This condition forebode delirium and death, unless stayed by the only means at hand. It was in very truth a pitiful alternative offered to the sufferers.

With sickening anguish the first morsels were prepared and given to Lemuel Murphy, but for him they were too late. Not one touched flesh of kindred body. Nor was there need of restraining hand, or warning voice to gauge the small quantity which safety prescribed to break the fast of the starving. Death would have been preferable to that awful meal, had relentless fate not said: "Take, eat that ye may live. Eat, lest ye go mad and leave your work undone!"

All but the Indians obeyed the mandate, and were strengthened and reconciled to prepare the remaining flesh to sustain them a few days longer on their journey.

Hitherto, the wanderers had been guided partly by the fitful sun, partly by Lewis and Salvador, the Indians who had come with Stanton from Sutter's Fort. In the morning, however, when they were ready to leave that spot, which was thereafter known as the "Camp of Death," Salvador, who could speak a little English, insisted that he and Lewis were lost, and, therefore, unable to guide them farther.

Nevertheless, the party at once set out and travelled instinctively until evening. The following morning they wrapped pieces of blanket around their cracked and swollen feet and again struggled onward until late in the afternoon, when they encamped upon a high ridge. There they saw beyond, in the distance, a wide plain which they believed to be the Sacramento Valley.

This imaginary glimpse of distant lowland gave them a peaceful sleep. The entire day of December 31 was spent in crossing a cañon, and every footstep left its trace of blood in the snow.

When they next encamped, Mr. Eddy saw that poor Jay Fosdick was failing, and he begged him to summon up all his courage and energy in order to reach the promised land, now so near. They were again without food; and William Foster, whose mind had become unbalanced by the long fast, was ready to kill Mrs. McCutchen or Miss Graves. Mr. Eddy confronted and intimidated the crazed sufferer, who next threatened the Indian guides, and would have carried out his threat then, had Mr. Eddy not secretly warned them against danger and urged them to flee. But nothing could save the Indians from Foster's insane passion later, when he found them on the trail in an unconscious and dying condition.

January 1, 1847, was, to the little band of eight, a day of less distressing trials; its members resumed travel early, braced by unswerving will-power. They stopped at midday and revived strength by eating the toasted strings of their snowshoes. Mr. Eddy also ate his worn out moccasins, and all felt a renewal of hope upon seeing before them an easier grade which led to night-camp where the snow was only six feet in depth. Soothed by a milder temperature, they resumed their march earlier next morning and descended to where the snow was but three feet deep. There they built their camp-fire and slightly crisped the leather of a pair of old boots and a pair of shoes which constituted their evening meal, and was the last of their effects available as food.

An extraordinary effort on the third day of the new year brought them to bare ground between patches of snow. They were still astray among the western foothills of the Sierras, and sat by a fire under an oak tree all night, enduring hunger that was almost maddening.

Jay Fosdick was sinking rapidly, and Mr. Eddy resolved to take the gun and steal away from camp at dawn. But his conscience smote him, and he finally gave the others a hint of his intention of going in search of game, and of not returning unless successful. Not a moving creature nor a creeping thing had crossed the trail on their journey thither; but the open country before them, and minor marks well known to hunters, had caught Mr. Eddy's eye and strengthened his determination. Mrs. Pike, in dread and fear of the result, threw her arms about Mr. Eddy's neck and implored him not to leave them, and the others mingled their entreaties and protestations with hers. In silence he took his gun to go alone. Then Mary Graves declared that she would keep up with him, and without heeding further opposition the two set out. A short distance from camp they stopped at a place where a deer had recently lain.

With a thrill of emotion too intense for words, with a prayer in his heart too fervent for utterance, Mr. Eddy turned his tearful eyes toward Mary and saw her weeping like a child. A moment later, that man and that woman who had once said that they knew not how to pray, were kneeling beside that newly found track pleading in broken accents to the Giver of all life, for a manifestation of His power to save their starving band. Long restrained tears were still streaming down the cheeks of both, and soothing their anxious hearts as they arose to go in pursuit of the deer. J.Q. Thornton says:

> They had not proceeded far before they saw a large buck about eighty yards distant. Mr. Eddy raised his rifle and for some time tried to bring it to bear upon the deer, but such was his extreme weakness that he could not. He breathed a little, changed his manner of holding the gun, and made another effort. Again his weakness prevented him from being able to hold upon it. He heard a low, suppressed sobbing behind him, and, turning around, saw Mary Graves weeping and in great agitation, her head bowed, and her hands upon her face. Alarmed lest she should cause the deer to run, Mr. Eddy begged her to be quiet, which she was, after exclaiming, "Oh, I am afraid you will not kill it."
>
> He brought the gun to his face the third time, and elevated the muzzle above the deer, let it descend until he saw the animal through the sight, when the rifle cracked. Mary immediately wept aloud,

exclaiming, "Oh, merciful God, you have missed it!" Mr. Eddy assured her that he had not; that the rifle was upon it the moment of firing; and that, in addition to this, the animal had dropped its tail between its legs, which this animal always does when wounded.

His belief was speedily confirmed. The deer ran a short distance, then fell, and the two eager watchers hastened to it as fast as their weakened condition would allow. Mr. Eddy cut the throat of the expiring beast with his pocket-knife, and he and his companion knelt down and drank the warm blood that flowed from the wound.

The excitement of getting that blessed food, and the strength it imparted, produced a helpful reaction, and enabled them to sit down in peace to rest a while, before attempting to roll their treasure to the tree near-by, where they built a fire and prepared the entrails.

Mr. Eddy fired several shots after dark, so that the others might know that he had not abandoned them. Meanwhile, Mr. and Mrs. Foster, Mrs. McCutchen, and Mrs. Pike had moved forward and made their camp half-way between Mr. Eddy's new one and that of the previous night. Mr. Fosdick, however, being too weak to rise, remained at the first camp. His devoted wife pillowed his head upon her lap, and prayed that death would call them away together.

Mr. Thornton continues:

The sufferer had heard the crack of Mr. Eddy's rifle at the time he killed the deer, and said, feebly, "There! Eddy has killed a deer! Now, if I can only get to him I shall live!"

But in the stillness of that cold, dark night, Jay Fosdick's spirit fled alone. His wife wrapped their only blanket about his body, and lay down on the ground beside him, hoping to freeze to death. The morning dawned bright, the sun came out, and the lone widow rose, kissed the face of her dead, and, with a small bundle in her hand, started to join Mr. Eddy. She passed a hunger-crazed man on the way from the middle camp, going to hers, and her heart grew sick, for she knew that her loved one's body would not be spared for burial rites.

She found Mr. Eddy drying his deer meat before the fire, and later saw him divide it so that each of his companions in the camps should have an equal share.

The seven survivors, each with his portion of venison, resumed travel on the sixth and continued in the foothills a number of days, crawling up the ascents, sliding down the steeps; often harassed by fears of becoming lost near the goal, yet unaware that they were astray.

The venison had been consumed. Hope had almost died in the heart of the bravest, when at the close of day on the tenth of January, twenty-five days from the date of leaving Donner Lake, they saw an Indian village at the edge of a thicket they were approaching. As the sufferers staggered forward, the Indians were overwhelmed at sight of their misery. The warriors gazed in stolid silence. The squaws wrung their hands and wept aloud. The larger children hid themselves, and the little ones clung to their mothers in fear. The first sense of horror having passed, those mothers fed the unfortunates. Some brought them unground acorns to eat, while others mixed the meal into cakes and offered them as fast as they could cook them on the heated stones. All except Mr. Eddy were strengthened by the food. It sickened him, and he resorted to green grass boiled in water.

The following morning the chief sent his runners to other *rancherias, en route* to the settlement, telling his people of the distress of the pale-faces who were coming toward them, and who would need food. When the Forlorn Hope was ready to move on, the chief led the way, and an Indian walked on either side of each sufferer supporting and helping the unsteady feet. At each *rancheria* the party was put in charge of a new leader and fresh supporters.

On the seventeenth, the chief with much difficulty procured, for Mr. Eddy, a gill of pine nuts which the latter found so nutritious that the following morning, on resuming travel, he was able to walk without support. They had proceeded less than a mile when his companions sank to the ground completely unnerved. They had suddenly given up and were willing to die. The Indians appeared greatly perplexed, and Mr. Eddy shook with sickening fear. Was his great effort to come to naught? Should his wife and babes die while he stood guard over those who would no longer help themselves? No, he would push ahead and see what he yet could do!

The old chief sent an Indian with him as a guide and support. Relieved of the sight and personal responsibility of his enfeebled companions, Mr. Eddy felt a renewal of strength and determination. He pressed onward, scarcely heeding his dusky guide. At the end of five miles they met another Indian, and Mr. Eddy, now conscious that his feet were giving out, promised the stranger tobacco, if he would go with them and help to lead him to the "white man's house."

And so that long, desperate struggle for life, and for the sake of loved ones, ended an hour before sunset, when Mr. Eddy, leaning heavily upon the Indians, halted before the door of Colonel M.D. Richey's home, thirty-five miles from Sutter's Fort.

The first to meet him was the daughter of the house, whom he asked for bread. Thornton says:

She looked at him, burst out crying, and took hold of him to assist him into the room. He was immediately placed in bed, in which he lay unable to turn his body during four days. In a very short time he had food brought to him by Mrs. Richey, who sobbed as she fed the miserable and frightful being before her. Shortly, Harriet, the daughter, had carried the news from house to house in the neighborhood, and horses were running at full speed from place to place until all preparations were made for taking relief to those whom Mr. Eddy had left in the morning.

William Johnson, John Howell, John Rhodes, Mr. Keiser, Mr. Sagur, Racine Tucker, and Joseph Varro assembled at Mr. Richey's immediately. The females collected the bread they had, with tea, sugar, and coffee, amounting to as much as four men could carry. Howell, Rhodes, Sagur, and Tucker started at once, on foot, with the Indians as guides, and arrived at camp, between fifteen and eighteen miles distant, at midnight.

Mr. Eddy had warned the outgoing party against giving the sufferers as much food as they might want, but, on seeing them, the tender-hearted men could not deny their tearful begging for "more." One of the relief was kept busy until dawn preparing food which the rest gave to the enfeebled emigrants. This overdose of kindness made its victims temporarily very ill, but caused no lasting harm.

Early on the morning of January 18, Messrs. Richey, Johnson, Varro, and Keiser, equipped with horses and other necessaries, hurried away to bring in the refugees, together with their comrades who had gone on before. By ten o'clock that night the whole of the Forlorn Hope were safe in the homes of their benefactors. Mr. Richey declared that he and his party had retraced Mr. Eddy's track six miles, by the blood from his feet; and that they could not have believed that he had travelled that eighteen miles, if they themselves had not passed over the ground in going to his discouraged companions.

The kindness and sympathy shown Mr. Eddy by the good people in the neighborhood of the Richey and Johnson ranches encouraged his efforts in behalf of his fellow-sufferers in the mountains. While the early sunlight of January 19 was flooding his room with cheer and warmth, he dictated a letter to Mr. John Sinclair, Alcalde of the Upper District of California, living near Sutter's Fort, in which he stated as briefly as possible the conditions and perils surrounding the snow-bound travellers, and begged him to use every means in his power toward their immediate rescue.

Bear River was running high, and the plain between it and Sutter's Fort seemed a vast quagmire, but John Rhodes volunteered to deliver the letter. He was ferried over the river on a raft formed of two logs lashed together with strips of rawhide. Then he rolled his trousers above the knee and with his shoes in his hand, started on his mission. He saw no white faces until he reached Sinclair's, where the letter created a painful interest and won ready promises of help.

It was dark when he reached Sutter's Fort, nevertheless from house to house he spread the startling report: "Men, women, and little children are snow-bound in the Sierras, and starving to death!"

Captain Kerns in charge at the Fort, pledged his aid, and influence to the cause of relief. Captain Sutter, who had already twice sent supplies, first by Stanton and again by McCutchen and Reed, in their unsuccessful attempt to cross the mountains, at once agreed to coöperate with Alcalde Sinclair.

While Captain Kerns at Sutter's Fort was sending messengers to different points, and Mrs. Sinclair was collecting clothing to replace the tattered garments of the members of the Forlorn Hope, her husband despatched an open letter to the people of San Francisco, describing the arrival of the survivors of the Forlorn Hope, and the heart-rending condition of those remaining in the mountains. He urged immediate action, and offered his services for individual work, or to coöperate with Government relief, or any parties that might be preparing to go out with Messrs. Reed and McCutchen, who were known to be endeavoring to raise a second expedition.

The letter was taken to the City Hotel in San Francisco, and read aloud in the dining-room. Its contents aroused all the tender emotions known to human nature. Some of the listeners had parted from members of the Donner Party at the Little Sandy, when its prospects appeared so bright, and the misfortunes which had since befallen the party seemed incredible. Women left the room sobbing, and men called those passing, in from the street, to join the knots of earnest talkers. All were ready and willing to do; but, alas, the obstacles which had prevented Mr. Reed getting men for the mountain work still remained to be overcome.

Existing war between Mexico and the United States was keeping California in a disturbed condition. Most of the able-bodied male emigrants had enlisted under Captain Frémont as soon as they reached the country, and were still on duty in the southern part of the province; and the non-enlisted were deemed necessary for the protection of the colonies of American women and children encamped on the soil of the enemy. Moreover, all felt that each man who should attempt to cross the snow belt would do so at the peril of his life.

Mr. Reed, who in the late Autumn had sent petitions to the Military Governor and to Lieutenant Washington A. Bartlett of the United States Navy, Alcalde of the town and district of San Francisco, but as yet had obtained nothing, now appeared before each in person, and was promised assistance. Captain Mervine of the United States Navy, and Mr.

Richardson, United States Collector, each subscribed fifty dollars to the cause on his own account.

As a result of these appeals, Alcalde Bartlett called a public meeting; and so intense was the feeling that Mr. Dunleary, "the first speaker, had scarcely taken his seat on the platform when the people rushed to the chairman's table from all parts of the house with their hands full of silver dollars," and could hardly be induced to stay their generosity until the meeting was organized.

A treasurer and two committees were appointed; the one to solicit subscriptions, and the other to purchase supplies. The Alcalde was requested to act with both committees. Seven hundred dollars was subscribed before the meeting adjourned. Seven hundred dollars, in an isolated Spanish province, among newly arrived immigrants, was a princely sum to gather.

Messrs. Ward and Smith, in addition to a generous subscription, offered their launch *Dice mi Nana*, to transport the expedition to Feather River, and Mr. John Fuller volunteered to pilot the launch.

It was decided to fit out an expedition, under charge of Past Midshipman Woodworth, who had tendered his services for the purpose, he to act under instructions of the Military Governor and coöperate with the committee aiding Reed.

Soon thereafter "Old Trapper Greenwood" appeared in San Francisco, asking for assistance in fitting out a following to go to the mountains with himself and McCutchen, Mr. George Yount and others in and around Sonoma and Napa having recommended him as leader. Donations of horses, mules, beef, and flour had already been sent to his camp in Napa Valley. Furthermore, Lt. William Maury, U.S.N., Commander at the port; Don Mariano G. Vallejo, Ex-Commandante-General of California; Mr. George Yount, and others subscribed the sum of five hundred dollars in specie toward outfitting Greenwood and the men he should select to cross the mountains.

Greenwood urged that he should have ten or twelve men on whom he could rely after reaching deep snow. These, he said, he could secure if he had the ready money to make advances and to procure the necessary warm clothing and blankets. He had crossed the Sierras before, when the snow lay deep on the summit, and now proposed to drive over horses and kill them at the camps as provisions for the sufferers. If this scheme should fail, he and his sons with others would get food to the camp on snowshoes. Thornton says:

> *The Governor-General of California, after due form, and trusting to the generosity and humanity of the Government which he represented, appropriated four hundred dollars on Government account toward outfitting this relief party. Furthermore, in compliance with an application from Alcade Bartlee (for the committee), Captain Mervine, of the U.S. frigate* Savannah, *furnished from the ship's stores ten days' full rations for ten men. The crews of the* Savannah *and the sloop* Warren, *and the marines in garrison at San Francisco, increased the relief fund to thirteen hundred dollars. Messrs. Mellus and Howard tendered their launch to carry the party up the bay to Sonoma, and Captain Sutter proffered his launch* Sacramento *for river use.*
>
> *It was now settled that the "Reed-Greenwood party" should go to Johnson's ranch by way of Sonoma and Napa, and Woodworth with his men and supplies, including clothing for the destitute, should go by boat to Sutter's Landing; there procure pack animals, buy beef cattle, and hurry on to the snow-belt; establish a relay camp, slaughter the cattle, and render all possible aid toward the immediate rescue of the snow-bound.*

Meanwhile, before Alcalde Sinclair's letter had time to reach San Francisco, he and Captain Sutter began outfitting the men destined to become the "First Relief." Agilla Glover and R. S. Moutrey volunteered their services, declaring their willingness to undertake the hazardous journey for the sake of the lives they might save.

To hasten recruits for service, Captain Sutter and Alcalde Sinclair promised that in case the Government should fail to grant the sum, they themselves would become responsible for the payment of three dollars per day to each man who would get food through to the snow-bound camps. Accordingly, Aguilla Glover and R. S. Moutrey, driving pack animals well laden with warm clothing, blankets, and food supplies, left the Fort at sunrise on the morning of February the first, and on the third reached Johnson's ranch, where they joined Messrs. Tucker, Johnson, Richey and others, who, being anxious to assist in the good work, had killed, and were fire-drying, beef to take up the mountains. Here two days were spent making pack-saddles, driving in horses, and getting supplies in shape. Indians were kept at the handmill grinding wheat. Part of the flour was sacked, and part converted into bread by the women in the vicinity.

On the morning of the fifth of February, Alcalde Sinclair rode to Johnson's ranch, and all things being ready, he appointed Racine Tucker Captain of the company, and in touching words commended the heroic work of its members, and bade them godspeed on their errand of mercy. When ready to mount, he shook hands with each man, and recorded the names in a note-book as follows:

Racine Tucker, Aguilla Glover, R. S. Moutrey, John Rhodes, Daniel Rhodes, Edward Coffemeir, D. Richey, James Curtis, William Eddy, William Coon, George Tucker, Adolph Brenheim, and John Foster.

This party is generally known as the "First Relief." Their route to the snow-belt lay through sections of country which had become so soft and oozy that the horses often sank in mire, flank deep; and the streams were so swollen that progress was alarmingly slow. On the second day they were driven into camp early by heavy rains which drenched clothing, blankets, and even the provisions carefully stored under the saddles and leather saddle-covers. This caused a delay of thirty-six hours, for everything had to be sun or fire dried before the party could resume travel.

Upon reaching Mule Springs, the party found the snow from three to four feet deep, and, contrary to expectations, saw that it would be impossible to proceed farther with the horses. Mr. Eddy was now ill of fever, and unfit to continue the climb; whereupon his companions promised to bring out his loved ones if he would return with Joe Varro, whom Mr. Johnson had sent along to bring the pack animals home after they should cease to be of use.

At Mule Springs, the party built a brush store-house for the extra supplies and appointed George Tucker and William Coon camp-keepers.

Then they prepared packs containing jerked beef, flour, and bread, each weighing between forty and seventy-five pounds, according to the temperament and strength of the respective carriers. The following morning ten men started on their toilsome march to Bear Valley, where they arrived on the thirteenth, and at once began searching for the abandoned wagon and provisions which Reed and McCutchen had cached the previous Autumn, after their fruitless attempt to scale the mountains. The wagon was found under snow ten feet in depth; but its supplies had been destroyed by wild beasts. Warned by this catastrophe, the First Relief decided to preserve its supplies for the return trip by hanging them in parcels from ropes tied to the boughs of trees.

The ten kept together courageously until the fifteenth; then Mr. M. D. Richey, James Curtis, and Adolph Brenheim gave up and turned back. Mr. Tucker, fearing that others might become disheartened and do likewise, guaranteed each man who would persevere to the end, five dollars per diem, dating from the time the party entered the snow. The remaining seven pushed ahead, and on the eighteenth, encamped on the summit overlooking the lake, where the snow was said to be forty feet in depth.

The following morning Aguilla Glover and Daniel Rhodes were so oppressed by the altitude that their companions had to relieve them of their packs and help them on to the cabins, which, as chronicled in a previous chapter, the party reached on the nineteenth of February, 1847.

After the departure of the First Relief we who were left in the mountains began to watch and pray for the coming of the Second Relief, as we had before watched and prayed for the coming of the First.

Sixteen-year-old John Baptiste was disappointed and in ill humor when Messrs. Tucker and Rhodes insisted that he, being the only able-bodied man in the Donner camp, should stay and cut wood for the enfeebled, until the arrival of other rescuers. The little half-breed was a sturdy fellow, but he was starving too, and thought that he should be allowed to save himself.

After he had had a talk with father, however, and the first company of refugees had gone, he became reconciled to his lot, and served us faithfully. He would take us little ones up to exercise upon the snow, saying that we should learn to keep our feet on the slick, frozen surface, as well as to wade through slush and loose drifts.

Frequently, when at work and lonesome, he would call Georgia and me up to keep him company, and when the weather was frosty, he would bring "Old Navajo," his long Indian blanket, and roll her in it from one end, and me from the other, until we would come together in the middle, like the folds of a paper of pins, with a face peeping above each fold. Then he would set us upon the stump of the pine tree while he chopped the trunk and boughs for fuel. He told us that he had promised father to stay until we children should be taken from camp, also that his home was to be with our family forever. One of his amusements was to rake the coals together nights, then cover them with ashes, and put the large camp kettle over the pile for a drum, so that we could spread our hands around it, "to get just a little warm before going to bed."

For the time, he lived at Aunt Betsy's tent, because Solomon Hook was snow-blind and demented, and at times restless and difficult to control. The poor boy, some weeks earlier, had set out alone to reach the settlement, and after an absence of forty-eight hours was found close to camp, blind, and with his mind unbalanced. He, like other wanderers on that desolate waste, had become bewildered, and, unconsciously, circled back near to the starting-point.

Aunt Betsy came often to our tent, and mother frequently went to hers, and they knelt together and asked for strength to bear their burdens. Once, when mother came back, she reported to father that she had discovered bear tracks quite close to camp, and was solicitous that the beast be secured, as its flesh might sustain us until rescued.

As father grew weaker, we children spent more time upon the snow above camp. Often, after his wound was dressed and he fell into a quiet slumber, our ever-busy, thoughtful mother would come to us and sit on the tree trunk. Sometimes she brought paper and wrote; sometimes she sketched the mountains and the tall tree-tops, which now looked like small trees growing up through the snow. And often, while knitting or sewing, she held us spell-bound with wondrous tales of "Joseph in Egypt," of "Daniel in the den of lions," of "Elijah healing the widow's son," of dear little Samuel, who said, "Speak Lord, for Thy servant heareth," and of the tender, loving Master, who took young children in his arms and blessed them.

With me sitting on her lap, and Frances and Georgia at either side, she referred to father's illness and lonely condition, and said that when the next "Relief" came, we little ones might be taken to the settlement, without either parent, but, God willing, both would follow later. Who could be braver or tenderer than she, as she prepared us to go forth with strangers and live without her? While she, without medicine, without lights, would remain and care for our suffering father, in hunger and in cold, and without her little girls to kiss good-morning and good-night. She taught us how to gain friends among those whom we should meet, and what to answer when asked whose children we were.

Often her eyes gazed wistfully to westward, where sky and mountains seemed to meet, and she told us that beyond those snowy peaks lay California, our land of food and safety, our promised land of happiness, where God would care for us. Oh, it was painfully quiet some days in those great mountains, and lonesome upon the snow. The pines had a whispering homesick murmur, and we children had lost all inclination to play.

The last food which I remember seeing in our camp before the arrival of the Second Relief was a thin mould of tallow, which mother had tried out of the trimmings of the jerked beef brought us by the First Relief. She had let it harden in a pan, and after all other rations had given out, she cut daily from it three small white squares for each of us, and we nibbled off the four corners very slowly, and then around and around the edges of the precious pieces until they became too small for us to hold between our fingers.

It was the first of March, about ten days after the arrival of the First Relief, before James Reed and William McCutchen succeeded in reaching the party they had left long months before. They, together with Brit Greenwood, Hiram Miller, Joseph Jondro, Charles Stone, John Turner, Matthew Dofar, Charles Cady, and Nicholas Clark constituted the Second Relief.

They reported having met the First Relief with eighteen refugees at the head of Bear Valley, three having died *en route* from the cabins.

Among the survivors Mr. Reed found his wife, his daughter Virginia, and his son James F. Reed, Jr. He learned there from his anxious wife that their two younger children, Martha J. and Thomas K. Reed, had also left the cabin with her, but had soon given out and been carried back and left at the mountain camp by Messrs. Glover and Moutrey, who then retraced their steps and rejoined the party.

Consequently this Reed-Greenwood party, realizing that this was no time for tarrying, had hurried on to the lake cabins, where Mr. Reed had the happiness of finding his children still alive. There he and five companions encamped upon the snow and fed and soothed the unfortunates. Two members continued on to Aunt Betsy's abode, and Messrs. Cady and Clark came to ours.

This Relief had followed the example of its predecessor in leaving supplies at marked caches along the trail for the return trip. Therefore, it reached camp with a frugal amount for distribution. The first rations were doled out with careful hand, lest harm should come to the famishing through overeating, still, the rescuers administered sufficient to satisfy the fiercest cravings and to give strength for the prospective journey.

While crossing Alder Creek Valley to our tent that first afternoon, Messrs. Cady and Clark had seen fresh tracks of a bear and cubs, and in the evening the latter took one of our guns and went in pursuit of the game which would have been a godsend to us. It was dark when he returned and told my mother that he had wounded the old bear near the camp, but that she had escaped with her young through the pines into a clump of tamarack, and that he would be able to follow her in the morning by the blood-stains on the snow.

Meanwhile, the two men who had come to Aunt Betsy's with food thought it best not to tell her that her son William had died *en route* to the settlement with the First Relief. They selected from among her children in camp, Solomon, Mary, and Isaac, as able to follow a leader to the lake cabins, and thence to go with the outgoing Second Relief, across the mountains. Hopefully, that mother kissed her three children good-bye, and then wistfully watched them depart with their rescuers on snowshoes. She herself was strong enough to make the journey, but remained because there was no one to help to carry out her two youngest children.

Thirty-one of the company were still in the camps when this party arrived, nearly all of them children, unable to travel without assistance, and the adults were too feeble to give much aid to the little ones upon the snow. Consequently, when my father learned that the Second Relief comprised only ten men, he felt that he himself would never reach the settlement. He was willing to be left alone, and entreated mother to leave him and try to save herself and us children. He reminded her that his life was almost spent, that she could do little for him were she to remain, and that in caring for us children she would be carrying on his work.

She who had to choose between the sacred duties of wife and mother, thought not of self. She looked first at her helpless little children, then into the face of her suffering and helpless husband, and tenderly, unhesitatingly, announced her determination to remain and care for him until both should be rescued, or death should part them.

Perplexities and heartaches multiplied with the morning hours of the following day. Mr. Clark, being anxious to provide more food, started early to hunt the wounded bear. He had not been gone long, when Mr. Stone arrived from the lake cabins and told Mr. Cady that the other members of the Relief had become alarmed at gathering storm clouds, and had resolved to select at once the ablest among the emigrants and hasten with them across the summit, and to leave Clark, Cady, and himself to cut the necessary fuel for the camps, and otherwise assist the sufferers until the Third Relief should reach them.

Cady and Stone, without waiting to inform Clark, promptly decided upon their course of action. They knew the scarcity of provisions in camp, the condition of the trail over the mountains, the probability of long, fierce March storms, and other obstacles which might delay future promised relief, and, terror-stricken, determined to rejoin their party, regardless of opposition, and return to the settlement.

Mother, fearing that we children might not survive another storm in camp, begged Messrs. Cady and Stone to take us with them, offering them five hundred dollars in coin, to deliver us to Elitha and Leanna at Sutter's Fort. The agreement was made, and she collected a few keepsakes and other light articles, which she wished us to have, and which the men seemed more than willing to carry out of the mountains. Then, lovingly, she combed our hair and helped us to dress quickly for the journey. When we were ready, except cloak and hood, she led us to the bedside, and we took leave of father. The men helped us up the steps and stood us up on the snow. She came, put on our cloaks and hoods, saying, as if talking to herself, "I may never see you again, but God will take care of you."

Frances was six years and eight months old and could trudge along quite bravely, but Georgia, who was little more than five, and I, lacking a week of four years, could not do well on the heavy trail, and we were soon taken up and carried. After travelling some distance, the men left us sitting on a blanket upon the snow, and went ahead a short distance where they stopped and talked earnestly with many gesticulations. We watched them, trembling lest they leave us there to freeze. Then Frances said,

"Don't feel afraid. If they go off and leave us, I can lead you back to mother by our foot tracks on the snow."

After a seemingly long time, they returned, picked us up and took us on to one of the lake cabins, where without a parting word, they left us.

The Second Relief Party, of which these men were members, left camp on the third of March. They took with them seventeen refugees—the Breen and Graves families, Solomon Hook, Isaac and Mary Donner, and Martha and Thomas, Mr. Reed's two youngest children.

How can I describe that fateful cabin, which was dark as night to us who had come in from the glare of day? We heard no word of greeting and met no sign of welcome, but were given a dreary resting-place near the foot of the steps, just inside the open doorway, with a bed of branches to lie upon, and a blanket to cover us. After we had been there a short time, we could distinguish persons on other beds of branches, and a man with bushy hair reclining beside a smouldering fire.

Soon a child began to cry, "Give me some bread. Oh, give me some meat!"

Then another took up the same pitiful wail. It continued so long that I wept in sympathy, and fastened my arms tightly around my sister Frances' neck and hid my eyes against her shoulder. Still I heard that hungry cry, until a husky voice shouted,

"Be quiet, you crying children, or I'll shoot you."

But the silence was again and again broken by that heart-rending plea, and again and again were the voices hushed by the same terrifying threat. And we three, fresh from our loving mother's embrace, believed the awful menace no vain threat.

We were cold, and too frightened to feel hungry, nor were we offered food that night, but next morning Mr. Reed's little daughter Mattie appeared carrying in her apron a number of newly baked biscuits which her father had just taken from the hot ashes of his camp fire. Joyfully she handed one to each inmate of the cabin, then departed to join those ready to set forth on the journey to the settlement. Few can know how delicious those biscuits tasted, and how carefully we caught each dropping crumb. The place seemed drearier after their giver left us, yet we were glad that her father was taking her to her mother in California.

Soon the great storm which had been lowering broke upon us. We were not exposed to its fury as were those who had just gone from us, but we knew when it came, for snow drifted down upon our bed and had to be scraped off before we could rise. We were not allowed near the fire and spent most of our time on our bed of branches.

Dear, kind Mrs. Murphy, who for months had taken care of her own son Simon, and her grandson George Foster, and little James Eddy, gave us a share of her motherly attention, and tried to feed and comfort us. Affliction and famine, however, had well nigh sapped her strength and by the time those plaintive voices ceased to cry for bread and meat, her willing hands were too weakened to do much for us.

I remember being awakened while there by two little arms clasped suddenly and tightly about me, and I heard Frances say,

"No, she shall not go with you. You want to kill her!"

Near us stood Keseberg, the man with the bushy hair. In limping past our sleeping place, he had stopped and said something about taking me away with him, which so frightened my sisters that they believed my life in danger, and would not let me move beyond their reach while we remained in that dungeon. We spoke in whispers, suffered as much as the starving children in Joseph's time, and were more afraid than Daniel in the den of lions.

How long the storm had lasted, we did not know, nor how many days we had been there. We were forlorn as children can possibly be, when Simon Murphy, who was older than Frances, climbed to his usual "look out" on the snow above the cabin to see if any help were coming. He returned to us, stammering in his eagerness:

"I seen—a woman—on snow shoes—coming from the other camp! She's a little woman—like Mrs. Donner. She is not looking this way—and may pass!"

Hardly had he spoken her name, before we had gathered around him and were imploring him to hurry back and call our mother. We were too excited to follow him up the steps.

She came to us quickly, with all the tenderness and courage needed to lessen our troubles and soften our fears. Oh, how glad we were to see her, and how thankful she appeared to be with us once more! We heard it in her voice and saw it in her face; and when we begged her not to leave us, she could not answer, but clasped us closer to her bosom, kissed us anew for father's sake, then told how the storm had distressed them. Often had they hoped that we had reached the cabins too late to join the Relief—then in grieving anguish felt that we had, and might not live to cross the summit.

She had watched the fall of snow, and measured its depth; had seen it drift between the two camps making the way so treacherous that no one had dared to cross it until the day before her own coming; then she induced Mr. Clark to try to ascertain if Messrs. Cady and Stone had really got us to the cabins in time to go with the Second Relief.

We did not see Mr. Clark, but he had peered in, taken observations, and returned by nightfall and described to her our condition.

John Baptiste had promised to care for father in her absence. She left our tent in the morning as early as she could see the way. She must have stayed with us over night, for I went to sleep in her arms, and they were still around me when I awoke; and it seemed like a new day, for we had time for many cherished talks. She veiled from us the ghastliness of death, telling us Aunt Betsy and both our little cousins had gone to heaven. She said Lewis had been first to go, and his mother had soon followed; that she herself had carried little Sammie from his sick mother's tent to ours the very day we three were taken away; and in order to keep him warm while the storm raged, she had laid him close to father's side, and that he had stayed with them until "day before yesterday."

I asked her if Sammie had cried for bread. She replied, "No, he was not hungry, for your mother saved two of those little biscuits which the relief party brought, and every day she soaked a tiny piece in water and fed him all he would eat, and there is still half a biscuit left."

How big that half-biscuit seemed to me! I wondered why she had not brought at least a part of it to us. While she was talking with Mrs. Murphy, I could not get it out of my mind. I could see that broken half-biscuit, with its ragged edges, and knew that if I had a piece, I would nibble off the rough points first. The longer I waited, the more I wanted it. Finally, I slipped my arm around mother's neck, drew her face close to mine and whispered,

"What are you going to do with the half-biscuit you saved?"

"I am keeping it for your sick father," she answered, drawing me closer to her side, laying her comforting cheek against mine, letting my arm keep its place, and my fingers stroke her hair.

The two women were still talking in subdued tones, pouring the oil of sympathy into each others' gaping wounds. Neither heard the sound of feet on the snow above; neither knew that the Third Relief Party was at hand, until Mr. Eddy and Mr. Foster came down the steps, and each asked anxiously of Mrs. Murphy, "Where is my boy?"

Each received the same sorrowful answer—"Dead."

It will be remembered that Mr. Eddy, being ill, was dropped out of the First Relief at Mule Springs in February, and sent back to Johnson's Ranch to await the return of this party, which had promised to bring out his family. Who can realize his distress when it returned with eighteen refugees, and informed him that his wife and little Maggie had perished before it reached the camps, and that it had been obliged to leave his baby there in care of Mrs. Murphy?

Disappointed and aggrieved, the afflicted father immediately set out on horseback, hoping that he would meet his child on the trail in charge of the Second Relief, which it seemed reasonable to expect would follow closely in the footsteps of the first. He was accompanied by Mr. Foster, of the Forlorn Hope, who had been forced to leave his own little son at the camp in charge of Mrs. Murphy, its grandmother.

On the evening of the second day, the two reached Woodworth's camp, established as a relay station pursuant to the general plan of rescue originally adopted. They found the midshipman in snug quarters with several men to do his bidding. He explained that the lack of competent guides had prevented his venturing among the snow peaks. Whereupon, Mr. Eddy earnestly assured him that the trail of those who had already gone up outlined the way.

After much deliberation, Woodworth and his men agreed to start out next morning for the mountain camps, but tried to dissuade Mr. Eddy from accompanying them on account of his apparent depleted condition. Nevertheless both he and Mr. Foster remained firm, and with the party, left the relay camp, crossed the low foothills and encamped for the night on the Yuba River.

At dusk, Woodworth was surprised by the arrival of two forlorn-looking individuals, whom he recognized as members of the Reed-Greenwood Relief, which had gone up the mountain late in February and was overdue. The two implored food for themselves, also for their seven companions and three refugees, a mile back on the trail, unable to come farther.

When somewhat refreshed, they were able to go more into detail, and the following explanation of their plight was elicited:

"One of our men, Clark, is at Donner's Camp, and the other nine of us left the cabins near the lake on the third of March, with seventeen of the starving emigrants. The storm caught us as we crossed the summit, and ten miles below, drove us into camp. It got so bad and lasted so long that our provisions gave out, and we almost froze to death cutting wood. We all worked at keeping the fires until we were completely exhausted, then seeing no prospects of help coming to us, we left, and made our way down here, bringing Reed's two children and Solomon Hook, who said he could and would walk. The other fourteen that we brought over the summit are up there at what we call Starved Camp. Some are dead, the rest without food."

Woodworth and two followers went at once with provisions to the near-by sufferers, and later brought them down to camp.

Messrs. Reed and Greenwood stated that every available means had been tried by them to get the seventeen unfortunates well over the summit before the great storm reached its height. They said the physical condition of the refugees was such, from the very start, that no persuasion, nor warnings, nor threats could quicken their feeble steps. All but three of the number were children, with their hands and feet more or less frozen. Worse still, the caches on which the party had relied for sustenance had been robbed by wild animals, and the severity of the storm had forced all into camp, with nothing more than a breastwork of brush to shelter them. Mrs. Elisabeth Graves died the first night, leaving to the party the hopeless task of caring for her emaciated babe in arms, and her three other children between the ages of nine and five years. Soon, however, the five-year-old followed his mother, and the number of starving was again lessened on the third night when Isaac Donner went to sleep beside his sister and did not waken. The storm had continued so furiously that it was impossible to bury the dead. Days and nights were spent in steadfast struggling against the threatening inevitable, before the party gave up; and Greenwood and Reed, taking the two Reed children and also Solomon Hook, who walked, started down the mountain, hoping to save their own lives and perhaps get fresh men to complete the pitiful work which they had been forced to abandon.

When Messrs. Reed and Greenwood closed their account of the terrible physical and mental strain their party had undergone, "Mr. Woodworth asked his own men of the relay camp, if they would go with him to rescue those unfortunates at 'Starved Camp,' and received an answer in the negative."

The following morning there was an earnest consultation, and so hazardous seemed the trail and the work to be done that for a time all except Eddy and Foster refused to go farther. Finally, John Stark stepped forward, saying,

"Gentlemen, I am ready to go and do what I can for those sufferers, without promise of pay."

By guaranteeing three dollars per day to any man who would get supplies to the mountain camps, and fifty dollars in addition to each man who should carry a helpless child, not his own, back to the settlement, Mr.

Eddy secured the services of Hiram Miller, who had just come down with the Second Relief; and Mr. Foster hired, on the same terms, Mr. Thompson from the relay camp. Mr. Woodworth offered like inducements, on Government account, to the rest of his men, and before the morning was far advanced, with William H. Eddy acting as leader, William Foster, Hiram Miller, Mr. Thompson, John Stark, Howard Oakley, and Charles Stone (who had left us little ones at the lake camp) shouldered their packs and began the ascent.

Meanwhile how fared it at Starved Camp? Mr. and Mrs. Breen being left there with their own five suffering children and the four other poor, moaning little waifs, were tortured by situations too heart-rending for description, too pitiful to seem true. Suffice it to relate that Mrs. Breen shared with baby Graves the last lump of loaf sugar and the last drops of tea, of that which she had denied herself and had hoarded for her own babe. When this was gone, with quivering lips she and her husband repeated the litany and prayed for strength to meet the ordeal,—then, turning to the unburied dead, they resorted to the only means left to save the nine helpless little ones.

When Mr. Eddy and party reached them, they found much suffering from cold and crying for "something to eat," but not the wail which precedes delirium and death.

This Third Relief settled for the night upon the snow near these refugees, who had twice been in the shadow of doom; and after giving them food and fire, Mr. Eddy divided his force into two sections. Messrs. Stark, Oakley, and Stone were to remain there and nurture the refugees a few hours longer, then carry the small children, and conduct those able to walk to Mule Springs, while Eddy and three companions should hasten on to the cabins across the summit.

Section Two, spurred on by paternal solicitude, resumed travel at four o'clock the following morning, and crossed the summit soon after sunrise. The nearer they approached camp, the more anxious Messrs. Eddy and Foster became to reach the children they hoped to find alive. Finally, they rushed ahead, as we have seen, to the Murphy cabin. Alas! only disappointment met them there.

Even after Mrs. Murphy had repeated her pitiful answer, "Dead," the afflicted fathers stood dazed and silent, as if waiting for the loved ones to return.

Mr. Eddy was the first to recover sufficiently for action. Presently Simon Murphy and we three little girls were standing on the snow under a clear blue sky, and saw Hiram Miller and Mr. Thompson coming toward camp.

The change was so sudden it was difficult to understand what had happened. How could we realize that we had passed out of that loathsome cabin, never to return; or that Mrs. Murphy, too ill to leave her bed, and Keseberg, too lame to walk, by reason of a deep cleft in his heel, made by an axe, would have to stay alone in that abode of wretchedness?

Nor could we know our mother's anguish, as she stepped aside to arrange with Mr. Eddy for our departure. She had told us at our own camp why she would remain. She had parted from us there and put us in charge of men who had risked much and come far to do a heroic deed. Later she had found us, abandoned by them, in time of direst need, and in danger of an awful death, and had warmed and cheered us back to hope and confidence. Now, she was about to confide us to the care of a party whose leader swore either to save us or die with us on the trail. We listened to the sound of her voice, felt her good-bye kisses, and watched her hasten away to father, over the snow, through the pines, and out of sight, and knew that we must not follow. But the influence of her last caress, last yearning look of love and abiding faith will go with us through life.

The ordeal through which she passed is thus told by Colonel Thornton, after a personal interview with Mr. Eddy:

Mrs. George Donner was able to travel. But her husband was in a helpless condition, and she would not consent to leave him while he survived. She expressed her solemn and unalterable purpose, which no danger or peril could change, to remain and perform for him the last sad office of duty and affection. She manifested, however, the greatest solicitude for her children, and informed Mr. Eddy that she had fifteen hundred dollars in silver, all of which she would give him, if he would save the lives of the children.

He informed her that he would not carry out one hundred dollars of all she had, but that he would save her children or die in the effort. The party had no provisions to leave for the sustenance of these unhappy, unfortunate beings.

After remaining about two hours, Mr. Eddy informed Mrs. Donner that he was constrained by force of circumstances to depart. It was certain that George Donner would never rise from the miserable bed upon which he had lain down, worn by toil and wasted by famine.

A woman was probably never before placed in circumstances of greater or more peculiar trial; but her duty and affection as a wife triumphed over all her instincts of reason.

The parting scene between parent and children is represented as being one that will never be forgotten, so long as life remains or memory performs its functions.

My own emotions will not permit me to attempt a description which language, indeed, has not power to delineate. It is sufficient to say that it was affecting beyond measure; and that the last words uttered by Mrs. Donner in tears and sobs to Mr. Eddy were, "Oh, save, save my children!"

When we left the lake cabin, we still wore the clothing we had on when we came from our tent with Messrs. Cady and Stone. Georgia and I were clad in quilted petticoats, linsey dresses, woollen stockings, and well-worn shoes. Our cloaks were of a twilled material, garnet, with a white thread interwoven, and we had knitted hoods to match. Frances' clothing was as warm; instead of cloak, however, she wore a shawl, and her hood was blue. Her shoes had been eaten by our starving dog before he disappeared, and as all others were buried out of reach, mother had substituted a pair of her own in their stead.

Mr. Foster took charge of Simon Murphy, his wife's brother, and Messrs. Eddy and Miller carried Georgia and me. Mr. Eddy always called Georgia "my girl," and she found great favor in his eyes, because in size and looks she reminded him of his little daughter who had perished in that storm-bound camp.

Our first stop was on the mountain-side overlooking the lake, where we were given a light meal of bread and meat and a drink of water. When we reached the head of the lake, we overtook Nicholas Clark and John Baptiste who had deserted father in his tent and were hurrying toward the settlement. Our coming was a surprise to them, yet they were glad to join our party.

After our evening allowance of food we were stowed snugly between blankets in a snow trench near the summit of the Sierras, but were so hungry that we could hardly get to sleep, even after being told that more food would do us harm.

Early next morning we were again on the trail. I could not walk at all, and Georgia only a short distance at a time. So treacherous was the way that our rescuers often stumbled into unseen pits, struggled among snow drifts, and climbed icy ridges where to slip or fall might mean death in the yawning depth below.

Near the close of this most trying day, Hiram M. Miller put me down, saying wearily, "I am tired of carrying you. If you will walk to that dark thing on the mountain-side ahead of us, you shall have a nice lump of loaf sugar with your supper."

My position in the blanket had been so cramped that my limbs were stiff and the jostling of the march had made my body ache. I looked toward the object to which he pointed. It seemed a long way off; yet I wanted the sugar so much that I agreed to walk. The wind was sharp. I shivered, and at times could hardly lift my feet; often I stumbled and would have fallen had he not held my hand tightly, as he half led, half drew me onward. I did my part, however, in glad expectation of the promised bit of sweetness. The sun had set before we reached our landmark, which was a felled and blackened tree, selected to furnish fuel for our night fire. When we children were given our evening allowance of food, I asked for my lump of sugar, and cried bitterly on being harshly told there was none for me. Too disappointed and fretted to care for anything else, I sobbed myself to sleep.

Nor did I waken happy next morning. I had not forgotten the broken promise, and was lonesome for mother. When Mr. Miller told me that I should walk that day as far as Frances and Georgia did, I refused to go forward, and cried to go back. The result was that he used rough means before I promised to be good and do as he commanded. His act made my sister Frances rush to my defence, and also, touched a chord in the fatherly natures of the other two men, who summarily brought about a more comfortable state of affairs.

When we proceeded on our journey, I was again carried by Mr. Miller in a blanket on his back as young children are carried by Indians on long journeys. My head above the blanket folds bobbed uncomfortably at every lurch. The trail led up and down and around snow peaks, and under overhanging banks that seemed ready to give way and crush us.

At one turn our rescuers stopped, picked up a bundle, and carefully noted the fresh human foot prints in the snow which indicated that a number of persons were moving in advance. By our fire that night, Mr. Eddy opened the bundle that we had found upon the snow, and to the surprise of all, Frances at once recognized in it the three silk dresses, silver spoons, small keepsakes, and articles of children's clothing which mother had intrusted to the care of Messrs. Cady and Stone.

The spoons and smaller articles were now stowed away in the pockets of our rescuers for safekeeping on the journey; and while we little girls dressed ourselves in the fresh underwear, and watched our discarded garments disappear in the fire, the dresses, which mother had planned should come to us later in life, were remodelled for immediate use.

Mr. Thompson pulled out the same sharp pocket-knife, coarse black thread, and big-eyed needle, which he had used the previous evening, while making Frances a pair of moccasins out of his own gauntlet gloves. With the help of Mr. Eddy, he then ripped out the sleeves, cut off the waists about an inch above the skirt gathers, cut slits in the skirts for armholes, and tacked in the sleeves. Then, with mother's wish in mind, they put the dove-colored silk on Frances, the light brown on Georgia, and the dark coffee-brown on me. Pleats and laps in the skirt bands were necessary to fit them to our necks. Strings were tied around our waists, and the skirts tacked up until they were of walking length. These ample robes served for cloaks as well as dresses for we could easily draw our hands back through the sleeves and keep our arms warm beneath the folds. Thus comfortably clad, we began another day's journey.

Before noon we overtook and passed Messrs. Oakley, Stone, and Stark, having in charge the following refugees from Starved Camp: Mr. and Mrs. Patrick Breen and their five children; Mary Donner, Jonathan Graves, Nancy Graves, and baby Graves. Messrs. Oakley and Stone were in advance, the former carrying Mary Donner over his shoulder; and the latter baby Graves in his arms. Great-hearted John Stark had the care of all the rest. He was broad-shouldered and powerful, and would stride ahead with two weaklings at a time, deposit them on the trail and go back for others who could not keep up. These were the remnant of the hopeful seventeen who had started out on the third of March with the Second Relief, and with whom mother had hoped we children would cross the mountains.

It was after dark when our own little party encamped at the crossing of the Yuba River. The following morning Lieutenant Woodworth and attendants were found near-by. He commended the work done by the Third Relief; yet, to Mr. Eddy's dismay, he declared that he would not go to the rescue of those who were still in the mountains, because the warmer weather was melting the snow so rapidly that the lives of his men would be endangered should he attempt to lead them up the trail which we had just followed down. He gave our party rations, and said that he would at once proceed to Johnson's Ranch and from there send to Mule Springs the requisite number of horses to carry to the settlement the persons now on the trail.

Our party did not resume travel until ten o'clock that morning; nevertheless, we crossed the snow line and made our next camp at Mule Springs. There we caught the first breath of spring-tide, touched the warm, dry earth, and saw green fields far beyond the foot of that cold, cruel mountain range. Our rescuers exclaimed joyfully, "Thank God, we are at last out of the snow, and you shall soon see Elitha and Leanna, and have all you want to eat."

Our allowance of food had been gradually increased and our improved condition bore evidence of the good care and kind treatment we had received. We remained several days at Mule Springs, and were comparatively happy until the arrival of the unfortunates from Starved Camp, who stretched forth their gaunt hands and piteously begged for food which would have caused death had it been given to them in sufficient quantities to satisfy their cravings.

When I went among them I found my little cousin Mary sitting on a blanket near Mr. Oakley, who had carried her thither, and who was gently trying to engage her thoughts. Her wan face was wet with tears, and her hands were clasped around her knee as she rocked from side to side in great pain. A large woollen stocking covered her swollen leg and frozen foot which had become numb and fallen into the fire one night at Starved Camp and been badly maimed before she awakened to feel the pain. I wanted to speak to her, but when I saw how lonesome and ill she looked, something like pain choked off my words.

Her brother Isaac had died at that awful camp and she herself would not have lived had Mr. Oakley not been so good to her. He was now comforting her with the assurance that he would have the foot cared for by a doctor as soon as they should reach the settlement; and she, believing him, was trying to be brave and patient.

We all resumed travel on horseback and reached Johnson's Ranch about the same hour in the day. As we approached, the little colony of emigrants which had settled in the neighborhood the previous Autumn crowded in and about the two-roomed adobe house which Mr. Johnson had kindly set apart as a stopping place for the several relief parties on their way to and from the mountains. All were anxious to see the sufferers for whose rescue they had helped to provide.

Survivors of the Forlorn Hope and of the First Relief were also there awaiting the arrival of expected loved ones. There Simon Murphy, who came with us, met his sisters and brother; Mary Graves took from the arms of Charles Stone, her slowly dying baby sister; she received from the hands of John Stark her brother Jonathan and her sister Nancy, and heard of the death of her mother and of her brother Franklin at Starved Camp. That house of welcome became a house of mourning when Messrs. Eddy and Foster repeated the names of those who had perished in the snows. The scenes were so heart-rending that I slipped out of doors and sat in the sunshine waiting for Frances and Georgia, and thinking of her who had intrusted us to the care of God.

Before our short stay at the Johnson Ranch ended, we little girls had a peculiar experience. While standing in a doorway, the door closed with a bang upon two of my fingers. My piercing cry brought several persons to the spot, and one among them sat down and soothed me in a motherly way. After I was myself again, she examined the dress into which Messrs. Thompson and Eddy had stitched so much good-will, and she said:

"Let me take off this clumsy thing, and give you a little blue dress with white flowers on it." She made the change, and after she had fastened it in the back she got a needle and white thread and bade me stand closer to her so that she might sew up the tear which exposed my knees. She asked why I looked so hard at her sewing, and I replied,

"My mother always makes little stitches when she sews my dresses."

No amount of pulling down of the sleeves or straightening out of the skirt could conceal the fact that I was too large for the garment. As I was leaving her, I heard her say to a companion, "That is just as good for her, and this will make two for my little girl." Later in the day Frances and Georgia parted with their silks and looked as forlorn as I in calico substitutes.

Oh, the balm and beauty of that early morning when Messrs. Eddy, Thompson, and Miller took us on horseback down the Sacramento Valley. Under the leafy trees and over the budding blossoms we rode. Not rapidly, but steadily, we neared our journey's end. Toward night, when the birds had stopped their singing and were hiding themselves among bush and bough, we reached the home of Mr. and Mrs. John Sinclair on the American River, thirty-five miles from Johnson's Ranch and only two and a half from Sutter's Fort.

That hospitable house was over-crowded with earlier arrivals, but as it was too late for us to cross the river, sympathetic Mrs. Sinclair said that she would find a place for us. Having no bed to offer, she loosened the rag-carpet from one corner of the room, had fresh straw put on the floor, and after supper, tucked us away on it, drawing the carpet over us in place of quilts.

We had bread and milk for supper that night, and the same good food next day. In the afternoon we were taken across the river in an Indian canoe. Then we followed the winding path through the tules to Sutter's Fort, where we were given over to our half-sisters by those heroic men who had kept their pledge to our mother and saved our lives.

Two

Zero Dark Storm

Christopher Van Tilburg, MD

ON A BITTER COLD, MIDDLE-OF-WINTER, MIDDLE-OF-THE-NIGHT, MID-dle-of-the-storm Sunday, no one hears the call for help.

While a beefy, dark storm pulverizes Mount Hood, a mountain res-cue page zings to four dozen cell phones in the Hood River Valley, a quaint, picturesque fruit-growing and outdoor recreation community in north central Oregon.

But no one hears the page. No one responds to the call for help. It is deathly quiet.

The 911 call comes sometime after midnight. A backcountry skier is in distress at the Tilly Jane Guard Station, a rustic shelter tucked in a thick forest on the remote north flank of Mount Hood.

Mount Hood, I'll remind readers, is a gargantuan, ice-clad, rocky, snow-covered volcano that sticks up in the middle of the vast Mount Hood National Forest, which has miles and miles and acres and acres of evergreen conifers: the stands are mainly Douglas fir, but are spiced with western hemlock, western red cedar, larch, and lodgepole and ponderosa pine. The thick understory is hearty crop of every imaginable shade of greenery—vine maple, big leaf maple, Oregon grape, white oak, broad-leaf ferns, Old Man's Beard lichen—and rocks—basalt and andesite boulders, crags, cliffs, and promontories deposited by volcanic eruptions eons ago.

And Mount Hood is a big mountain towering over the land. The peak has several purported heights. In 1867 Lt. Col. Robert Williamson calculated the elevation at 11,225 feet. In 1980, the US Geodetic Survey measured 11,239 feet using the National Geodetic Vertical Datum of 1929. A 1986 US National Geodetic Survey measurement was adjusted in 1991 to 11,249 feet using the North American Vertical Datum of 1988. A group of surveyors unofficially measured 11,240 feet in 1993 using Global Positioning System from the summit. But mountaineers and cartographers and geologists are funny, in the way they need to know the exact height. When you climb to the summit, soak in the panoramic view, and ski down on creamy smooth snow, in my opinion, the actual height really doesn't matter. It's just one gigantic, ominous mountain.

Mount Hood—named after British Admiral Lord Samuel Hood by Lt. William Broughton when he spied it from the Columbia River in 1792, but originally called Wy'East by the indigenous people—has four general regions. The south has Timberline Lodge and Summit ski areas and the bustling year-round ski and snowboard community of Government Camp. The east has Mount Hood Meadows Mountain Resort, one of the busiest ski and snowboard areas in the western United States. The west is much less visited, accessible by only one potholed road. The north has the one-chairlift Cooper Spur Mountain Resort and the Cloud Cap–Tilly Jane Historic District.

It is here, in the Cloud Cap–Tilly Jane Historic District, where a collection of antique buildings are clustered at 6,000 feet. The US Forest Service Tilly Jane Guard Station was built in 1934 by the Civilian Conservation Corps as a backcountry cabin for snow surveys and fire protection. Long since defunct for government operations, it's a popular hut for backcountry skiers to rent in the winter. This area is accessible in the winter by skis or snowshoes via the 2-mile Tilly Jane Trail, which was hewn from the forest during 1938–39 by Hood River mountaineers Percy Bucklin, Bill Cochran, Harold Wells, and Walter Applegren.

Other antique buildings of the same era still remain in the heavily wooded Tilly Jane area. The relatively dilapidated, but still functional, A-frame is another winter backcountry ski hut available for rent. The American Legion Cookhouse, currently with a collapsing roof, was also built around the same time; it was used by Legionnaires who held annual cookouts and summit climbs from 1927 to 1948.

A mile through the woods from these three Tilly Jane cabins are two other buildings at Cloud Cap Saddle, a prominent outcropping of basalt and andesite. To the south, this saddle overlooks the Hood River Valley and, on a clear day, Mount St. Helens, Mount Adams, and Mount Rainier. To the north stands the giant north face of Mount Hood. The Cloud Cap Saddle buildings predate the Tilly Jane structures by a good four decades. The Snowshoe Club Hut is a century-old private hut perched in a clearing on the saddle. And in a sparse collection of lodgepole pines sits our historic mountain rescue cabin, 130-year-old Cloud Cap Inn, where currently two dozen members of our ninety-year-old volunteer mountain rescue team, the Crag Rats, are sleeping after a day of powder skiing and avalanche-rescue training.

Earlier that day, the victim, her husband, and another couple had rented the Tilly Jane Guard Station for a weekend outing of backcountry skiing. The skiing that day had been excellent: light, dry, deep powder snow. The weather was blustery: windy, spatters of snow, and intermittent clouds, which moved eerily and rapidly across Ghost Ridge so that occasional sunbreaks lit up the forest in sparkly sunlight. After skiing all day, the woman jolted awake after midnight with excruciating back pain, so debilitating that she was only able to alleviate the pain by resting on her side, curled up in a ball, on the floor of the Guard Station.

Fortunately, the husband found cell reception—despite the thick trees, thick storm clouds, and being many miles distant from a cell tower—and called 911. The Hood River County dispatcher, after checking with the sheriff's deputy on duty, dispatched the Crag Rats by using our cell phone text messaging system.

But none of us hears the callout text.

Our mountain rescue group is in deep.

We Crag Rats are deeply sleeping in the middle of a deep, dark storm after skiing deep powder all day. We are exhausted and hunkered in our sleeping bags in the bunks of our cabin, Cloud Cap Inn, or for us, *the cabin*. This old structure was constructed in 1889, a mile from the Tilly Jane buildings, on this outcropping of rock at 6,000 feet with a spectacular in-your-face view of Mount Hood's north side. The sight of Mount Hood's north face includes Cooper Spur ridge on the left horizon, the giant serac- and crevasse-filled Eliot Glacier and steep, sheer Eliot Glacier Headwall (a 2,500-foot nearly sheer cliff) in the center, and Cathedral Ridge on the right skyline. The cabin was originally built as a private bed-and-breakfast in 1889, well before the Civilian Conservation Corps erected the other buildings in the historic district. Several owners ran the inn intermittently and with limited success, considering guests came from Hood River 35 miles away, via horse and buggy. Often they came up the Columbia River via ferry from The Dalles, 20 miles to the east, or from Portland, 60 miles to the west. After a short trial and failure as a B&B, the cabin was sold to the Forest Service in 1942 for a few thousand dollars. After the Forest Service took it over, the lodge eventually succumbed to weather and vandalism. It fell into a state of disrepair. It was in danger of being razed by 1954: the Forest Service was set to burn it. When the Crag Rats heard about the plan to destroy Cloud Cap Inn, our group, with support from Hood River County Historical Society, struck a deal with the Forest Service. The Crag Rats would repair and maintain the building in exchange for using it as a base for snow surveys and mountain rescue. That was six decades ago. Although we call it *our* cabin, it is owned by the Forest Service and we lease it under a special-use permit. We've maintained the cabin ever since—putting thousands and thousands of hours and dollars into maintenance and repair—as our mountain rescue base for missions and training on the north side of Mount Hood. Originally, the cabin was also used as a base for snow surveys, in which Crag Rats would take manual measurements of the depth of the snowpack to gauge the summer water supply. Those surveys have long been discontinued with the advent of modern electronic devices.

We ski this mountain year-round, all seasons, every month, due to the permanent glaciers and snowfields. Every winter we take a long weekend to train, ski, and foster general camaraderie. We affectionately still call this weekend *The Winter Outing*. The Winter Outing begins on a Wednesday in the third week of February with a group of self-described old-timers who open up the cabin, fire up the woodstoves, tell stories, and pack in food via snowcat. The outing ramps up on Friday and Saturday when other members ski up the mountain, after being released from household, work, and family duties. If the snow is excellent, we mostly ski, and do a bit of training such as avalanche-rescue simulation, snow cave building, crevasse rescue training, or *cabineering*, hanging out in the cabin. The Winter Outing culminates with a big dinner on Saturday night.

This particular year, the snow quality is superb. We ski deep powder all day on Friday and Saturday: the wind and intermittent spats of snow showers keep filling in our track so nearly every run we have fresh, untracked snow. Because the storm brings wind and poor visibility above timberline, which is for the most part at 6,000 feet on Mount Hood, we choose to ski the thick trees below the cabin, Ghost Ridge, which is a slope often too low in elevation to maintain good snow. Bernie Wells, long-term member and probably the Crag Rat who knows the most about the cabin, drives our snowcat up and down Ghost Ridge, shuttling skiers back uphill.

That afternoon, since later in the year we have a mountain rescue recertification coming up, we run avalanche-rescue simulations. Our parent organization is the national Mountain Rescue Association. We belong to a subsection, Oregon Mountain Rescue Council, which includes all five mountain rescue teams in our state: Corvallis Mountain Rescue, Eugene Mountain Rescue, Portland Mountain Rescue, Deschutes County Sheriff's Office Search and Rescue Team, and us. As a council, we are responsible for certifying each other in high angle (cliffs), avalanche, crevasse, and ground search-and-rescue techniques. This year, we're up for avalanche-rescue recertification, so we take the time to drill on a rescue scenario on the Back Lawn, a wide, smooth, low-angle snow-covered slope just below the cabin.

After the rescue simulation Bernie and his son Todd set up the rope tow. A generator attached to a pulley is set up at the back door of the cabin. A 1,000-foot rope tied in a loop is stretched out down the back lawn and threaded into a pulley attached to a 15-foot-high steel water survey tower. We fire up the generator, which pulls the loop rope, and we have a backwoods rope tow.

About the time we all hunker down in the cabin for dinner, the sky darkens and the storm thickens. We share a giant vat of chili that Joe McCulloch brewed up. By bedtime, we are all exhausted. The sky is a full-on storm: the windows of the old cabin rattle and the rafters creak as wind finds every nook to pierce the century-old log walls. The tempera-ture drops. Sometime after 10:00 p.m., we crawl deep into our sleeping bags. I find space in a back room in the east wing: the air is stale and bitter cold. I'm several rooms removed from the fireplace and woodstoves that keep the main room of the cabin toasty.

So, when the text message pings our phones, no one hears the text message, even though our crew sleeps 1 mile away from the Guard Sta-tion, where the woman is curled up in a ball on the floor and the husband is pacing around waiting for dispatch to call him back.

Fortunately, someone at dispatch in our small county gets ahold of a Crag Rat down in the valley by phone, perhaps Bill Pattison, an octoge-narian who has been a member for six decades. He's calm and collected: he's been doing this rescue business a long time. A dispatcher learns that the Crag Rats are at The Winter Outing and starts old-school communi-cation: phone calls.

"Try calling Don," says Bill to dispatch.

Somehow, Don Pattison, son of Bill, hears his phone ring. Don bolts awake, answers the phone, and quickly musters key players. He first jostles Rick Ragan to fire up our snowcat. Rick is a soft-spoken, level-headed, bearded, senior member of our group. He was an original snow ranger on Mount Hood and later became a Forest Service wildland firefighter. Now retired from the Forest Service, he brings a calm sense of expertise to our crew, both with rescues and the challenging task of navigating multiple agencies we work with: sheriff's office, Forest Service, and fire department.

A few other Crag Rats tumble out of bed to help organize the rescue, including Scott Hukari and Dale Crockett. Don wades from the front room, warmed still by smoldering fires in the cast-iron stove and the fireplace, to the frigid east wing of the cabin, where boards creak loudly underfoot. He's apparently looking for me. I'm deep in my sleeping bag, in a back room.

"Doc, we have a callout. Guard Station. Ragan is firing up the snow-cat," he says in staccato due to bitter cold as he walks into the small room in the east wing—it's the size of a dorm room, with two bunks and a stack of Rubbermaid bins. The bins, one for each Crag Rat, are where we store our personal sleeping bags, toothbrushes, and extra clothes, so we can ski up in the winter with just a small day pack.

"Now? Seriously?" My brain is fuzzy for a second as I am staring into the white light of Don's headlamp, which lights up his face in the pitch black room, like the scene from a low-budget horror film. Then, a second later, I jolt awake, sit up, and get pulverized by the bitter cold when my sleeping bag falls off my shoulders. Accustomed to being called in the middle of the night after two decades of working as an emergency physician, I wake up instantly.

My brain clears; the bitter cold helps. It's cold. Really cold.

Paul Crowley, a retired circuit court judge, is in the bunk across the room and also sits up.

"I'll come," he says matter-of-factly. He immediately turns on a headlamp and starts searching for ski clothing.

"What's the story?" I ask.

"Someone at the Guard Station," says Don again. "Rick's warming up the cat."

"Ok, let me get dressed," I say. I click on my headlamp and watch vapor pouring out of my mouth. I'm breathing hard just from the frigid air temperature. I had slept in my long underwear and ski socks, so I just need to pull on ski pants, layers of fleece and down, and my parka. I wiggle into ski clothing while still in my sleeping bag. I have a headache. I'm thirsty. I'm cold. I'm tired.

When I snake out of bed, sit up, and crowbar my feet into foam-and-plastic backcountry ski boots, I am greeted with another shock: the boots are freezing cold. Usually I leave them warming by the fire in the front room, but with the big crowd in the cabin, I'd brought them into the tiny back room in the east wing. Cold ski boots: good way to get frostbite.

Paul and I grab our ski packs and bumble through the cabin, bumping into bunks of sleeping Crag Rats, prospective members, and friends of Crag Rats. In the front room, I find a bustle of activity and bright lights from the propane and solar systems we have at the cabin. Ragan is outside with the snowcat, which is growling laboriously, trying to warm up in the cold. Others ready their gear: Portland firefighter and Crag Rat Tim Mortenson and Don join us as we quickly organize our ski gear and retrieve our clothing, which had been hung in the rafters of the main room above the fire to dry after skiing. Scott and Dale don't come on the rescue but get out of their bunks, pull on clothing, and help us get out the door. The cabin is more than a hundred years old, dusty, and creaky. We've got two woodstoves and a fireplace. Either Dale or Scott has just refueled the fires from our stash of fruitwood from the Hood River Valley, world-renowned for pear, apple, and cherry orchards.

In full winter ski regalia—helmet, goggles, parka, layers of fleece and down, skis, boots, and backpack full of avalanche-rescue and winter-survival gear—I step outside in the middle of the night, in the middle of the storm.

This will, as readers will come to learn, become a recurring scenario: night rescue. Often cold, sometimes stormy, and always dark. Outside, I get chilled to my core. And visibility is horrible because the storm has reached full potential. The sky is *puking*, big flakes of snow falling from the night. The wind blows the snow in all directions in whirlwinds. I put on goggles just to walk 20 feet from the cabin to the snowcat. I squeeze through the back door of the metal box wearing my backpack. Inside the back of the snowcat, we have a bit of respite from the weather, but the wind still finds a way to leak through the cracks of the walls and send a deep chill. The metal compartment smells of gasoline. Miscellaneous ropes and bungee cords litter the floor, as we had used the snowcat earlier that day to shuttle skiers up Ghost Ridge. The rudimentary bench has no padding, so as I plop down, the metal conducts heat and sucks the energy out of me through my thin ski pants.

It's cold. It's dark. We are tired. We are hungry. And I have a small, nagging headache. Nothing like starting out a rescue feeling lousy. It's the middle of the night, in the middle of a storm. If it sounds like I'm being repetitious, it's because this is exactly the way it seems at the time. Cold, then more cold, then colder. Wind, then more wind. Darkness, and more darkness. It is everywhere in repeated and larger doses.

This is a mountain rescue mission. This is what we do, the Crag Rats. We are the nine-decades-old, all-volunteer mountain rescue team for Hood River County. Even though we specialize in high-angle cliff, crevasse, avalanche, and snow rescue, we function as the all-purpose, all-terrain search-and-rescue team for the entire county. When we get called for rescues, we operate under the authority and direction of the Hood River County Sheriff's Office. This will be one of thirty missions for the average year—many of which are in foul weather, half of which are on the mountain, and a third of which are at night.

We pile into the snowcat and shut the back door with a slam, as Ragan guns the throttle. Ragan navigates the trusty 1988 LMC 1800 snowcat as we lumber out of the Cloud Cap Inn parking area, squeeze though a tight gap where the road goes between the cabin and a 50-foot cliff, and plow down the snow-drifted road, as all the while the machine is belching and burping, tossing us around in the back. Although the ski trail to the Tilly Jane Guard Station is about a half-mile from Cloud Cap directly through the woods, we have to take a wider path with the snowcat: the road. Rick drives a mile from Cloud Cap Saddle on the snow-covered road to a fork, and then a mile back up another road to the Tilly Jane area. As the heavy machine plows through the drifts, the snowcat struggles with a deep guttural moan like a growling dog about to pick a fight.

The Crag Rats have had many snowcats over the years; currently we have a second-hand Logan Manufacturing Company machine. The LMCs were made from 1978 to 2000, originally owned by the Thiokol snowcat division but later renamed LMC when the company was bought by John DeLorean, the same guy who made the car that bears his last name that appeared in the film *Back to the Future*.

Ragan can barely see through the storm. The windshield wipers are full speed, a defrost fan is on high power, and the headlights are on max. Every few minutes he wipes condensation from the front window with a rag. But the night is dark and the snow is blowing wildly. Visibility is 20 feet or less. We careen through the blackness a half-mile to the Tilly Jane Guard Station. It takes twenty minutes of expert driving.

When we arrive, Ragan aims the snowcat lights on the Guard Station and we wade through the deep snow, like walking through thick mud, to the front door. Inside, we find the woman curled up in a ball on the floor.

"We're search and rescue," I say, matter-of-fact. "I'm the doc, Van Tilburg," I introduce myself. I almost always use my first and last name, but in the middle of the night, in the middle of the storm, I'm going to be as brief as possible. Staccato. Get to the point quickly. The first task, which I try to complete within about twenty seconds of entering the room, is to determine whether this is a critical situation.

"What happened?" I ask. At the same time, I see the woman is flushed and sweating from pain, but her color is good, she's breathing okay, and she's alert. All good signs.

"I have pain in my stomach, started out of the blue," she says. I kneel down and do three things at once: I look to see if she's breathing normally, I check her pulse, which is ninety beats per minute and strong at the wrist, and feel her skin, which is cool and sweaty. I check her abdomen: she winces in pain.

In mountain rescue, patients are usually stable, since it takes so long for us to reach them, or dead, unfortunately. Rarely are we able to respond immediately. Normally, the Crag Rats respond from home and our response takes some time. Several things happen before we're even dispatched. The 911 center gets the call, gathers information, and calls a sheriff's deputy, usually one of three trained in search and rescue. The sheriff's deputy then needs to figure out three key things, which sometimes takes five minutes and sometimes several hours: What is the emergency? Where is the victim? What resources do we need?

In this case, a 911 call via phone answered the questions quite quickly. Woman in trouble. At Tilly Jane Guard Station. Need Crag Rats to evacuate. Fortunately, we were already on the mountain, which eliminated the second major time suck that occurs after someone calls 911: the Crag Rats' response. For most missions, we are at home or work. So we need to gather our gear from home, muster at the county yard where we store our truck, drive up the mountain, organize ourselves at the staging area, receive an assignment from the sheriff's deputy running the rescue, and then climb up the mountain.

Lucky for the woman, Bill answered the phone and then Don answered the phone.

My job, as medical lead for this rescue, is to determine in the first few minutes if the patient is critical and needs an immediate response, or if the patient is non-critical and we can take a bit of time. A critical patient in the backcountry, with no medical gear and no chance of a helicopter evacuation due to the storm, would be a dire situation.

This woman, however, is not about to die. First, she is talking, although obviously struggling due to the pain. She's got a steady, strong pulse at ninety beats per minute in her wrist, which means her blood pressure is at least 90 mm Hg systolic. (The top number, systolic, is responsible for pumping blood to the vital organs and tissue to deliver vital oxygen and pick up toxic carbon dioxide. The bottom number, diastolic, is when the heart relaxes, rests, rejuvenates.) I don't carry a blood-pressure cuff in the field because space and weight in my medical pack are limited and the actual number isn't as critical as the clinical assessment.

"No injury?"

"No," gasp.

"Sudden onset?"

"Yes," gasp, wince.

Abdominal pain is a difficult symptom to diagnose in the ER, more so in the backcountry with no medical supplies or equipment. I should know—my accident is still quite fresh and I have a zipper scar down the center of my abdomen as a perpetual, indelible reminder. The abdomen is packed with many organs from several organ systems. The nerves are jumbled so that pain in one area may signify an injury in that area, or the pain can be referred from another area. My spleen injury presented as left shoulder pain, lower-lung pneumonia can show up as belly pain, and appendicitis can show up as left-side pain, even though the appendix is on the right side. The digestive system alone could have multiple life-threatening conditions: gallstones blocking the exit ducts, gallbladder infection, liver inflammation, stomach ulcer that's bleeding or ruptured, twisted intestine, blocked intestine, appendicitis, or injury from trauma such as a liver or bowel laceration. The urinary system could have any number of issues: a blocked duct from a stone, a lacerated kidney, or an infection. In females, there's a host of problems that can occur specific to female parts: twisted ovary, ovarian cyst, gynecologic infection. Men can have abdominal pain from acute prostate infection or twisted testicle. Abdominal pain is one of the most difficult *differential diagnoses*, the list of all possible problems.

"Any medical problems?" I ask.

"Two babies. And a hysterectomy but they left one ovary. Feels like it twisted. It happened once before." It is always good to talk to patients and always good when they know what the problem is. "I think I have another twisted ovary."

The woman is not in shock, even though general popular usage of the term sometimes refers to severe pain. She is breathing, mentating, and pumping blood to her tissues. But at any time she could turn critical.

At this point, all we can do is evacuate the patient. I have no medical gear suitable to fix this woman: IV fluids and pain medication would be useful.

So, four of us rescuers bend over the woman, lift her up by the arms and legs, and carry her in a seated position. It is not a gentle process but a rough one: we have no choice. We have to squeeze out the tiny door of the cabin, wade through knee-deep snow, lift the patient up and over the transom of the snowcat, and wiggle her into the back of the LMC. We are trying to be gentle and concerned for her pain and well-being. But it's not easy. Did I mention it's also in the middle of the night, in the middle of a storm? Darkness pierced only by tiny headlamps and the old LMC lights, with snow falling, wind blowing, deep snow drifting. Coldness and blackness. And we are fatigued.

Once inside the snowcat, we rescuers pile in. The woman curls in the position of comfort: on her side in the fetal position on the floor. We make room for the husband and backpacks.

When we are all in the snowcat, Ragan pauses. He doesn't like something about the way the snowcat sounds. It idles at a low hum that perks up to a growl when Ragan juices the throttle. Sounds okay to me, but I'm a medical guy, not a mechanical one. Ragan gets on the radio.

"Ragan to Cloud Cap," he says.

"Cloud Cap," answers Scott Hukari, staffing the radio all night.

"Can you have someone warm up the sheriff's snowcat?" Since we have been training at the winter outing, we'd had both our LMC snowcat and the sheriff's snowcat up at Cloud Cap. Ragan, thinking ahead, wants a backup plan. "The LMC sounds funny."

"Will do," says Scott, who then clambers into the storm to warm up the second snowcat, parked outside the cabin.

Then, with Ragan at the controls, we start the long, harrowing descent down the mountain.

One might picture a snowcat at a ski resort, grooming the runs. These tend to be state-of-the-art snowcats with hi-fi sound systems, warm heaters, and plush seats. And often in ski resorts, even if visibility is limited, the ski runs are well defined. The LMC, however, is a different animal: a sturdy backcountry work machine, purchased secondhand. It is simple, small, and burly. But driving the beast is no easy task—it's physically strenuous. Ragan has a throttle to control speed. Steering is rudimentary: Ragan grips handles like joysticks that activate brakes: one lever for each of the tracks. Pull the right lever, activate the right track brake, and the snowcat turns right, for example. Top speed is maybe 15 miles an hour on firm, smooth, flat snow. We're moving much slower due partly to lack of visibility and partly to the deep, thick drifts of snow. Maybe 4 miles per hour. If we didn't have the snowcat, the only other option would be to put the woman in a specialized toboggan called an Akja (ah-key-uh). The Akja is a fiberglass toboggan that has two 4-foot-long aluminum handles at each end. These handles allow rescuers to ski down the Tilly Jane trail while carrying and sliding the toboggan, with one rescuer in front and one in back.

Luckily, we've got the snowcat. And luckily, we are already on the mountain.

In addition to the rigors of driving, navigating is a problem in the storm. The 9-mile-long Cloud Cap Road, which allows access to the Cloud Cap–Tilly Jane Historic District, is closed to car travel for most of the year. It is gated from the first snow in November until late spring when the snow melts and the road dries out. In winter, the snow-covered road is used by snowmobilers and cross-country skiers. The road begins at Tilly Jane Trailhead, and starts out heading west, meandering around corners and bends, mostly on the 4,000-foot contour. After 4 miles, the road turns south up the mountain. But here, the road is not straight. The road ascends via a dozen steep, rocky, narrow switchbacks, and gains 2,000 vertical feet in another 4 miles, a 22 percent grade. Near the top, the road forks. The right-hand fork heads a mile to Cloud Cap Saddle Campground, Cloud Cap Inn, and the Snowshoe Club Hut. The left-hand fork heads to Tilly Jane Campground and the A-Frame, Guard Station, and American Legion Cookhouse. In the winter with the snowcat, we take a shortcut, the Wagon Road Trail #642, which is the original path to Cloud Cap Inn used when guests would come down the Columbia River on a ferry and then take a horse and buggy 30 miles from the Columbia River to the cabin. This old road cuts directly to Cloud Cap Inn, bypassing most of the switchbacks. In summer, it is steep, narrow, and full of downed timber: pretty much impassable. But in winter, it's still steep and narrow, but the gully fills with snow and gives us a more direct route to the cabin via snowcat.

But we have a visibility problem due to the storm as well as the Gnarl Ridge forest fire in 2008. The Wagon Road is difficult to find. The burned snags that look like silver spears poking from the snow, the thick drifts, and the zero-dark-thirty storm make everything look the same. The Wagon Road is not marked like the usual cross-country trails, which have blue diamond trail markers, called blazes, hammered into the trees every 100 feet.

The snowcat snarls as Ragan navigates it down the mountain. Every ten minutes he stops, gets out of the cab, stands on the track, and peers through the blinding snow to get his bearings. He tries to find the Wagon Road, or at least confirm he's on the right path. Even if we miss the Wagon Road, heading due north, down the mountain, we will eventually reach the flat east-west section of Cloud Cap Road. There, we need to take an abrupt right-hand turn to the east to head back to the Tilly Jane Trailhead and an awaiting ambulance. Yet, that is a potential problem too: we are at risk for missing the Cloud Cap Road altogether by driving right across it. If we miss the road we will end up driving north, down the mountain, into thick, steep drainages of Crystal Spring Creek. That would get us basically nowhere but into a thick forest.

Then the snowcat gets stuck. As Ragan revs the motor, the tracks spin and auger us into a snowbank. We sink into a giant hole that is being created by the spinning tracks.

Then the snowcat begins to list, 20 degrees to the right on an embankment.

Then the snowcat slides back into a giant snag of dead timber. I wonder for a second if a snowcat can roll. Right at the same time, someone speaks aloud, "These things are really hard to roll."

Ragan spends ten minutes expertly jockeying the LMC back and forth, like doing a 50-point turn, until he is able to get the tracks to pack down the snow and gain purchase. He gets the snowcat unstuck, drives out of the hole, and continues across a snowfield that may or may not be the Wagon Road, which may or may not be above the Cloud Cap Road exit.

Ragan is an expert at this—there's no one I'd rather have behind the controls of the LMC.

In clear weather on firm snow, the 9-mile drive down the Wagon Road and out Cloud Cap Road takes forty-five minutes. This descent takes us two hours. We get down Wagon Road, and then exit east on the relatively flat Cloud Cap Road, where we are all relieved a bit. Faster now, perhaps 10 miles an hour, Ragan motors to the trailhead. We lumber into Tilly Jane Trailhead at 4:30 a.m.—the woman still in pain, still curled in a ball, still with no treatment. A sheriff's deputy and Parkdale Fire volunteers wait with an ambulance.

I must admit, at one point in this harrowing descent—probably when the snowcat felt like it was going to tip over and roll down the hill, in the middle of the night, in the middle of a storm, in the middle of the wilderness—I had been a bit concerned. Okay, call it frightened, or scared. We were taking a bit of a risk. But we'd made it down, safely. Our job is mostly complete.

After unloading the patient into the Parkdale ambulance, I sign out the patient to the paramedics and Ragan drives us back up the mountain. With the coming of the glow of dawn and the slight abatement of the storm, it is easier to drive the LMC uphill. Plus the route is now packed down so Ragan can follow our tracks. By 6:00 a.m. we arrive at the cabin at daybreak, pile out of the LMC, and find that Scott and Dale have cooked a full hot breakfast for us. After recounting the rescue and eating, I ski with a few Crag Rats down to my car parked at Tilly Jane Trailhead.

The snow is excellent quality: light, dry, fresh. I am back to my car a little before noon, then drive 30 miles home down the twisty Highway 35.

Once home, I dump my gear in my mud room, scarf some snacks, and jump in the shower. Out of the shower, I feel slightly more awake. I'm ready to get some real food, settle down to relax for the evening, check in with my kids, and go to bed early.

Then, my phone buzzes again just as I'm thinking of lying down for a quick nap.

Kids? Nope.

My new romantic interest, Margaret? Nope.

Parents? Nope.

Another mountain rescue callout? But of course. Blood drains from my head, hands. I get dizzy and shake my head to clear my brain. I have ten seconds of dread, knowing my evening is ruined. And then I decide to respond to the rescue, and adrenaline kicks in again.

Injury. Tilly Jane. Need responders. Snowcat still at trailhead.

This time, a person is injured at the Tilly Jane A-Frame, the building that is 100 yards from the Guard Station. Not only had I just returned home, but the entire crew had just closed up Cloud Cap Inn, just returned to the trailhead, and just loaded the snowcat on the trailer at the Tilly Jane Trailhead. They had planned to leave the snowcat parked on the trailer at Tilly Jane Trailhead and fetch it the next day. All Crag Rats had returned home after spending between one and four nights at Cloud Cap Inn.

I grab my gear, still packed from the night before. I quickly dig out my empty water bottle and wet clothing. I pull on clean, dry ski clothes—long-underwear tops and bottoms, ski pants, fleece sweater, puffy vest, calf-high ski socks. I grab my ski boots, still dank from the weekend: they stink badly. I hunt around for dry gloves and a clean hat. I fill my water bottle and grab a handful of energy bars.

And I head back up the mountain.

I drive back up Highway 35 to Tilly Jane Trailhead and meet the crew: Bernie Wells is here to drive the LMC, equally skilled as Ragan. Bernie is a long-time member and current treasurer, a relatively permanent position. He's the soft-spoken owner of Wells Construction, now mostly taken over by his son Todd. Bernie knows more about the Crag

Rats than most, having devoted thousands of hours of his personal time into maintaining Cloud Cap Inn, the Hut (our meeting hall in Hood River), our relationships with the Forest Service, and the lore of our group. Bernie, Ragan, and Bill Pattison make up the core of our elders.

A half-dozen Crag Rats have responded, mostly fresh from not attending The Winter Outing. We clamber in the snowcat and head up the mountain. Back up Cloud Cap Road. Back up Old Wagon Road. Back up to the Guard Station. At least it's still light out and the storm has abated. The sky glows blue and yellow as the sun begins to drift toward setting; we are running low on daylight. It's easier driving now since the track up the Wagon Road is packed down from the multiple snowcat trips that day, from both the rescue and The Winter Outing.

At the Guard Station we park the snowcat, slap climbing skins on our skis (adhesive on one side, the strips of fabric stick to our skis to provide traction for skiing uphill), click into ski bindings, and ski 100 yards to Tilly Jane A-frame. The snowcat can't make it to the front door of the A-Frame because of Tilly Jane Creek. From the Guard Station, we have to ski 20 feet down into Tilly Jane Creek, cross a bridge, which is buried in 4 feet of snow (luckily we know where the bridge crosses the creek), and then ski 20 feet out of Tilly Jane Creek. Past the amphitheater and past the dilapidated cookhouse, we arrive at the A-Frame. Inside, a dozen people are huddling around a young boy. The boy is lying on a picnic table and is attended by two bystanders who happen to be summer river guides.

"Hi, Doc Van Tilburg," I say. "What happened?"

"Sledding, careened out of control, and hit a tree," says one of the river guides. "We've taken pulse and blood pressure every fifteen minutes for two hours: he's stable," says the guide, showing me a first-responder notebook with the log of vital signs. This is ideal data: I instantly know this is not a helicopter evacuation for the same reason as the woman I'd examined earlier that morning. Pulse: stable. Blood pressure: stable. Good color. Talking and breathing normally. Chest and hips have no apparent injury. His abdomen is slightly tender.

"How you feeling?" I ask.

"Okay. My side hurts." The differential diagnosis—the list of possible causes for his pain in the setting of trauma—includes rib fracture, spleen laceration, liver laceration, compression fracture of his lumbar spine, and pelvis fracture.

I have a bag of IV fluids in my jacket that the volunteer firefighter handed me when leaving the snowcat. But considering that the boy has been stable for two hours, he's lying on a dirty picnic table in a dirty, dark cabin, and pediatric IV starts are difficult because kids' veins are small, I defer putting in the IV. Not to mention, I'm not nearly as skilled as a nurse or paramedic at placing tiny catheters into tiny veins.

"Are your parents around?"

"No," says the boy.

"He's here with a Boy Scout troop," says a man. "I'm the leader. He was sledding and hit a tree. I'm so sorry about this."

"Look, don't worry. He's stable. We'll get him down the mountain," I reassure him.

We carry the boy outside, put him in a litter, and ski him over to Tilly Jane Creek. Before crossing the bridge, I ask Walter Burkhardt to set up a safety rope. Even though we only descend 20 feet into the creek, the entrance to the creek is a steep side hill and we have to traverse the off-camber hill 20 yards upstream to get to the snow-covered bridge. So, to keep the litter from sliding down into the creek before we reach the bridge, we want a rope.

We pause for Walter to set up the rope, and then descend into the creek, cross the bridge, and struggle up the opposite bank—pushing, dragging, and shoving the litter uphill through the deep snow—to the waiting snowcat. We pile in and head back down the mountain. Down the Wagon Road. Down Cloud Cap Road. At Tilly Jane Trailhead, for the second time in twelve hours, we transfer a patient from the LCM to an ambulance and Parkdale volunteer firefighters. They are probably just as exhausted as we are. For the second time in a day, I went up and down the mountain. For the second time in a day, I return home from a mountain rescue mission utterly exhausted.

If we get a third callout, I'm not going.

THREE

Faint of Heart at Yosemite Falls

Andrea Lankford

NEAR THE DOOR TO THE YOSEMITE VALLEY RANGER STATION SAT A huge cross section of an ancient tree. According to the sign, the sequoia had been a thousand years old when it fell in 1919. Plastic labels tacked into the wood pointed out rings of tree growth that corresponded to the years of major human events, such as the Battle of Hastings in 1066, the signing of the Declaration of Independence in 1776, the start of the Civil War in 1861, and the year Yosemite became a national park—1890. During the summer of 1993, park ranger Mary Litell passed this exhibit so often during the course of her workday that, before too long, she forgot it was there.

One deceptively calm evening, after passing the tree exhibit on her way home from work, Mary crossed the street and walked along the backside of the Pioneer Cemetery. There, underneath the shade of five evergreens, a large but otherwise unpretentious hunk of granite marked the grave of Yosemite's first park ranger—Galen Clark, who became the park's first civilian guardian in 1867. From Clark's grave, with three good kicks you could have sent a pinecone into the yard of the cabin Mary shared with two male coworkers. But tonight the ranger would not make it home before dark. Just as she turned the corner near Clark's headstone, she heard the screaming.

Behind the Park Service corral, a colossal wall of granite formed a natural amphitheater that intensified the panicked cries for help coming from a ledge three hundred feet above the ground. The anguish in those screams quickened the ranger's pulse and sent a jolt of empathic fear into the hearts of the patrol horses resting in their stables. Sprinting toward the sound, Mary ran into a group of neighborhood kids, children of park employees. The kids had been playing in the woods behind their houses. Now they carried haunted expressions on their faces. "He fell," they said, pointing to the cliffs.

Later it became clear what happened. Hours earlier, two young men, brothers, had leaned as far as they dared over the handrails to watch the water plunge over Yosemite Falls. From the trail they spotted what looked like a shortcut down to the valley. They stepped off the trail. The farther they went, the more difficult the route became until the brothers were scaling the rocky benches under the Lost Arrow Spire. Here there were no handrails, and the mellow feeling from the marijuana the men smoked at the overlook had long since faded. The decomposed granite was flaking off in their hands. Their feet were sending rocks crashing down the nearly vertical slab. When one of them fell, his brother started screaming.

Mary ran up the bouldered slope. Where the granite became scree, she met rescuers Rick Folks and Mike Ray. At the base of the cliff they found something caught in the lower branches of an oak. The large mass tangled up in the tree branches was a man—a very messed-up man. No way was he alive.

Mary yelled up at the man's brother, who was still screaming, and told him to stay put; the rangers would come and get him. Using her park radio, she described the situation to the dispatcher as Mike Ray climbed up to where the tree branches met the scree. Mary watched Ray reach his fingers toward the crumpled man's throat to confirm that this was indeed a fatality.

The rescuers were startled when the man inhaled a wheezy breath.

Mike Ray had aspirations of becoming an emergency-room doctor and knew exactly what to do. He opened the man's airway. Then, using his own body as a backboard to protect the patient's spine, he curled the man out of the tree. Two paramedic rangers arrived, and within minutes an airway tube was down the patient's throat, an IV line was in his vein, his body was on a stretcher, and he was being carried down through the difficult terrain. The ranger-medics worked their injured patient with an urgent calm. Their steady voices told Mary and the other less-experienced rangers what to do.

Mary and five rescuers carried the basket stretcher down the rugged slope. The critically injured man had been unconscious until now. He began to squirm. A medic shouted, "Grab his hands!" Before anyone could stop him, the patient grabbed the plastic airway tube the medics had slid down his throat and pulled it out of his own mouth. He said, "Jesus." Then his heart stopped beating. The rangers initiated CPR, but it was obvious to all but the newbies that this one wasn't going to have a happy ending.

That night the doctor at the park clinic told Mary that even if the guy had fallen onto a table in front of a team of trauma specialists prepped for surgery, he still wouldn't have made it.

It was disappointing. Mary was a cross-wearing Catholic. She had hoped for one of those times when God slaps his palm on his forehead and says, "Oh, shit, John Smith? I meant John Schmidt!" so he sends in a couple of rangers to correct his mistake. She had seen a miracle like this only a week earlier when the dispatcher had reported a severely injured man "under the Green Dragon." No one had been optimistic about that guy making it either. "Green Dragons" were those diesel-fueled, tour guide–equipped, open-air trams that caterpillar the valley roads all day, slowing traffic and pulling a long chain of green-and-yellow cars filled with tourists. If a man was under one of those, his number had been called.

Emergency sirens echoed off the valley walls as the rangers raced to find the green dragon with the man under it. There were several to check, and they were scattered all over Yosemite Village. But every tour guide the rangers contacted swore up and down they hadn't run over any stray tourists that day. Precious lifesaving minutes ticked by. Rangers radioed in their frustrations to dispatchers who were very confused. Then Mary got an idea.

Minutes later she found him lying unconscious under bloodstained granite along a rock-climbing route called "the Green Dragon."

The guy should have died. In a race against the setting sun, the rangers medically stabilized the climber and got him flown out of the valley before the stroke of darkness turned the park helicopter into a pumpkin. As she watched the rescue helicopter fly into the sunset, Mary decided this ranger gig was a keeper.

Mary was a ranger who had to learn things the hard way. Like Rule Number One: Measure your head before you order your ranger hat—or you'll have to stuff paper towels inside the headband to keep the hat from falling down over your eyes. Rule Number Two: If you must wear mascara to work, make it waterproof—the guys will laugh at you when you turn into a raccoon during a water-sprayed rescue mission under Yosemite Falls. Rule Number Three: Say "I don't know" if a park visitor asks a question and you don't know the answer. There will always be a crowd standing around you when a camper asks, "Oh, ranger, what kind of squirrel is that?" If you draw a blank and say, "Uh. A bushy-tailed squirrel?" a guy with a video camera will be there to say, "It's called a California gray squirrel," the disgust dripping from his voice.

Mary Litell was no Jane Goodall. That's for certain. But then rangers would have more time for studying the natural history of Yosemite squirrels if people would just stop falling off cliffs. But people will continue to fall off cliffs as long as leaves continue to fall off trees. And over the years, layers upon layers of stories about people falling off cliffs have accumulated into fat files of multicolored papers stuffed into brown cardboard boxes stacked head-high in a walk-in closet inside the special agent's office. And these stories, which the rangers once typed onto quadruplicate-copy government forms and now type into government computers, are as surreal and melodramatic as any of the so-called legends the Ahwahneechee and their descendants passed down orally from generation to generation over the past two hundred years.

A young Swiss woman traveled to America with her bold and athletic boyfriend, a Czechoslovakian climber. During their days at Yosemite, the Czech climber grabbed his ropes and climbing equipment and set out to climb the Lost Arrow Spire over the course of several days. Before he left, the climber asked his girlfriend to occasionally monitor his progress through a pair of binoculars.

On days one and two, the climber's girlfriend eyed the cliff face, watching her lover ascend the route. On day three she lost sight of him. On day four she spotted a rock climber's haul bag hanging from the rock. On day five she saw no sign of her boyfriend, and the haul bag was in the same spot as it had been before. On day six, when she saw that the haul bag had not moved, the girlfriend was beyond concerned; she was frantic.

Back at camp, a visibly anxious woman convinced two Hungarian climbers to hike with her to the cliff above the spire. At the top, one Hungarian rappelled down the rock alongside the Czechoslovakian's route. The Hungarian found the Czech's gear, a shirt, a hammer, and an anchor set in the granite. Attached to the anchor was a daisy chain (a length of multilooped webbing climbers use to attach themselves and their gear to anchors). The daisy chain appeared to have been cut or smashed in two. The Hungarian ascended back up the rope and ran down the trail to notify the park rangers.

Within minutes of receiving this report, Mary Litell was in the park rescue helicopter, her eyes scanning the Lost Arrow Spire for clues. She spotted a pile of red and black rags lying on the rocks below and asked the pilot to move in closer. The winds were "squirrelly" that day, making the maneuver difficult for the pilot. He hovered as close as he dared to the granite, tilting the helicopter to give Mary a better look. The rotor wash shooed away a flock of crows that had been sitting on the pile of rags, revealing to Mary that the rags weren't rags. They were a human body. Leaning out of the helicopter door, the webbing of her seat belt the only thing keeping her from falling, she snapped an instant photo of the scene.

Back at the rescue cache, Mary showed this photograph to me, the incident commander. (After two summers at Cape Hatteras and four years in Zion National Park, I had transferred to Yosemite. Now a permanent full-time ranger, I was given the leadership role for this particular mission.) As I studied the photograph, Mary informed me that this climber must have fallen eight hundred feet several days ago while climbing the Lost Arrow Spire. Then she pointed to the snapshot of a tattered lump of clothing and decomposing flesh and said, "I don't think he's going to make it."

A rescue helicopter dropped a recovery team near the body before flying Mary to the top of the cliff to find the victim's girlfriend. Mary was looking for a woman with long blond hair and wearing blue shorts, a yellow shirt, and skinny sandals. But instead of the girlfriend, Mary spotted thirty people dressed from head to toe in black, a pack of ninjas standing in a circle and tossing around nunchakus at the edge of the cliff. What the hell? The pilot landed the helicopter, and Mary walked out to investigate. When she returned, the ranger had a driver's license in her back pocket and a dozen nunchakus cradled in her arms. "You're not going to believe this," she told the pilot. "A guy was teaching a martial arts class in the Yosemite backcountry."

At the park morgue, a concrete room adjacent to the search and rescue (SAR) cache, two park rangers waited for the body to arrive. In Yosemite the federal government has exclusive jurisdiction, giving the NPS full responsibility over legal issues such as enforcing laws and investigating deaths inside the park. A handful of rangers are therefore trained to perform as coroners.

If you are thinking people do not become park rangers to do coroner duty, you would be right. Nevertheless, the job must be done. Rangers trained for coroner duty receive no additional pay. However, the experience might help a ranger compete for a better paying job as an NPS special agent.

After the body recovery team rolled the gurney with the Czech climber's remains into the morgue, the ranger-coroners delicately searched for wallets, jewelry, and other objects of evidence or identification.

When the helicopter landed in Ahwahnee Meadow, Mary got out, walked to her patrol car, and dumped all the nunchakus into the trunk. The incident commander sent her to Sunnyside Campground, where the girlfriend was waiting for someone from the NPS to contact her. Like most rangers, Mary would have rather juggled knives while attached to a flaming rope dangling over a mile-high cliff than do a death notification. This was going to be her first.

At Sunnyside Campground, Mary walked up to the dead climber's girlfriend. Surely the girlfriend suspected the worst, but until someone in uniform said it out loud, she was holding onto a glimmer of hope. Mary saw her words put out that glimmer in the girlfriend's eyes. But it was the ranger, not the grieving girlfriend, who first broke down into tears. The two women hugged. The girlfriend said this had happened to her before, years ago in Europe. He, too, was a rock climber. He, too, fell to his death while scaling a cliff.

Later that night, after the recovery mission had wound down, the wayward martial arts instructor met Mary in front of the ranger station. Along with his driver's license, Mary handed him a ticket for conducting commercial operations without a permit inside a national park. Then the ranger apologized. She had to confiscate his nunchakus as evidence since they were deadly weapons, the possession of which was illegal in a national park as well as a felony in California.

The loss of his weapons seemed to matter little to the martial arts instructor. He shrugged and said, "Will you have dinner with me tonight?"

"Sorry," Mary said. "I'm too busy."

Collateral duties are common for a ranger. While some rangers are trained to be coroners, others are trained to be critical incident stress counselors. These ranger-counselors conduct critical incident stress debriefings (CISDs) and often function as a NPS liaison and/or counselor for families. Like coroner detail, certification as a grief sponge involves a couple of weeks of additional training and no additional pay. When CISD "peer counselors" lead group "stress debriefings," you can talk about your feelings and cry if you want to. But the rangers with the weather-beaten Stetsons don't say much during these sessions. They appear to be able to walk it off, shrug it off, laugh it off, and forget it. I saw an example of this coping mechanism when I showed up for work the next morning. Tacked to the bulletin board in the briefing room was the photo Mary had taken from the helicopter. On the white border under this snapshot of a corpse at the base of the Lost Arrow Spire, written in black marker, were the words "Canceled Czech."

I, too, relied on jokes to dismiss the many tragedies we saw. I was another ranger who had to learn things the hard way. Rule Number 313: Tombstone humor is a Band-Aid placed over what may become a deep and festering wound.

Four

Escape from Death Valley

William Lewis Manly

THIS NIGHT WE HAD ANOTHER MEETING TO DECIDE UPON OUR COURSE and determine what to do. At this meeting no one was wiser than another, for no one had explored the country and knew what to expect. The questions that now arose were "How long can we endure this work in this situation? How long will our oxen be able to endure the great hardship on the small nourishment they receive? How long can we provide ourselves with food?"

We had a few small pieces of dry bread. This was kept for the children, giving them a little now and then. Our only food was in the flesh of the oxen, and when they failed to carry themselves along we must begin to starve. It began to look as if the chances of leaving our bones to bleach upon the desert were the most prominent ones.

One thing was certain we must move somewhere at once. If we stay here we can live as long as the oxen do, and no longer, and if we go on it is uncertain where to go, to get a better place. We had guns and ammunition to be sure, but of late we had seen no living creature in this desert wild. Finally Mr. Bennett spoke and said:—

"Now I will make you a proposition. I propose that we select two of our youngest, strongest men and ask them to take some food and go ahead on foot to try to seek a settlement, and food, and we will go back to the good spring we have just left and wait for their return. It will surely not take them more than ten days for the trip, and when they get back we shall know all about the road and its character and how long it will take us to travel it. They can secure some other kind of food that will make us feel better, and when the oxen have rested a little at the spring we can get out with our wagons and animals and be safe. I think this is the best and safest way."

"Now what do you all say?" After a little discussion all seemed to agree that this was the best, and now it remained to find the men to go. No one offered to accept the position of advance messengers. Finally Mr. Bennett said he knew one man well enough to know that he would come back if he lived, and he was sure he would push his way through. "I will take Lewis (myself) if he will consent to go." I consented, though I knew it was a hazardous journey, exposed to all sorts of things, Indians, climate and probable lack of water, but I thought I could do it and would not refuse. John Rogers a large strong Tennessee man was then chosen as the other one and he consented also.

Now preparations began, Mr. Arcane killed the ox which had so nearly failed, and all the men went to drying and preparing meat. Others made us some new mocassins out of rawhide, and the women made us each a knapsack.

Our meat was closely packed, and one can form an idea how poor our cattle were from the fact that John and I actually packed seven-eighths of all the flesh of an ox into our knapsacks and carried it away. They put in a couple of spoonfuls of rice and about as much tea. This seemed like robbery to the children, but the good women said that in case of sickness even that little bit might save our lives. I wore no coat or vest, but took half of a light blanket, while Rogers wore a thin summer coat and took no blanket. We each had a small tin cup and a small camp kettle holding a quart. Bennett had me take his seven-shooter rifle, and Rogers had a good double barreled shot gun. We each had a sheath knife, and our hats were small brimmed, drab affairs fitting close to the head and not very conspicuous to an enemy as we might rise up from behind a hill into possible views. We tried on our packs and fitted the straps a little so they would carry easy. They collected all the money there was in camp and gave it to us. Mr. Arcane had about $30 and others threw in small amounts from forty cents upward. We received all sorts of advice. Capt. Culverwell was an old sea faring man and was going to tell us how to find our way back, but Mr. Bennett told the captain that he had known Lewis as a hunter for many years, and that if he went over a place in the daytime he could find his way back at night every time. Others cautioned us about the Indians and told us how to manage. Others told us not to get caught in deep snow which we might find on the mountains.

This advice we received in all the kindness in which it was given, and then we bade them all good bye. Some turned away, too much affected to approach us and others, shook our hands with deep feeling, grasping them firmly and heartily hoping we would be successful and be able to pilot them out of this dreary place into a better land. Every one felt that a little food to make a change from the poor dried meat would be acceptable. Mr. and Mrs. Bennett and J. B. Arcane and wife were the last to remain when the others had turned away. They had most faith in the plan and felt deeply. Mrs. Bennett was the last, and she asked God to bless us and bring some food to her starving children.

We were so much affected that we could not speak and silently turned away and took our course again up the canyon we had descended the night before.

After a while we looked back and when they saw us turn around, all the hats and bonnets waved us a final parting.

Those left in the camp were Asabel, Bennett and Sarah his wife, with three children, George, Melissa, and Martha; J. B. Arcane and wife with son Charles. The youngest children were not more than two years old. There were also the two Earhart brothers, and a grown son, Capt. Culverwell, and some others I cannot recall; eleven grown people in all, besides a Mr. Wade, his wife and three children who did not mingle with our party, but usually camped a little distance off, followed our trail, but seemed to shun company. We soon passed round a bend of the cañon, and then walked on in silence.

We both of us meditated some over the homes of our fathers, but took new courage in view of the importance of our mission and passed on as fast as we could.

By night we were far up the mountain, near the perpendicular rough peak, and far above us on a slope we could see some bunches of grass and sage brush. We went to this and found some small water holes. No water ran from them they were so small. Here we staid all night. It did not seem very far to the snowy peak to the north of us. Just where we were seemed the lowest pass, for to the south were higher peaks and the rocks looked as if they were too steep to be got over.

Through this gap came a cold breeze, and we had to look round to get a sheltered place in which to sleep. We lay down close together, spoon fashion, and made the little blanket do as cover for the both of us. In the morning we filled our canteens, which we had made by binding two powder cans together with strips of cloth, and started for the summit near by. From this was the grandest sight we ever beheld. Looking east we could see the country we had been crawling over since November 4th. "Just look at the cursed country we have come over!" said Rogers as he pointed over it. To the north was the biggest mountain we ever saw, peaks on peaks and towering far above our heads, and covered with snow which was apparently everlasting.

This mountain seemed to have very few trees on it, and in extent, as it reached away to the north seemed interminable. South was a nearly level plain, and to the west I thought I could dimly see a range of mountains that held a little snow upon their summits, but on the main range to the south there was none. It seemed to me the dim snowy mountains must be as far as 200 miles away, but of course I could not judge accurately. After looking at this grand, but worthless landscape long enough to take in its principal features we asked each other what we supposed the people we left behind would think to see mountains so far ahead. We knew that they had an idea that the coast range was not very far ahead, but we saw at once to go over all these mountains and return within the limits of fifteen days which had been agreed upon between us, would probably be impossible, but we must try as best we could, so down the rocky steep we clambered and hurried on our way. In places the way was so steep that we had to help each other down, and the hard work made us perspire freely so that the water was a prime necessity. In one place near here, we found a little water and filled our canteens, besides drinking a good present supply. There were two low, black rocky ranges directly ahead of us which we must cross.

When part way down the mountain a valley or depression opened up in that direction up which it seemed as if we could look a hundred miles. Near by and a short distance north was a lake of water and when we reached the valley we crossed a clear stream of water flowing slowly toward the lake.

Being in need of water, we rushed eagerly to it and prepared to take a big drink, but the tempting fluid was as salt as brine and made our thirst all the more intolerable. Nothing grew on the bank of this stream and the bed was of hard clay, which glistened in the sun.

We now began the ascent of the next ridge, keeping a westernly course, and walked as fast as we could up the rough mountain side. We crossed the head of a cañon near the summit about dark, and here we found a trail, which from indications we knew to be that of the Jayhawkers, who had evidently been forced to the southward of the course they intended to take. They had camped here and had dug holes in the sand in search of water, but had found none.

We staid all night here and dug around in some other places in the bottom of the cañon, in the hope to have better luck than they did, but we got no water anywhere.

We seemed almost perishing for want of water, the hard exercise made us perspire so freely. In the morning we started on, and near the summit we came to the dead body of Mr. Fish, laying in the hot sun, as there was no material near here with which his friends could cover the remains. This Mr. Fish was the man who left camp some two weeks before in company with another and who carried the long whiplash wound about his body, in hope he could somewhere be able to trade it for bread. No doubt in this very place where he breathed his last, his bones still lie.

As we came in sight of the next valley, we could see a lake of water some distance south of our western course.

We had followed the Jayhawkers trail thus far, but as we found no water in small holes in the rocks as we were likely to do when we were the first to pass, we decided to take a new route in the hope to find a little water in this way, for we had no hope of finding it in any other. This valley we now crossed seemed to come to an end about ten miles to the north of us. To the south it widened out, enclosing the lake spoken of. This valley was very sandy and hard to walk over. When about halfway across we saw some ox tracks leading toward the lake, and in the hope we might find the water drinkable we turned off at right angles to our course and went that way also. Long before we reached the water of the lake, the bottom became a thin, slimy mud which was very hard on our mocassins. When we reached the water we found it to be of a wine color, and so strongly alkaline as to feel slippery to the touch, and under our feet.

This side trip, had cost us much exertion and made us feel more thirsty than ever.

We turned now west again, making for a cañon, up which we passed in the hope we should at some turn find a little basin of rain water in some rock. We traveled in it miles and miles, and our mouths became so dry we had to put a bullet or a small smooth stone in and chew it and turn it around with the tongue to induce a flow of saliva. If we saw a spear of green grass on the north side of a rock, it was quickly pulled and eaten to obtain the little moisture it contained.

Thus we traveled along for hours, never speaking, for we found it much better for our thirst to keep our mouths closed as much as possible, and prevent the evaporation. The dry air of that region took up water as a sponge does. We passed the summit of this ridge without finding any water, and on our way down the western side we came to a flat place where there was an Indian hut made of small brush. We now thought there surely must be some water near and we began a thorough search. The great snow mountain did not seem far off, but to the south and southwest a level or inclined plain extended for a long distance. Our thirst began to be something terrible to endure, and in the warm weather and hard walking we had secured only two drinks since leaving camp.

We were so sure that there must be water near here that we laid our knapsacks down by the little hut and looked around in every possible place we could think of. Soon it got dark and then we made a little fire as a guide and looked again. Soon the moon arose and helped us some, and we shouted frequently to each other so as not to get lost.

We were so nearly worn out that we tried to eat a little meat, but after chewing a long time, the mouth would not moisten it enough so we could swallow, and we had to reject it. It seemed as if we were going to die with plenty of food in our hand, because we could not eat it.

We tried to sleep but could not, but after a little rest we noticed a bright star two hours above the horizon, and from the course of the moon we saw the star must be pretty truly west of us. We talked a little, and the burden of it was a fear that we could not endure the terrible thirst a while longer. The thought of the women and children waiting for our return made us feel more desperate than if we were the only ones concerned. We thought we could fight to the death over a water hole if we could only secure a little of the precious fluid. No one who has ever felt the extreme of thirst can imagine the distress, the dispair, which it brings. I can find no words, no way to express it so others can understand.

The moon gave us so much light that we decided we would start on our course, and get as far as we could before the hot sun came out, and so we went on slowly and carefully in the partial darkness, the only hope left to us being that our strength would hold out till we could get to the shining snow on the great mountain before us. We reached the foot of the range we were descending about sunrise. There was here a wide wash from the snow mountain, down which some water had sometime run after a big storm, and had divided into little rivulets only reaching out a little way before they had sunk into the sand.

We had no idea we could now find any water till we at least got very near the snow, and as the best way to reach it we turned up the wash although the course was nearly to the north. The course was up a gentle grade and seemed quite sandy and not easy to travel. It looked as if there was an all day walk before us, and it was quite a question if we could live long enough to make the distance. There were quite strong indications that the water had run here not so very long ago, and we could trace the course of the little streams round among little sandy islands. A little stunted brush grew here but it was so brittle that the stems would break as easy as an icicle.

In order to not miss a possible bit of water we separated and agreed upon a general course, and that if either one found water he should fire his gun as a signal. After about a mile or so had been gone over I heard Roger's gun and went in his direction. He had found a little ice that had frozen under the clear sky. It was not thicker than window glass. After putting a piece in our mouths we gathered all we could and put it into the little quart camp kettle to melt. We gathered just a kettle full, besides what we ate as we were gathering, and kindled a little fire and melted it.

I can but think how providential it was that we started in the night for in an hour after the sun had risen that little sheet of ice would have melted and the water sank into the sand. Having quenched our thirst we could now eat, and found that we were nearly starved also. In making this meal we used up all our little store of water, but we felt refreshed and our lives renewed so that we had better courage to go on.

We now took our course west again taking a bee line for a bluff that lay a little to the south of the big snow mountain. On and on we walked till the dark shadow of the great mountain in the setting sun was thrown about us, and still we did not seem more than half way to the bluff before us.

All the way had been hill and very tiresome walking. There was considerable small brush scattered about, here and there, over this steeply inclined plain.

We were still several miles from the base of this largest of the mountains and we could now see that it extended west for many miles. The buttes to the south were low, black and barren, and to the west as far as we could see there were no mountains with any snow. As the sun got further down we could see a small smoke curling up near the base of the mountain, and we thought it must be some signal made by the Indians, as we had often seen them signal in that way, but we stopped and talked the matter over, and as we were yet a long way from the bluff which had been our objective point, we concluded we would investigate the smoke signal a little closer. So we set off toward it in the dusk and darkness and when within about a mile we found we were in a tract that had been somewhat beaten. Feeling with my fingers I was quite sure I could distinguish ox tracks, and then was quite sure that we had overtaken the Jayhawkers, or at least were on their trail. And then I thought perhaps they had fallen among the Indians, who now might be feasting on their oxen and it became necessary to use great caution in approaching the little smoke.

We took a circuitous route and soon saw that the persons were on a little bench above us and we kept very cautious and quiet, listening for any sounds that might tell us who they were.

If they were Indians we should probably hear some of their dogs, but we heard none, and kept creeping closer and closer, till we were within fifty yards without hearing a sound to give us any idea of who they were.

We decided to get our guns at full cock and then hail the camp, feeling that we had a little the advantage of position. We hailed and were answered in English. "Don't Shoot" said we and they assured us they had no idea of such a thing, and asked us to come in. We found here to our surprise, Ed Doty, Tom Shannon, L. D. Stevens, and others whom I do not recollect, the real Jayhawkers. They gave us some fresh meat for supper, and near the camp were some water holes that answered well for camp purposes.

Here an ox had given out and they had stopped long enough to dry the meat, while the others had gone on a day ahead.

Coming around the mountain from the north was quite a well defined trail, leading to the west and they said they were satisfied some one lived at the end of it, and they were going to follow it if it led to Mexico or anywhere else. They said that Mr. Brier and his family were still on behind, and alone. Every one must look out for himself here, and we could not do much for another in any way.

We inquired of them about the trail over which they had come, and where they had found water, and we told them of our experience in this respect. We then related how our train could not go over the mountains with wagons, how they had returned to the best spring, and that we started to go through to the settlements to obtain relief while they waited for our return. We explained to them how they must perish without assistance. If we failed to get through, they could probably live as long as the oxen lasted and would then perish of starvation. We told them how nearly we came to the point of perishing that very morning, of thirst, and how we were saved by finding a little patch of ice in an unexpected place, and were thus enabled to come on another day's travel.

These men were not as cheerful as they used to be and their situation and prospects constantly occupied their minds. They said to us that if the present trail bore away from the mountain and crossed the level plain, that there were some of them who could not possibly get along safely to the other side. Some were completely discouraged, and some were completely out of provisions and dependent on those who had either provisions or oxen yet on hand. An ox was frequently killed, they said, and no part of it was wasted. At a camp where there was no water, for stewing, a piece of hide would be prepared for eating by singeing off the hair and then roasting in the fire. The small intestines were drawn through the fingers to clean them, and these when roasted made very fair food.

They said they had been without water for four or five days at a time and came near starving to death, for it was impossible to swallow food when one became so thirsty. They described the pangs of hunger as something terrible and not to be described. They were willing to give us any information we desired and we anxiously received all we could, for on our return we desired to take the best possible route, and we thus had the experience of two parties instead of one. They told us about the death of Mr. Fish and Mr. Isham, and where we would find their bodies if we went over their trail.

In the morning we shouldered our packs again and took the trail leading to the west, and by night we had overtaken the advance party of the Jayhawkers, camped in a cañon where there was a little water, barely sufficient for their use. We inquired why they did not take the trail leading more directly west at the forks, and they said they feared it would lead them into deep snow which would be impassible. They said they considered the trail they had taken as altogether the safest one.

We met Bennett and Arcane's teamsters, and as we expected they were already out of grub and no way to get anymore. When the party killed an ox they had humbly begged for some of the poorest parts, and thus far were alive. They came to us and very pitifully told us they were entirely out, and although an ox had been killed that day they had not been able to get a mouthful. We divided up our meat and gave them some although we did not know how long it would be before we would ourselves be in the same situation.

Thus far we had not seen anything to shoot, big or little although we kept a sharp lookout.

The whole camp was silent, and all seemed to realize their situation. Before them was a level plain which had the appearance of being so broad as to take five or six days to cross. Judging by the look from the top of the mountain as we came over, there was little to hope for in the way of water. We thought it over very seriously. All the water we could carry would be our canteens full, perhaps two drinks apiece and the poor meat had so little nourishment that we were weak and unable to endure what we once could.

We were alone, Rogers and I, in interest at any rate, even if there were other men about. For the time it really seemed as if there was very little hope for us and I have often repeated the following lines as very closely describing my own feelings at that time.

Oh hands, whose loving, gentle grasp I loosed.
When first this weary journey was begun.
If I could feel your touch as once I could.
How gladly would I wish my work undone.
Harriet Keynon

During the evening, I had a talk with Capt. Asa Haines, in which he said he left a good home in Illinois, where he had everything he could wish to eat, and every necessary comfort, and even some to spare, and now he felt so nearly worn out that he had many doubts whether he could live to reach the mountains, on the other side. He was so deeply impressed that he made me promise to let his wife and family know how I found him and how he died, for he felt sure he would never see the California mines. I said I might not get through myself, but he thought we were so young and strong that we would struggle through. He said if he could only be home once more he would be content to stay. This was the general tenor of the conversation. There was no mirth, no jokes, and every one seemed to feel that he was very near the end of his life, and such a death as stood before them, choking, starving in a desert was the most dreary outlook I ever saw.

This camp of trouble, of forlorn hope, on the edge of a desert stretching out before us like a small sea, with no hope for relief except at the end of a struggle which seemed almost hopeless, is more than any pen can paint, or at all describe. The writer had tried it often. Picture to yourself, dear reader the situation and let your own imagination do the rest. It can never come up to the reality.

In the morning, as Rogers and I were about to start, several of the oldest men came to us with their addresses and wished us to forward them to their families if we ever got within the reach of mails. These men shed tears, and we did also as we parted. We turned silently away and again took up our march.

As we went down the cañon we came to one place where it was so narrow, that a man or a poor ox could barely squeeze through between the rocks, and in a few miles more reached the open level plain. When three or four miles out on the trail and not far from the hills we came to a bunch of quite tall willows. The center of the bunch had been cut out and the branches woven in so as to make a sort of corral. In the center of this was a spring of good water and some good grass growing around. This was pretty good evidence that some one had been here before. We took a good drink and filled our canteens anew, for we did not expect to get another drink for two or three days at least.

We took the trail again and hurried on as the good water made us feel quite fresh. After a few miles we began to find the bones of animals, some badly decayed and some well preserved. All the heads were those of horses, and it puzzled us to know where they came from. As we passed along we noticed the trail was on a slight up grade and somewhat crooked. If we stepped off from it the foot sank in about two inches in dirt finer than the finest flour. The bones were scattered all along, sometimes the bones of several animals together. Was it the long drive, poison water, or what? It was evident they had not been killed but had dropped along the way.

It was a dreary trail at best, and these evidences of death did not help to brighten it in the least. We wondered often where it led to and what new things would be our experience. After walking fast all day we came to quite an elevation, where we could stand and look in all directions. The low black range where we left the Jayhawkers was in sight, and this spur of the great snowy mountains extended a long way to the south, and seemed to get lower and lower, finally ending in low rocky buttes, a hundred miles away. Some may think this distance very far to see, but those who have ever seen the clear atmosphere of that region will bear me out in these magnificent distances. Generally a mountain or other object seen at a distance would be three or four times as far off as one would judge at first sight, so deceptive are appearances there. The broad south end of the great mountain which we first saw the next morning after we left the wagons, was now plain in sight, and peak after peak extending away to the north, all of them white with snow. Standing thus out in the plain we could see the breadth of the mountain east and west, and it seemed as though it must have been nearly a hundred miles. The south end was very abrupt and sank as one into a great plain in which we stood, twenty miles from the mountain's base.

To the northwest we could see a clay lake, or at least that was what we called it, and a line of low hills seemed to be an extension of the mountain in a direction swinging around to the south to enclose this thirsty, barren plain before us, which was bounded by mountains or hills on these sides. To the south this range seemed to get higher, and we could see some snow capped mountains to the south of our westerly course. The low mountains as those seen in the northwest direction is the same place now crossed by the Southern Pacific Railroad, and known as the Tehachipi pass, the noted loop, in which the railroad crosses itself, being on the west slope and Ft. Tejon being on the same range a little further south where the Sierra Nevada mountains and the Coast Range join. The first mountain bearing snow, south of our course was probably what is known as Wilson's peak, and the high mountains still farther south, the San Bernardino mountains. There were no names there known to us nor did we know anything of the topography of the country except that we supposed a range of mountains was all that separated us from California.

We were yet in the desert, and if we kept our due west course, we must cross some of the snow before us which if steep gave us some doubts whether we could get through or not.

We did not know exactly what the people left behind would do if we were gone longer than we intended, but if they started on it was quite plain to us they would be lost, and as seven days had already passed we were in serious trouble for fear we could not complete the trip in the time allotted to us. We surveyed the plain and mountains to learn its situation and then started, on following our trail. As we went on we seemed to be coming to lower ground, and near our road stood a tree of a kind we had not seen before. The trunk was about six or eight inches through and six or eight feet high with arms at the top quite as large as the body, and at the end of the arms a bunch of long, stiff bayonet shaped leaves.

It was a brave little tree to live in such a barren country. As we walked on these trees were more plenty and some were much larger than the first. As we came to the lowest part of the valley there seemed to be little faint water ways running around little clouds of stunted shrubs, but there was no signs that very much water ever run in them. We thought that these were the outlet of the big sandy lake which might get full of water and overflow through these channels after some great storm.

As this low ground was quite wide we lost our trail in crossing it, and we separated as we went along, looking to find it again, till nearly dark when we looked for a camping place. Fortunately we found a little pond of rain water, and some of our strange trees that were dead gave us good material for a fire, so that we were very comfortable indeed, having both drink and fire.

Starting on again our course was now ascending slightly, and we came across more and more of the trees, and larger ones than at first. We saw some that seemed to have broken down with their own weight. The bayonet shaped leaves seemed to fall off when old and the stalk looked so much like an old overgrown cabbage stump that we name them "Cabbage trees," but afterward learned they were a species of Yucca. We were much worried at losing our trail and felt that it would be quite unsafe to try to cross the mountain without finding it again, so we separated, Rogers going northwest, and I southwest, agreeing to swing round so as to meet again about noon, but when we met, neither of us had found a trail, and we were still about 10 miles from the foothills. Rogers said he had heard some of the people say that the trail leading from Salt Lake to Los Angeles crossed such a mountain in a low pass, with very high mountains on each side, and he supposed that the high mountain to the south must be the one where the trail crossed, but as this would take us fully fifty miles south of our course as we supposed it was we hesitated about going there, and concluded we would try the lowest place in the mountain first, and if we failed we could then go and try Roger's route, more to the south.

So we pushed on, still keeping a distance apart to look out for the trail, and before night, in the rolling hills, we saw here and there faint traces of it, which grew plainer as we went along, and about sundown we reached some water holes and from some old skulls of oxen lying around the ground showing that it had at some previous time been a camping ground. We found some good large sage brush which made a pretty good fire, and if we could have had a little fresh meat to roast we thought we were in a good position for supper. But that poor meat was pretty dry food. However it kept us alive, and we curled up together and slept, for the night was cool, and we had to make the little blanket do its best. We thought we ought to find a little game, but we had not seen any to shoot since we started.

In the morning the trail led us toward the snow, and as we went along, a brave old crow surprised us by lighting on a bush near the trail, and we surprised him by killing him with a charge of shot. "Here's your fresh meat," said Rogers as he put it into his knapsack to cook for supper, and marched on. As we approached the summit we could see, on the high mountains south of us, some trees, and when we came near the highest part of our road there were some juniper trees near it, which was very encouraging. We crossed over several miles of hard snow, but it moistened up our moccasins and made them soft and uncomfortable. After we had turned down the western slope we killed a small hawk. "Here's your meat" said I, as the poor thin fellow was stowed away for future grub, to cook with the crow.

When we got out of the snow we had lost the trail again but the hills on the sides were covered with large brush, and on a higher part of the mountain south, were some big trees, and we began to think the country would change for the better pretty soon. We followed down the ravine for many miles, and when this came out into a larger one, we were greatly pleased at the prospect, for down the latter came a beautiful little running brook of clear pure water, singing as it danced over the stones, a happy song and telling us to drink and drink again, and you may be sure we did drink, for it had been months and months since we had had such water, pure, sweet, free from the terrible alkali and stagnant taste that had been in almost every drop we had seen. Rogers leveled his shot gun at some birds and killed a beautiful one with a top knot on his head, and colors bright all down his neck. It was a California quail. We said birds always lived where human beings did, and we had great hopes born to us of a better land. I told John that if the folks were only there now I could kill game enough for them.

We dressed our three birds and got them boiling in the camp kettle, and while they were cooking talked over the outlook which was so flattering that our tongues got loose and we rattled away in strange contrast to the ominous silence of a week ago. While eating our stew of crow and hawk, we could see willows alders and big sage brush around and we had noticed what seemed to be cottonwoods farther down the cañon, and green trees on the slope of the mountain. We were sure we were on the edge of the promised land and were quite light hearted, till we began to tell of plans to get the good people out who were waiting for us beside the little spring in the desert. We talked of going back at once, but our meat was too near gone, and we must take them something to encourage them a little and make them strong for the fearful trip. As to these birds—the quail was as superb a morsel as ever a man did eat; the hawk was pretty fair and quite good eating; but that abominable crow! His flesh was about as black as his feathers and full of tough and bony sinews. We concluded we did not want any more of that kind of bird, and ever since that day, when I have heard people talk of "eating crow" as a bitter pill, I think I know all about it from experience.

There seemed to be no other way for us but to push on in the morning and try to obtain some relief for the poor women and children and then get back to them as fast as ever we could, so we shouldered our packs and went on down the cañon as fast as we could. We came soon to evergreen oaks and tall cottonwoods, and the creek bottom widened out to two hundred yards. There were trees on the south side and the brush kept getting larger and larger. There was a trail down this cañon, but as it passed under fallen trees we knew it could not have been the same one we had been following on the other side of the summit, and when we discovered a bear track in a soft place we knew very well it was not a trail intended for human beings, and we might be ordered out almost any moment.

On the high bold grassy point about four hundred yards we saw two horses that held their heads aloft and gave a snort, then galloped away out of sight. About 10 o'clock I felt a sudden pain in my left knee, keen and sharp, and as we went along it kept growing worse. I had to stop often to rest, and it was quite plain that if this increased or continued I was sure enough disabled, and would be kept from helping those whom we had left. Nerved with the idea we must get help to them, and that right soon, I hobbled along as well as I could, but soon had to say to Rogers that he had better go on ahead and get help and let me come on as best I could, for every moment of delay was a danger of death to our party who trusted us to get them help. Rogers refused to do this, he said he would stay with me and see me out, and that he could not do much alone, and had better wait till I got better. So we worked along through the tangled brush, being many times compelled to wade the stream to get along, and this made our moccasins soft and very uncomfortable to wear. I endured the pain all day, and we must have advanced quite a little distance in spite of my lameness, but I was glad when night came and we camped in the dark brushy cañon, having a big fire which made me quite comfortable all night, though it was quite cold, and we had to keep close together so as to use the blanket. I felt a little better in the morning and after eating some of our poor dried meat, which was about as poor as crow, and I don't know but a little worse, we continued on our way.

The tangle got worse and worse as we descended, and at times we walked in the bed of the stream in order to make more headway, but my lameness increased and we had to go very slow indeed. About noon we came to what looked like an excavation, a hole four feet square or more it looked to be, and on the dirt thrown out some cottonwood trees had grown, and one of the largest of these had been cut down sometime before. This was the first sign of white men we had seen and it was evidently an attempt at mining, no one knows how long ago. It encouraged us at any rate, and we pushed on through brush and briers, tangles of wild rose bushes and bushes of every sort, till all of a sudden we came out into an open sandy valley, well covered with sage brush and perhaps a hundred yards wide; probably more.

The hills on the south side had on them some oak trees and grassy spots, but the north side was thickly covered with brush. Our beautiful little brook that had kept us company soon sank into the dry sand out of sight, and we moved rather slowly along every little while we spoke of the chances of wagons ever getting through the road we had come, and the hope that my lameness might not continue to retard our progress in getting back to the place of our starting, that the poor waiting people might begin to get out of the terrible country they were in and enjoy as we had done, the beautiful running stream of this side of the mountain. If I did not get better the chances were that they would perish, for they never could come through alone, as the distance had proved much greater than we had anticipated, and long dry stretches of the desert were more than they would be prepared for. As it was we feared greatly that we had consumed so much time they would get impatient and start out and be lost.

I continued to hobble along down the barren valley as well as I could and here and there some tracks of animals were discovered, but we could not make out whether they were those of domestic cattle or elk. Soon, on the side of a hill, rather high up a pack of prairie wolves were snarling around the carcass of some dead animal, and this was regarded as another sign that more and better meat could be found, for these animals only live where some sort of game can be found, and they knew better than we that it was not for their health to go into the barren desert.

Before us now was a spur from the hills that reached nearly across our little valley and shut out further sight in that direction and when we came to it we climbed up over it to shorten the distance. When the summit was reached a most pleasing sight filled our sick hearts with a most indescribable joy. I shall never have the ability to adequately describe the beauty of the scene as it appeared to us, and so long as I live that landscape will be impressed upon the canvas of my memory as the most cheering in the world. There before us was a beautiful meadow of a thousand acres, green as a thick carpet of grass could make it, and shaded with oaks, wide branching and symmetrical, equal to those of an old English park, while all over the low mountains that bordered it on the south and over the broad acres of luxuriant grass was a herd of cattle numbering many hundreds if not thousands. They were of all colors shades and sizes.

Some were calmly lying down in happy rumination, others rapidly cropping the sweet grass, while the gay calves worked off their superfluous life and spirit in vigorous exercise or drew rich nourishment in the abundant mother's milk. All seemed happy and content, and such a scene of abundance and rich plenty and comfort bursting thus upon our eyes which for months had seen only the desolation and sadness of the desert, was like getting a glimpse of Paradise, and tears of joy ran down our faces. If ever a poor mortal escapes from this world where so many trials come, and joys of a happy Heaven are opened up to him, the change cannot be much more that this which was suddenly opened to us on that bright day which was either one of the very last of December 1849 or the first of January 1850, I am inclined to think it was the very day of the new year, but in our troubles, the accuracy of the calendar was among the least of our troubles. If it was, as I believe the beginning of the year, it was certainly a most auspicious one and one of the most hopeful of my life.

And *now if the others were only here*, was the burden of our thought, and a serious awakening from the dream of beauty and rich plenty spread out before us. This ring-streaked and speckled herd might be descended directly from Jacob's famous herd, blessed of the Lord, and while we could not keep our thoughts from some sad doubts as to the fate of those whom we had left behind, we tried to be generally hopeful and courageous and brightened up our steps to prepare for a relief and return to the hot dry plain beyond the mountains where they were awaiting us, no doubt with much tribulation.

I now thought of myself and my failing knee and we sat down under the shade of an oak to rest, and after a little, better feeling seemed to come. Down by a deep gully cut by the rains a yearling steer was feeding, and I took the rifle and crawled down near him and put first one ball through him, and then another, before he fell dead on the other side of the wash, when we sprang with all the agility of a deer. We quickly got some good meat and had it roasted and eaten almost quicker than can be told. We hardly realized how near starved we were till we had plenty before us again. We ate till we were satisfied for once, and for the first time in many long dreary weeks. We kindled a fire and commenced drying the meat, one sleeping while the other kept the fire, and changing off every few hours. What a rest that was! One who has never been nearly worn out and starved, down nearly to the point of death can never know what it is to rest in comfort. No one can tell. It was like a dream, a sweet, restful dream where troubles would drown themselves in sleep. How we felt the strength come back to us with that food and the long draughts of pure clear water.

The miserable dried meat in our knapsacks was put away and this splendid jerked beef put in its place. The wolves came to our camp and howled in dreadful disappointment at not getting a meal. Rogers wanted me to shoot the miserable howlers, but I let them have their concert out, and thought going without their breakfast must be punishment enough for them. As our moccasins were worn out we carefully prepared some sinews from the steer and made new foot gear from the green hide which placed us in shape for two or three week's walking.

The morning was clear and pleasant. We had our knapsacks filled with good food we had prepared, and were enjoying the cool breeze which came up the valley, when we heard faintly the bark of a dog, or at least we thought we did. If this were true there must be some one living not very far away and we felt better. I was still very lame and as we started along the walking seemed to make it worse again, so that it was all I could do to follow John on the trail down the valley. As we went along a man and woman passed us some distance on the left, and they did not seem to notice us, though we were in plain sight. They were curiously dressed. The woman had no hoops nor shoes, and a shawl wound about her neck and one end thrown over her head, was a substitute bonnet. The man had sandals on his feet, with white cotton pants, a calico shirt, and a wide rimmed, comical, snuff-colored hat. We at once put them down as Spaniards, or then descendants of Mexico, and if what we had read about them in books was true, we were in a set of land pirates, and blood thirsty men whom we might have occasion to be aware of. We had never heard a word of Spanish spoken, except perhaps a word or two upon the plains which some fellow knew, and how we could make ourselves known and explain who we were was a puzzle to us.

Difficulties began to arise in our minds now we were in an apparent land of plenty, but in spite of all we went along as fast as my lame knee would permit me to do. A house on higher ground soon appeared in sight. It was low, of one story with a flat roof, gray in color, and of a different style of architecture from any we had ever seen before. There was no fence around it, and no animals or wagons in sight, nor person to be seen. As we walked up the hill toward it I told John our moccasins made of green hide would betray us as having recently killed an animal, and as these people might be the owners and detain us by having us arrested for the crime, and this would be especially bad for us just now. We determined to face the people, and let the fact of our close necessities be a sufficient excuse for us, if we could make them understand our circumstances.

As we came near the house no person was seen, but a mule tied to a post told us there was some one about, and a man soon made an appearance, dressed about the same style as the one we had passed a short time before. As we came near we saluted him, bidding him good morning, and he in turn touched his hat politely, saying something in reply which we were not able to understand. I showed him that I was lame, and taking out some money pointed to the mule, but he only shook his head and said something I could not comprehend. Rogers now began looking around the house, which was built of sun-dried bricks about one by two feet in size, and one end was used as a storehouse. As he looked in, a man came to him and wanted a black, patent leather belt which Rogers wore, having a watch-pocket attached to it. He offered a quart or more of coarse corn meal, and Rogers made the trade.

We tried to inquire where we were or where ought to go, but could get no satisfactory answer from the man, although when we spoke San Francisco he pointed to the north. This was not very satisfactory to us and we seemed as badly lost as ever, and where or which way to go we did not seem very successful in finding out. So we concluded to go on a little way at least, and I hobbled off in the direction he pointed, which was down the hill and past a small, poorly fenced field which was sometimes cultivated, and across the stream which followed down the valley. Passing on a mile or two we stopped on a big patch of sand to rest.

I told Rogers I did not think this course would lead us to any place in a month, and just now a delay was ruinous to us and to those who were waiting for us, and it would not do for us to go off to the north to find a settlement. While I was expressing my opinion on matters and things, Rogers had wet up a part of his meal with water and put it to bake on the cover of his camp kettle. There was a fair sized cake for each of us, and it was the first bread of any kind we had eaten for months, being a very acceptable change from an exclusively meat diet. Looking up the valley we could see a cloud of dust, thick and high, and soon several men on horseback who came at a rushing gallop. I told Rogers they were after us, and believed them to be a murderous set who might make trouble for us. I hastily buried our little store of money in the sand, telling him that if they got us, they would not get our money. Putting our guns across our laps in an easy position we had them cocked and ready for business, and our knives where we could get them handy, and awaited their arrival.

They came on with a rush until within a short distance and halted for consultation just across the creek, after which one of them advanced toward us and as he came near us we could see he was a white man, who wished us good evening in our own language. We answered him rather cooly, still sitting in the sand and he no doubt saw that we were a little suspicious of the crowd. He asked us where we were from, and we told him our circumstances and condition and that we would like to secure some means of relief for the people we had left in the desert, but our means were very limited and we wanted to do the best we could. He said we were about 500 miles from San Francisco, not far from 100 miles from the coast and thirty miles from Los Angeles. We were much afraid we would not be able to get anything here, but he told us to go across the valley to a large live oak tree which he pointed out, and said we would find an American there, and we should wait there till morning. He said he would go back and stay at the house we had passed, and would do what he could to assist us to go to Los Angeles where we could get some supplies. Then he rode away, and as we talked it over we saw no way but to follow the directions of our newfound friend.

It seemed now that my lameness had indeed been a blessing. If I had been able to walk we would now have been well on toward the seashore, where we could have found no such friend as this who had appeared to us. The way seemed clearer to us, but the time for our return was almost up and there was no way of getting back in fifteen days as we had agreed upon, so there was great danger to our people yet. It seemed very likely to take us twenty four or thirty days at best, and while they probably had oxen enough to provide them food for so long a time they might take a notion to move on, which would be fatal.

At the big live oak tree we found an American camper, who was on his way to the gold mines. He was going a new route and said the mines could be reached much quicker than by going up the coast by way of San Francisco. A new company with wagons was soon to start out to break the road, and when they crossed the east end of the valley he would follow them. I think this man's name was Springer. He had come by way of the Santa Fe route, and the people of Los Angeles had told him this route was an easy one being often traveled by saddle horses, and if the company could make it possible for wagons they could have all the cattle they wanted to kill along the road as their pay for doing the work. Our new friend lay down early, and as he saw we were scant in blankets he brought some to us for our use, which were most thankfully received.

As soon as we were alone Rogers mixed up some more of the meal which we baked in our friend's frying pan, and we baked and ate and baked and ate again, for our appetites were ravenous, and the demand of our stomachs got the better of the judgment of our brains.

It was hard to find time to sleep, we were so full of the plans about the way, which we must manage to get relief for the people. We had many doubts if animals could ever come over the route we had come over, from deliberation we decided that by selecting a route with that idea in our minds, we could get mules and perhaps horses over the country. We perhaps could go more to the north and take the Jayhawkers trail, but this would take us fully a hundred miles farther and four or five days longer, at the best, and every moment of delay was to be carefully avoided as a moment of danger to our friends.

Thus again, our sleep was troubled from another cause. Being so long unaccustomed to vegetable food, and helped on, no doubt, by our poor judgment in gauging the quantity of our food, we were attacked by severe pains in the stomach and bowels, from which we suffered intensely. We arose very early and with a very light breakfast, for the sickness admonished us, we started back for the house we had first passed, at which our friend on horseback, said he would spend the night and where we were to meet him this morning. He said he could talk Spanish all right and would do all he could to help us.

Our suffering and trouble caused us to move very slowly, so that it was nine or ten o'clock before we reached the house, and we found they had two horses all ready for us to go to Los Angeles. There were no saddles for us, but we thought this would be a good way to cure my lameness. The people seemed to be friends to us in every way. We mounted, having our packs on our backs, and our guns before us, and with a friendly parting to the people who did not go, all four of us started on a trip of thirty miles to the town of Los Angeles.

When we reached the foot of the mountain which was very steep but not rocky, John and I dismounted and led our animals to the top, where we could see a long way west, and south, and it looked supremely beautiful. We could not help comparing it to the long wide, desert we had crossed, and John and myself said many times how we wished the folks were here to enjoy the pleasant sight, the beautiful fertile picture.

There appeared to be one quite large house in sight, and not far off, which the man told us was the Mission of San Fernando, a Roman Catholic Church and residence for priests and followers. The downward slope of the mountain was as steep as the other side and larger, and John and I did not attempt to mount till we were well down on the level ground again, but the other two men rode up and down without any trouble. We would let our leaders get half a mile or so ahead of us and then mount and put our horses to a gallop till we overtook them again. We had walked so long that riding was very tiresome to us, and for comfort alone we would have preferred the way on foot, but we could get along a little faster, and the frequent dismounting kept us from becoming too lame from riding.

We passed the Mission about noon or a little after, and a few miles beyond met a man on horseback who lived up to the north about a hundred miles. His name was French and he had a cattle range at a place called Tejon (Tahone). Our friends told him who we were, and what assistance we needed. Mr. French said he was well acquainted in Los Angeles and had been there some time, and that all the travelers who would take the Coast route had gone, those who had come by way of Salt

Lake had got in from two to four weeks before, and a small train which had come the Santa Fe Route was still upon the road. He said Los Angeles was so clear of emigrants that he did not think we could get any help there at the present time.

"Now," said Mr. French—"You boys can't talk Spanish and it is not very likely you will be able to get any help. Now I say, you boys turn back and go with me and I will give you the best I have, I will let you have a yoke of gentle oxen, or more if you need them, and plenty of beans, which are good food for I live on them; besides this I can give an Indian guide to help you back. Will that do?" After a moment we said we doubted if oxen could be got over the road, and if they were fat now they would soon get poor, and perhaps not stand it as well as the oxen which had became used to that kind of life, and of those they had in camp all they needed. We wanted to get something for the women and children to ride, for we knew they must abandon the wagons, and could not walk so far over that dry, rough country. "Well," said Mr. French:—"I will stop at the place you were this morning—I know them well—and they are good folks, and I am sure when I tell them what you want they will help you if they possibly can. This looks to me to be the most sensible course." After talking an hour our two companions advised us that the proposition of Mr. French seemed the most reasonable one that appeared. But for us to go clear back to his range would take up so much valuable time that we were almost afraid of the delay which might mean the destruction of our friends. French said he had a pack saddle, with him taking it home, and we could put it on one of our horses, and when we came back to Los Angeles could leave it at a certain saloon or place he named and tell them it belonged to him and to keep it for him. I have forgotten the name of the man who kept the saloon. We agreed to this, and bidding our two companions farewell, we turned back again with Mr. French.

When night came we were again at the Mission we had passed on the way down. We were kindly treated here, for I believe Mr. French told them about us. They sent an Indian to take our horses, and we sat down beside the great house. There were many smaller houses, and quite a large piece of ground fenced in by an adobe wall. The roof of the buildings was like that of our own buildings in having eaves on both sides, but the covering was of semi circular tiles made and burned like brick. Rows of these were placed close together, the hollow sides up, and then another course over the joints, placed with the round side up, which made a roof that was perfectly waterproof, but must have been very heavy. These tiles were about two feet long. All the surroundings, and general make up of the place were new to us and very wonderful. They gave us good dried meat to eat and let us sleep in the big house on the floor, which was as hard as granite, and we turned over a great many times before daylight, and were glad when morning came. We offered to pay them, but they would take nothing from us, and we left leading our horses over the steep mountain, and reaching the house again late in the day. They turned our horses loose and seemed disposed to be very friendly and disposed to do for us what they could.

We were very tired and sat down by the side of the house and rested, wondering how we would come out with our preparations. They were talking together, but we could not understand a word. A dark woman came out and gave each of us a piece of cooked squash. It seemed to have been roasted in the ashes and was very sweet and good. These were all signs of friendship and we were glad of the good feeling. We were given a place to sleep in the house, in a store room on a floor which was not soft. This was the second house we had slept in since leaving Wisconsin, and it seemed rather pent-up to us.

In the morning we were shown a kind of mill like a coffee mill, and by putting in a handful of wheat from a pile and giving the mill a few turns we were given to understand we should grind some flour for ourselves. We went to work with a will, but found it hard, slow work.

After a little, our dark woman came and gave us each a pancake and a piece of meat, also another piece of roasted squash, for our breakfast, and this, we thought, was the best meal we had ever eaten. The lady tried to talk to us but we could not understand the words, and I could convey ideas to her better by the sign language than any other way. She pointed out the way from which we came and wanted to know how many day's travel it might be away, and I answered by putting my hand to my head and closing my eyes, which was repeated as many times as there had been nights on our journey, at which she was much surprised that the folks were so far away. She then placed her hand upon her breast and then held it up, to ask how many women there were, and I answered her by holding up three fingers, at which she shrugged her shoulders and shook her head. Then pointing to a child by her side, four or five years old, and in the same way asked how many children, I answered by holding up four fingers, and she almost cried, opening her mouth in great surprise, and turned away.

I said to Rogers that she was a kind, well meaning woman, and that Mr. French had no doubt told her something of our story. Aside from her dark complexion her features reminded me of my mother, and at first sight of her I thought of the best woman on earth my own far off mother, who little knew the hardships we had endured. We went to work again at the mill and after a while the woman came again and tried to talk and to teach us some words of her own language. She place her finger on me and said *ombre* and I took out my little book and wrote down *ombre* as meaning man, and in the same way she taught me that *mujer*, was woman; *trigo*, wheat; *frijoles*, beans; *carne*, meat; *calazasa*, pumpkin; *caballo*, horse; *vaca*, cow; *muchacho*, boy, and several other words in this way.

I got hold of many words thus to study, so that if I ever came back I could talk a little and make myself understood as to some of the common objects and things of necessary use. Such friendly, human acts shown to us strangers, were evidences of the kindest disposition. I shall never forget the kindness of those original Californians. When in Walker's camp and finding he was friendly to Mormonism we could claim that we were also Mormons, but the good people though well known Catholics, did not so much as mention the fact nor inquire whether we favored that sect or not. We were human beings in distress and we represented others who were worse even than we, and those kind acts and great good will, were given freely because we were fellow human beings.

The provisions we prepared were, a sack of small yellow beans, a small sack of wheat, a quantity of good dried meat, and some of the coarse, unbolted flour we had made at the mills. They showed us how to properly pack the horse, which was a kind of work we had not been used to, and we were soon ready for a start. I took what money we had and put it on a block, making signs for them to take what the things were worth. They took $30, and we were quite surprised to get two horses, provisions, pack-saddles and ropes, some of the latter made of rawhide and some of hair, so cheaply, but we afterward learned that the mares furnished were not considered of much value, and we had really paid a good fair price for everything. To make it easy for us they had also fixed our knapsacks on the horses.

The good lady with the child, came out with four oranges and pointed to her own child and then to the East, put them in the pack meaning we should carry them to the children. With a hearty good bye from them, and a polite lifting of our hats to them we started on our return, down toward the gentle decline of the creek bottom, and then up the valley, the way we came. Toward night we came to a wagon road crossing the valley, and as we well knew we could not go up the tangled creek bed with horses we took this road to the north, which took a dry ravine for its direction, and in which there was a pack trail, and this the wagons were following. We kept on the trail for a few miles, and overtook them in their camp, and camped with them over night. We told them we considered our out-fit entirely too small for the purpose intended, which was to bring two women and four children out of the desert, but that being the best we could get, we were taking this help to them and hoped to save their lives. Our mission became well known and one man offered to sell us a poor little one-eyed mule, its back all bare of covering from the effect of a great saddle sore that had very recently healed. He had picked it up somewhere in Arizona where it had been turned out to die, but it seemed the beast had enough of the good Santa Ana stock in it to bring it through and it had no notion of dying at the present time, though it was scarcely more than a good fair skeleton, even then. The beast became mine at the price of $15, and the people expressed great sympathy with us and the dear friends we were going to try to save.

Another man offered a little snow-white mare, as fat as butter, for $15, which I paid, though it took the last cent of money I had. This little beauty of a beast was broken to lead at halter, but had not been broken in any other way. Rogers said he would ride her where he could, and before she got to the wagons she would be as gentle as a lamb. He got a bridle and tried her at once, and then there was a scene of rearing, jumping and kicking that would have made a good Buffalo Bill circus in these days. No use, the man could not be thrown off, and the crowd cheered and shouted to Rogers to—"Hold her level."

After some bucking and backing on the part of the mare and a good deal of whipping and kicking on the part of the man, and a good many furious clashes in lively, but very awkward ways, the little beast yielded the point, and carried her load without further trouble.

The people gave us a good supper and breakfast, and one man came and presented us with 25 pounds of unbolted wheat flour. They were of great assistance to us in showing us how to pack and sack our load, which was not heavy and could be easily carried by our two animals which we had at first. However we arranged a pack on the mule and this gave me a horse to ride and a mule to lead, while Rogers rode his milk-white steed and led the other horse. Thus we went along and following the trail soon reached the summit from which we could see off to the East a wonderful distance, probably 200 miles, of the dry and barren desert of hill and desolate valley over which we had come.

The trail bearing still to the north from this point, we left and turned due east across the country, and soon came to a beautiful lake of sweet fresh water situated well up toward the top of the mountain. This lake is now called Elizabeth Lake. Here we watered our animals and filled our canteens, then steered a little south of east among the Cabbage trees, aiming to strike the rain water hole where we had camped as we came over. We reached the water hole about noon and here found the Jayhawkers trail, which we took. They had evidently followed us and passed down the same brushy cañon while we having taken a circuitous route to the north, had gone around there. Getting water here for ourselves and horses, we went back to the trail and pushed on as fast as the animals could walk, and as we now knew where we could get water, we kept on till after dark, one of us walking to keep the trail, and some time in the night reached the Willow corral I have spoken of before. There was good water here, but the Jayhawker's oxen had eaten all the grass that grew in the little moist place around, and our animals were short of feed. One of us agreed to stand guard the fore part of the night and the other later, so that we might not be surprised by Indians and lose our animals. I took the first watch and let the blaze of the fire go out so as not to attract attention and as I sat by the dull coals and hot ashes I fell asleep. Rogers happened to wake and see the situation, and arose and waked me again saying that we must be more careful or the Indians would get our horses. You may be sure I kept awake the rest of my watch.

Next day we passed the water holes at the place where we had so stealthily crawled up to Doty's camp when coming out. These holes held about two pails of water each, but no stream run away from them. Our horses seemed to want water badly for when they drank they put their head in up to their eyes and drank ravenously.

Thirty miles from here to the next water, Doty had told us, and night overtook us before we could reach it, so a dry camp was made. Our horses began now to walk with drooping heads and slow, tired steps, so we divided the load among them all and walked ourselves. The water, when reached proved so salt the horses would not drink it, and as Doty had told us the most water was over the mountain ahead of us, we still followed their trail which went up a very rocky cañon in which it was hard work for the horses to travel. The horses were all very gentle now and needed some urging to make them go. Roger's fat horse no longer tried to unseat its rider or its pack, but seemed to be the most downhearted of the train. The little mule was the liveliest, sharpest witted animal of the whole. She had probably traveled on the desert before and knew better how to get along. She had learned to crop every spear of grass she came to, and every bit of sage brush that offered a green leaf was given a nip. She would sometimes leave the trail and go out to one side to get a little bunch of dry grass, and come back and take her place again as if she knew her duty. The other animals never tried to do this. The mule was evidently better versed in the art of getting a living than the horses.

Above the rough bed of the cañon the bottom was gravelly and narrow, and the walls on each side nearly perpendicular. Our horses now poked slowly along and as we passed the steep wall of the cañon the white animal left the trail and walked with full force, head first, against the solid rock. She seemed to be blind, and though we went quickly to her and took off the load she carried, she had stopped breathing by the time we had it done. Not knowing how far it was to water, nor how soon some of our other horses might fall, we did not tarry, but pushed on as well as we could, finding no water. We reached the summit and turned down a ravine, following the trail, and about dark came to the water they had told us about, a faint running stream which came out of a rocky ravine and sank almost immediately in the dry sand. There was water enough for us, but no grass. It seemed as if the horses were not strong enough to carry a load, and as we wanted to get them through if possible, we concluded to bury the wheat and get it on our return. We dug a hole and lined it with fine sticks, then put in the little bag and covered it with dry brush, and sand making the surface as smooth as if it had never been touched, then made our bed on it. The whole work was done after dark so the deposit could not be seen by the red men and we thought we had done it pretty carefully.

Next morning the little mule carried all the remaining load, the horses bearing only their saddles, and seemed hardly strong enough for that. There was now seven or eight miles of clean loose sand to go over, across a little valley which came to an end about ten miles north of us, and extended south to the lake where we went for water on our outward journey and found it red alkali. Near the Eastern edge of the valley we turned aside to visit the grave of Mr. Isham, which they had told us of. They had covered his remains with their hands as best they could, piling up a little mound of sand over it. Our next camp was to be on the summit of the range just before us, and we passed the dead body of Mr. Fish, we had seen before, and go on a little to a level sandy spot in the ravine just large enough to sleep on. This whole range is a black mass rocky piece of earth, so barren that not a spear of grass can grow, and not a drop of water in any place. We tied our horses to rocks and there they staid all night, for if turned loose there was not a mouthful of food for them to get.

In the morning an important question was to be decided, and that was whether we should continue to follow the Jayhawker's trail which led far to the north to cross the mountain, which stood before us, a mass of piled-up rocks so steep that it seemed as if a dog could hardly climb it. Our wagons were nearly due east from this point over the range, and not more than fifty miles away, while to go around to the north was fully a hundred miles, and would take us four or five days to make. As we had already gone so long we expected to meet them any day trying to get out, and if we went around we might miss them. They might have all been killed by Indians or they might have already gone. We had great fears on their account. If they had gone north they might have perished in the snow.

The range was before us, and we must get to the other side in some way. We could see the range for a hundred miles to the north and along the base some lakes of water that must be salt. To the south it got some lower, but very barren and ending in black, dry buttes. The horses must have food and water by night or we must leave them to die, and all things considered it seemed to be the quickest way to camp to try and get up a rough looking cañon which was nearly opposite us on the other side. So we loaded the mule and made our way down the rocky road to the ridge, and then left the Jayhawker's trail, taking our course more south so as to get around a salt lake which lay directly before us. On our way we had to go close to a steep bluff, and cross a piece of ground that looked like a well dried mortar bed, hard and smooth as ice, and thus got around the head of a small stream of clear water, salt as brine. We now went directly to the mouth of the cañon we had decided to take, and traveled up its gravelly bed. The horses now had to be urged along constantly to keep them moving and they held their heads low down as they crept along seemingly so discouraged that they would much rather lie down and rest forever than take another step. We knew they would do this soon in spite of all our urging, if we could not get water for them. The cañon was rough enough where we entered it, and a heavy up grade too, and this grew more and more difficult as we advanced, and the rough yellowish, rocky walls closed in nearer and nearer together as we ascended.

A perpendicular wall, or rather rise, in the rocks was approached, and there was a great difficulty to persuade the horses to take exertion to get up and over the small obstruction, but the little mule skipped over as nimbly as a well-fed goat, and rather seemed to enjoy a little variety in the proceedings. After some coaxing and urging the horses took courage to try the extra step and succeeded all right, when we all moved on again, over a path that grew more and more narrow, more and more rocky under foot at every moment. We wound around among and between the great rocks, and had not advanced very far before another obstruction, that would have been a fall of about three feet had water been flowing in the cañon, opposed our way. A small pile of lone rocks enabled the mule to go over all right, and she went on looking for every spear of grass, and smelling eagerly for water, but all our efforts were not enough to get the horses along another foot. It was getting nearly night and every minute without water seemed an age. We had to leave the horses and go on. We had deemed them indispensable to us, or rather to the extrication of the women and children, and yet the hope came to us that the oxen might help some of them out as a last resort. We were sure the wagons must be abandoned, and such a thing as women riding on the backs of oxen we had never seen, still it occurred to us as not impossible and although leaving the horses here was like deciding to abandon all for the feeble ones, we saw we must do it, and the new hope arose to sustain us for farther effort. We removed the saddles and placed them on a rock, and after a few moments hesitation, moments in which were crowded torrents of wild ideas, and desperate thoughts, that were enough to drive reason from its throne, we left the poor animals to their fate and moved along. Just as we were passing out of sight the poor creatures neighed pitifully after us, and one who has never heard the last despairing, pleading neigh of a horse left to die can form no idea of its almost human appeal. We both burst into tears, but it was no use, to try to save them we must run the danger of sacrificing ourselves, and the little party we were trying so hard to save.

We found the little mule stopped by a still higher precipice or perpendicular rise of fully ten feet. Our hearts sank within us and we said that we should return to our friends as we went away, with our knapsacks on our backs, and the hope grew very small. The little mule was nipping some stray blades of grass and as we came in sight she looked around to us and then up the steep rocks before her with such a knowing, intelligent look of confidence, that it gave us new courage. It was a strange wild place. The north wall of the cañon leaned far over the channel, overhanging considerably, while the south wall sloped back about the same, making the wall nearly parallel, and like a huge crevice descending into the mountain from above in a sloping direction.

We decided to try to get the confident little mule over this obstruction. Gathering all the loose rocks we could we piled them up against the south wall, beginning some distance below, putting up all those in the bed of the stream and throwing down others from narrow shelves above we built a sort of inclined plane along the walls gradually rising till we were nearly as high as the crest of the fall. Here was a narrow shelf scarcely four inches wide and a space of from twelve to fifteen feet to cross to reach the level of the crest. It was all I could do to cross this space, and there was no foundation to enable us to widen it so as to make a path for an animal. It was forlorn hope but we made the most of it. We unpacked the mule and getting all our ropes together, made a leading line of it. Then we loosened and threw down all the projecting points of rocks we could above the narrow shelf, and every piece that was likely to come loose in the shelf itself. We fastened the leading line to her and with one above and one below we thought we could help her to keep her balance, and if she did not make a misstep on that narrow way she might get over safely. Without a moment's hesitation the brave animal tried the pass. Carefully and steadily she went along, selecting a place before putting down a foot, and when she came to the narrow ledge leaned gently on the rope, never making a sudden start or jump, but cautiously as a cat moved slowly along. There was now no turning back for her. She must cross this narrow place over which I had to creep on hands and knees, or be dashed down fifty feet to a certain death. When the worst place was reached she stopped and hesitated, looking back as well as she could. I was ahead with the rope, and I called encouragingly to her and talked to her a little. Rogers wanted to get all ready and he said, "holler" at her as loud as he could and frighten her across, but I thought the best way to talk to her gently and let her move steadily.

I tell you, friends, it was a trying moment. It seemed to be weighed down with all the trials and hardships of many months. It seemed to be the time when helpless women and innocent children hung on the trembling balance between life and death. Our own lives we could save by going back, and sometimes it seemed as if we would perhaps save ourselves the additional sorrow of finding them all dead to do so at once. I was so nearly in despair that I could not help bursting in tears, and I was not ashamed of the weakness. Finally Rogers said, "Come Lewis" and I gently pulled the rope, calling the little animal, to make a trial. She smelled all around and looked over every inch of the strong ledge, then took one careful step after another over the dangerous place. Looking back I saw Rogers with a very large stone in his hand, ready to "holler" and perhaps kill the poor beast if she stopped. But she crept along trusting to the rope to balance, till she was half way across, then another step or two, when calculating the distance closely she made a spring and landed on a smooth bit of sloping rock below, that led up to the highest crest of the precipice, and safely climbed to the top, safe and sound above the falls. The mule had no shoes and it was wonderful how her little hoofs clung to the smooth rock. We felt relieved. We would push on and carry food to the people; we would get them through some way; there could be no more hopeless moment than the one just past, and we would save them all.

It was the work of a little while to transfer the load up the precipice, and pack the mule again, when we proceeded. Around behind some rocks only a little distance beyond this place we found a small willow bush and enough good water for a camp. This was a strange cañon. The sun never shown down to the bottom in the fearful place where the little mule climbed up, and the rocks had a peculiar yellow color. In getting our provisions up the precipice, Rogers went below and fastened the rope while I pulled them up. Rogers wished many times we had the horses up safely where the mule was, but a dog could hardly cross the narrow path and there was no hope. Poor brutes, they had been faithful servants, and we felt sorrowful enough at their terrible fate.

We had walked two days without water, and we were wonderfully refreshed as we found it here. The way up this cañon was very rough and the bed full of sharp broken rocks in loose pieces which cut through the bottoms of our moccasins and left us with bare feet upon the acute points and edges. I took off one of my buckskin leggins, and gave it to Rogers, and with the other one for myself we fixed the moccasins with them as well as we could, which enabled us to go ahead, but I think if our feet had been shod with steel those sharp rocks would have cut through.

Starting early we made the summit about noon, and from here we could see the place where we found a water hole and camped the first night after we left the wagons. Down the steep cañon we turned, the same one in which we had turned back with the wagons, and over the sharp broken pieces of volcanic rock that formed our only footing we hobbled along with sore and tender feet. We had to watch for the smoothest place for every step, and then moved only with the greatest difficulty. The Indians could have caught us easily if they had been around for we must keep our eyes on the ground constantly and stop if we looked up and around. But we at last got down and camped on some spot where we had set out twenty-five days before to seek the settlements. Here was the same little water hole in the sand plain, and the same strong sulphur water which we had to drink the day we left. The mule was turned loose dragging the same piece of rawhide she had attached to her when we purchased her, and she ranged and searched faithfully for food finding little except the very scattering bunches of sage brush. She was industrious and walked around rapidly picking here and there, but at dark came into camp and lay down close to us to sleep.

There was no sign that any one had been here during our absence, and if the people had gone to hunt a way out, they must either have followed the Jayhawker's trail or some other one. We were much afraid that they might have fallen victims to the Indians. Remaining in camp so long it was quite likely they had been discovered by them and it was quite likely they had been murdered for the sake of the oxen and camp equipage. It might be that we should find the hostiles waiting for us when we reached the appointed camping place, and it was small show for two against a party. Our mule and her load would be a great capture for them. We talked a great deal and said a great many things at that camp fire for we knew we were in great danger, and we had many doubts about the safety of our people, that would soon be decided, and whether for joy or sorrow we could not tell.

From this place, as we walked along, we had a wagon road to follow, in soft sand, but not a sign of a human footstep could we see, as we marched toward this, the camp of the last hope. We had the greatest fears the people had given up our return and started out for themselves and that we should follow on, only to find them dead or dying. My pen fails me as I try to tell the feelings and thoughts of this trying hour. I can never hope to do so, but if the reader can place himself in my place, his imagination cannot form a picture that shall go beyond reality.

We were some seven or eight miles along the road when I stopped to fix my moccasin while Rogers went slowly along. The little mule went on ahead of both of us, searching all around for little bunches of dry grass, but always came back to the trail again and gave us no trouble. When I had started up again I saw Rogers ahead leaning on his gun and waiting for me, apparently looking at something on the ground. As I came near enough to speak I asked what he had found and he said—"Here is Capt. Culverwell, dead." He did not look much like a dead man. He lay upon his back with arms extended wide, and his little canteen, made of two powder flasks, lying by his side. This looked indeed as if some of our saddest forebodings were coming true. How many more bodies should we find? Or should we find the camp deserted, and never find a trace of the former occupants.

We marched toward camp like two Indians, silent and alert, looking out for dead bodies and live Indians, for really we more expected to find the camp devastated by those rascals than to find that it still contained our friends. To the east we could plainly see what seemed to be a large salt lake with a bed that looked as if of the finest, whitest sand, but really a wonder of salt crystal. We put the dreary steps steadily one forward of another, the little mule the only unconcerned one of the party, ever looking for an odd blade of grass, dried in the hot dry wind, but yet retaining nourishment, which she preferred.

About noon we came in sight of the wagons, still a long way off, but in the clear air we could make them out, and tell what they were, without being able to see anything more. Half a mile was the distance between us and the camp before we could see very plainly, as they were in a little depression. We could see the covers had been taken off, and this was an ominous sort of circumstance to us, for we feared the depredations of the Indians in retaliation for the capture of their squashes. They had shot our oxen before we left and they have slain them this time and the people too.

We surely left seven wagons. Now we could see only four and nowhere the sign of an ox. They must have gone ahead with a small train, and left these four standing, after dismantling them.

No signs of life were anywhere about, and the thought of our hard struggles between life and death to go out and return, with the fruitless results that now seemed apparent was almost more than human heart could bear. When should we know their fate? When should we find their remains, and how learn of their sad history if we ourselves should live to get back again to settlements and life? If ever two men were troubled, Rogers and I surely passed through the furnace.

We kept as low and as much out of sight as possible, trusting very much to the little mule that was ahead, for we felt sure she would detect danger in the air sooner than we, and we watched her closely to see how she acted. She slowly walked along looking out for food, and we followed a little way behind, but still no decisive sign to settle the awful suspense in which we lived and suffered. We became more and more convinced that they had taken the trail of the Jayhawkers, and we had missed them on the road, or they had perished before reaching the place where we turned from their trail.

One hundred yards now to the wagons and still no sign of life, no positive sign of death, though we looked carefully for both. We fear that perhaps there are Indians in ambush, and with nervous irregular breathing we counsel what to do. Finally Rogers suggested that he had two charges in his shot gun and I seven in the Coll's rifle, and that I fire one of mine and await results before we ventured any nearer, and if there are any of the red devils there we can kill some of them before they get to us. And now both closely watching the wagons I fired the shot. Still as death and not a move for a moment, and then as if by magic a man came out from under a wagon and stood up looking all around, for he did not see us. Then he threw up his arms high over his head and shouted—"The boys have come. The boys have come!" Then other bare heads appeared, and Mr. Bennett and wife and Mr. Arcane came toward us as fast as ever they could. The great suspense was over and our hearts were first in our mouths, and then the blood all went away and left us almost fainting as we stood and tried to step. Some were safe perhaps all of those nearest us, and the dark shadow of death that had hovered over us, and cast what seemed a pall upon every thought and action, was lifted and fell away a heavy oppression gone. Bennett and Arcane caught us in their arms and embraced us with all their strength, and Mrs. Bennett when she came fell down on her knees and clung to me like a maniac in the great emotion that came to her, and not a word was spoken. If they had been strong enough they would have carried us to camp upon their shoulders. As it was they stopped two or three times, and turned as if to speak, but there was too much feeling for words, convulsive weeping would choke the voice.

All were a little calmer soon, and Bennett soon found voice to say:— "I know you have found some place, for you have a mule," and Mrs. Bennett through her tears, looked staringly at us as she could hardly believe our coming back was a reality, and then exclaimed:—"Good boys! O, you have saved us all! God bless you forever! Such boys should never die!" It was some time before they could talk without weeping. Hope almost died within them, and now when the first bright ray came it almost turned reason from its throne. A brighter happier look came to them than we had seen, and then they plied us with questions the first of which was:— "Where were you?"

We told them it must be 250 miles yet to any part of California where we could live. Then came the question:—"Can we take our wagons?" "You will have to walk," was our answer, for no wagons could go over that unbroken road that we had traveled. As rapidly and carefully as we could we told them of our journey, and the long distance between the water holes; that we had lost no time and yet had been twenty six days on the road; that for a long distance the country was about as dry and desolate as the region we had crossed east of this camp. We told them of the scarcity of grass, and all the reasons that had kept us so long away from them.

We inquired after the others whom we had left in camp when we went away, and we were told all they knew about them. Hardly were we gone before they began to talk about the state of affairs which existed. They said that as they had nothing to live on but their oxen it would be certain death to wait here and eat them up, and that it would be much better to move on a little every day and get nearer and nearer the goal before the food failed. Bennett told them they would know surely about the way when the boys returned, and knowing the road would know how to manage and what to expect and work for, and could get out successfully. But the general opinion of all but Mr. Bennett and Mr. Arcane and their families was, as expressed by one of them:—"If those boys ever get out of this cussed hole, they are d----d fools if they ever come back to help anybody."

Some did not stay more than a week after we were gone, but took their oxen and blankets and started on. They could not be content to stay idly in camp with nothing to occupy their minds or bodies. They could see that an ox when killed would feed them only a few days, and that they could not live long on them, and it stood them in hand to get nearer the western shore as the less distance the more hope while the meat lasted. Bennett implored them to stay as he was sure we would come back, and if the most of them deserted him he would be exposed to the danger of the Indians, with no hope of a successful resistance against them.

But the most seemed to think that to stay was to die, and it would be better to die trying to escape than to set idly down to perish. These men seemed to think their first duty was to save themselves, and if fortunate, help others afterward, so they packed their oxen and left in separate parties, the last some two weeks before. They said that Capt. Culverwell went with the last party. I afterward learned that he could not keep up with them and turned to go back to the wagons again, and perished, stretched out upon the sand as we saw him, dying all alone, with no one to transmit his last words to family or friends. Not a morsel to eat, and the little canteen by his side empty. A sad and lonely death indeed!

There was no end to the questions about the road we had to answer, for this was uppermost on their minds, and we tried to tell them and show them how we must get along on our return. We told them of the great snow mountains we had seen all to the north of our road, and how deep the snow appeared to be, and how far west it extended. We told them of the black and desolate ranges and buttes to the south, and of the great dry plains in the same direction. We told them of the Jayhawkers trail; of Fish's dead body; of the salt lake and slippery alkali water to which we walked, only to turn away in disappointment; of the little sheets of ice which saved our lives; of Doty's camp and what we knew of those gone before; of the discouraged ones who gave us their names to send back to friends; of the hawk and crow diet; of my lameness; of the final coming out into a beautiful valley, in the midst of fat cattle and green meadows, and the trouble to get the help arranged on account of not knowing the language to tell the people what we needed. They were deeply impressed that my lameness had been a blessing in disguise, or we would have gone on to the coast and consumed more time than we did in walking slowly to favor the crippled knee. Our sad adventures and loss of the horses in returning was sorrowfully told and we spoke of the provisions we had been able to bring on the little mule which had clambered over the rocks like a cat; that we had a little flour and beans, and some good dried meat with fat on it which we hoped would help to eke out the poorer fare and get them through at last. They were so full of compliments that we really began to think we had been brought into the world on purpose to assist some one, and the one who could forecast all things had directed us, and all our ways, so that we should save those people and bring them to a better part of God's footstool, where plenty might be enjoyed, and the sorrows of the desert forgotten. It was midnight before we could get them all satisfied with their knowledge of our experience.

FIVE

Trapped in an Instant: Death in Zion

Randi Minetor

THE NAMES OF THE FOURTEEN HIKERS IN THE NARROWS OF ZION Canyon on July 27, 1998, did not become part of the record reported in the *Salt Lake Tribune* two days later, but their gruesome find certainly did—and the report, at least in the short term, chilled many a hiker's enthusiasm for braving the waters of the North Fork of the Virgin River.

The Virgin River sculpts a dramatic and compelling corridor through the heart of Zion National Park, one that lures otherwise cautious hikers to take on a challenge entirely different from the ones they find on dry land. Here sandstone walls stretch upward for a thousand feet or more, allowing a glistening ribbon of water to find its way between them with only twenty or thirty feet of tolerance on either side. Sunlight generally forsakes this slim waterway, making this a dim or even murky journey—but when a shaft of natural light casts a momentary glow on a towering wall, the effect can be so remarkable that hikers pause to admire the play of sun and shadow against the folds of sandstone glowing in shades of vermillion, white gold, and mahogany.

On the floor of the canyon, the Virgin River polishes the rocks in its bed into slippery spheres, making a hike through even ankle-deep water tricky at best. The effect is like walking on "buttered bowling balls," as my husband phrased it during our most recent hike through the canyon. Every hiker knows—or discovers, much to his or her chagrin—that a sturdy walking stick is an absolute must, providing a necessary third point of contact with the ground while the hiker feels for a stable foothold with each cautious step forward. In Springdale, the park's entrance town, a viable industry has developed to provide Narrows hikers with canyoneering shoes, neoprene socks, walking sticks, dry suits in winter (when the water temperature drops to thirty-four degrees Fahrenheit), and wet suits in summer to help prevent soaking-wet hikers from developing hypothermia in the chilly shade of the upper canyon.

The bulk of the visitor traffic begins at the south end of the canyon where the park shuttle stops at the Temple of Sinawava, with hikers beginning their journey on the easy Riverside Walk. At the end of the mile-long paved path, it's time to plunge into the water and hike in the river to the canyon's narrowest point, about two and a half miles up the canyon. Here delighted visitors discover the slot canyons, gorgeous examples of the interplay of water, sandstone, and light as the walls stand barely twenty feet apart. "This is the slot canyon that all other slot canyons are compared to," writes photographer Joe Braun on his website, Joe's Guide to Zion National Park.

For casual hikers eager to see the best that Zion has to offer, this short but strenuous trek offers tremendous rewards in multiple megabytes of photos, access to hidden natural wonders that cannot be seen from any road, and bragging rights: Only the bravest visitors venture past the end of the Riverside Walk to see the magic in the heart of Zion Canyon.

Those who crave a more challenging experience of the canyon take the route less traveled, beginning at the north end at Chamberlain's Ranch. The daunting sixteen-mile route usually takes two days (though some power hikers finish it in one) and involves an overnight stay at one of the twelve designated campsites along the North Fork of the Virgin River. The park requires hiking parties to obtain a permit to hike the Narrows from the north end, and to make a reservation to use one of the campsites. This allows the park to control the number of people who hike the Narrows at any one time—but equally important, the permit and campsite reservation give the rangers a fairly good idea of where hikers are at any given time. If anything goes wrong and the hikers do not arrive safely at the end of the hike within a few hours of their expected time, search and rescue crews can deduce how far along the party might be.

Why the concern? While hiking the Narrows at its most shallow may result in an unplanned dunking into the water or, at worst, a twisted ankle, there's a greater danger from the middle of July to the end of August. Just as Zion's shuttle buses become jammed with passengers and the trails are crowded with day-trippers and visitors from around the world, torrential thunderstorms begin to pop up regularly in the mountains north of the park. Hikers in the Narrows report looking up past the canyon walls to see bright blue sky even as rain drenches the land twenty or thirty miles away. As the rain falls and the runoff from the desert and mountains swells the volume of the Virgin River, all that water flows into Zion Canyon.

Once inside, the volume of water becomes concentrated as it squeezes between the monolithic walls. The water level rises instantly, racing down the canyon at rates as high as four thousand cubic feet per second—and as the canyon becomes even narrower, the water level rises again. What may have begun as a few extra inches of water high in the mountains now speeds down the center of the canyon, reaching well over hikers' heads and creating a deadly situation for people who have been lulled into a sense of security by the patches of clear blue sky they see above them. If they are caught on low ground, they may be swept away by the current's force.

Because of Zion's unique topography, hikers also may find themselves without the ability to climb to safety. Floodwaters cover all the riverbed sandbars and scraps of land at the bottom of the canyon, and walls scoured by centuries of such floods offer no ledges or even footholds to help people climb to a higher point on the rock face. Hikers, climbers, and canyoneering enthusiasts, including some lifelong experts, have found themselves trapped on a point too low for safety. Others manage to scramble up to a point above the water, remaining stranded on a ledge until the water recedes. This can take many hours, an uncomfortable situation for hikers who thought they were on a day trip and who did not pack enough extra food, dry clothing, and water to last into another day.

So on Monday afternoon, July 27, 1998, when 0.47 inches of rain fell at Zion National Park headquarters and the Lava Point area west of the Narrows received 0.37 inches, parties of hikers—fourteen people in all—became trapped overnight about two miles upriver from the Temple of Sinawava parking area. They managed to scramble to higher ground as the water level rose three feet in a matter of minutes, and as the flow increased from 110 cubic feet to 740 cubic feet per second, making wading in the roiling river impossible. They made makeshift camps, getting as comfortable as they could while keeping a close eye on the current for any sign that the depth might become passable once again.

That's how the hikers spotted the body.

It floated by them at about 5:00 p.m., battered significantly by rocks it had encountered in the swift current. No medical expertise was required to determine that the person had most likely drowned in the flash flood.

Immediately seeing the need to retrieve this person's remains, several of the hikers worked together to reach the body, bring it to a patch of ground, and secure it there. It remained in place until early Tuesday morning, when the river had returned to a manageable level and the hikers could make their way out of the canyon. They reported their find to the first ranger they could locate.

When Zion's search and rescue squad entered the Narrows, it located the body where the hikers had secured it. Determining who the victim was, however, became a tricky process. "There was no identification on the man, and we haven't heard any reports about a missing person," park spokesman Denny Davies told the *Salt Lake Tribune*. The recovery team ventured an educated guess that the man was in his forties, and that he weighed between 230 and 250 pounds. Washington County sheriff Glenwood Humphries noted that the body had taken a severe beating in the swiftly flowing current, making it that much harder to achieve a solid identification. Whoever this person was, he had not obtained a permit from the park to hike the canyon, and he had not made an advance reservation for a campsite. His identity was a complete mystery.

On Tuesday evening, however, park investigators found an unlocked vehicle parked in Zion Canyon with two wallets in it, and they matched one of the driver's license photos with the unidentified body. They determined that the victim was twenty-seven-year-old Ramsey E. Algan of Long Beach, California. Two other hikers who had emerged from the canyon after the flash flood confirmed what seemed to be the case: Algan had been hiking with another man, and that man had not returned to his car either. Park search and rescue teams now had to face the fact that they had another hiker to find—and the chances were slim that they would find him alive.

On Wednesday, July 29, Acting Chief Ranger David Buccello coordinated the second search along the Virgin River, breaking the searchers into teams to explore five sectors of the park. He also engaged the assistance of Rocky Mountain Rescue Dogs from Salt Lake City. "The search dogs can be a great help in searching the debris piles left after such a flood," Buccello said in a statement released by the National Park Service. South of the park, Washington County sheriff's deputy Kurt Wright led search efforts on the chance that the second man's body might have been carried downstream and beyond the park's boundaries on the strong storm current.

On Wednesday morning, July 30, searchers discovered the body of the second man about a mile and a half upstream from where Algan's body was first spotted. Paul Garcia, a thirty-one-year-old man from Paramount, California, was located in a debris pile where his body had snagged during the flash flood.

Park officials were quick to use this tragedy to reinforce the message that those planning to hike the Narrows need to check with park rangers at a visitor center or ranger station before venturing up or down the Virgin River. "We cannot stress too strongly that visitors need to heed these flash flood warnings and plan alternate trips that don't include slot canyons," acting park superintendent Eddie Lopez told the *Salt Lake Tribune*. He urged hikers to get updated weather information before venturing into any narrow or slot canyon, and to delay their hike if thunderstorms were predicted.

TO HIKE OR NOT TO HIKE

Park rangers at Zion move quickly to put a range of warnings in place when flash floods are possible in the Narrows. Hikers who apply for permits at ranger stations receive sincere and concerned discouragement from rangers if rainstorms are in the forecast, and signs are posted at the Narrows trailheads, warning hikers that flooding may be imminent. "Unfortunately, many people ignore the warnings and enter the Narrows," spokesperson Davies told the *Deseret News* on the day Algan's body was retrieved. When asked if the victim should have known a flash flood warning was in effect, Davies responded simply: "Yes."

Why would anyone hike the Narrows when there's a flash flood in the forecast? For vacationers who have planned a hike up or down the Narrows as a central part of their Zion visit, timing can become a greater priority than the potential for danger. The special challenges of hiking, climbing, or canyoneering in the Narrows make it a bucket-list experience for many visitors—and after months or even years of planning, scrapping the hike because of rain may feel like the coward's way out.

The potential for life-threatening danger is very real, however. To date, fifteen people have perished in the Narrows when they were caught in flash floods, and many others have sustained injuries in their scramble to get out of the path of rushing water. There is no way to tally how many hikers have been forced to wait for hours or even overnight after they've succeeded in reaching higher ground—and untold numbers of these hikers made plans only for a day hike or for a single night in camp, finding themselves without sufficient food, water, warm clothing, or dry items to make their unscheduled extra time in the Narrows as bearable as possible.

With the wealth of information outlets available today, it's easy for would-be Narrows hikers to get the weather updates they need to determine if they should postpone their excursion for a day or two to avoid flash flood activity. Zion National Park provides a number of links to water level information and flash flood forecasts, including the National Weather Service Forecast Office's page on all of southern Utah's parks. There's even a link to the US Geological Survey's flow rate data for the Virgin River, so serious water information enthusiasts can delve into the trends in cubic feet per second. For people who just want to check the forecast, links to the National Weather Service (weather.gov) provide radar maps and the percentage chance of rain.

Descriptions of the Narrows hikes found on the park's website make it clear that this is not a hike for the timid. "Hiking the Zion Narrows means hiking in the Virgin River," the website explains. "At least 60% of the hike is spent wading, walking, and sometimes swimming in the stream. There is no maintained trail; the route is the river. The current is swift, the water is cold, and the rocks underfoot are slippery. Flash flooding and hypothermia are constant dangers. Good planning, proper equipment, and sound judgment are essential for a safe and successful trip."

There is no way to judge how many people's lives have been saved by the availability of data, the emphatic warning signs, and the advice of rangers in the park; we rarely hear about people who are dissuaded from making a dangerous hike into the wilderness. We do know, however, that while people find themselves trapped by a flash flood in the Narrows every year, only a handful of these floods have led to hikers' deaths.

THE FLASH FLOOD OF 1961

"If Linda hadn't heard the roar," John Dearden of Park City, Utah, told the Provo *Daily Herald*, "nobody would have been alive."

Some describe the summer storms in southwest Utah as monsoons, sudden bursts of hard, pelting rain that flood dry creek beds until roads and bridges disappear under the flow. On Sunday, September 17, 1961, a cloudburst followed by steady rain dumped a whopping 0.79 inches of rain on parts of Utah, saturating the ground in advance of the more powerful storm to come. Monday's rain inundated Zion National Park and the surrounding area with an additional 1.33 inches, washing out the main bridge at the park's south entrance near Springdale and closing Highway 15 from St. George. Water engorged the Virgin River as the rain sluiced over the sandy soil and spilled down the riverbanks. As the rain continued to fall, the river swelled and gathered speed—and the force of it rushed into the Narrows.

Inside the canyon on Sunday morning, twenty-six hikers on a tour conducted by SOCOTWA Expeditions were well along an eighteen-mile hike they had begun on Saturday morning. Expecting clear weather— as reported by the local weather service when group leaders checked on Saturday morning—they had arrived by bus from Salt Lake City and entered the canyon from the Navajo Lake area in Dixie National Forest, heading south along the North Fork of the river. Nineteen teens and seven adults made their way along the spectacular slot canyons, keeping an unhurried pace between the two-thousand-foot-high canyon walls. They camped in the Narrows on Saturday night and continued on Sunday morning, entering an area well known for having no alternate routes and few opportunities to reach high ground.

They reached the confluence of Kolob Creek with the Virgin River at about noon on Sunday, and leader Robert Perry, an Air National Guardsman, led nine of the hikers on a side trip into Orderville Canyon. That's when Linda McIntyre let out a yell, and Perry heard the flood coming toward them. "The first indication of trouble was a thunderlike noise he heard in back of the group," the *Salt Lake Tribune* reported. When he turned around, Perry saw "a wall of muddy water, bristling with driftwood, tree trunks and limbs."

Perry decided that they should turn back. "We got to the mouth of the canyon and found Carla Larson standing knee deep in water," he told the *Tribune*. The girl was stranded on a high spot in the river, with deep water all around her. "We had to swim about ten yards to get to her. Someone asked, 'what next.'" Several group members provided their backpacks as flotation devices, and they towed Carla to higher ground and comparative safety.

"We knew a terrific flood had come down through the canyon," said Perry, "but we didn't realize how bad it was." Inexplicably, the weather was still clear. Half an hour would pass before the rain arrived in the Narrows—and then "you couldn't see a hundred yards across the gulch," he said. "I've been in hurricanes before, but they couldn't hold a candle to this storm."

Perry led his party up Orderville Canyon and found high ground, where they made a shelter from their ponchos and "huddled together in wet sleeping bags for warmth."

They passed a terrifying night in Orderville Canyon, with no idea how the other sixteen people in their tour were faring in the storm and flood.

"The rain-swollen stream suddenly grew to a 14-foot crest," the *Daily Herald* reported, "and bore down on them in a canyon only 12 feet wide in places."

Luckily, the group had reached an area of the Narrows where the walls provided some hand- and footholds, as well as ledges where they could escape the massive torrent of river water. Perched on sandbars and shelves of rock with the river rushing just below them, the members of the party could not see who had found their way up the canyon walls and who may have been swept away by the raging water. They remained pinned down throughout the night, hopeful that all of their friends and guides had scrambled to safety.

"The water came up to within a foot of us—we couldn't have gone any further, the rock wall was straight up," said Dearden.

Hiker Lyle Moss told the *Salt Lake Tribune* that he and two other hikers managed to climb up on top of a sandbar, but the water came to within six inches of where they were standing.

"Long-time residents of the area say it was the heaviest rainstorm to hit the Zion Park area in nearly 25 years," the *Tribune* reported. "Rain gauges at park headquarters caught one and 43 hundredths inches of precipitation during the storm."

Twenty-two hours passed before the water had finally receded enough for the hikers to make their way out. On the ground at last, they found the riverbed muddier than when they began and loaded with debris—fallen branches, twigs, and dirt that formed irregular dams and obstacles to their progress. The ten who had passed the night in Orderville Canyon met up with nine other members of the party about a mile and a half downstream, and they began to hear the fate of some of the others. One group of boys and girls had found safety on the opposite side of the canyon from Lyle Moss, and they watched in horror as forty-eight-year-old Walter Scott, the leader of the group, and two younger boys drifted by in a current moving at an estimated twenty-five miles per hour.

When nineteen of the original twenty-six hikers emerged from the Narrows at the Riverside Walk on Monday afternoon, they found that search and rescue crews were already looking for them. Tour bus driver Dave Randall had arrived at the Temple of Sinawava on Sunday afternoon to pick up the hikers and take them home to Salt Lake—and when the tour group did not arrive, Randall moved quickly to notify park officials.

The hikers also learned that two of their comrades had already been pulled from the river. Young Vance Justett, a thirteen-year-old Springdale resident, discovered Walter Scott's body in Springdale on Monday when the boy went to the river to see how much damage the flood had done. He told Washington County deputy sheriff Dick Barnes that he saw a pair of legs in a pile of driftwood that the water had swept onto the shore. "So swift was the torrent that Mr. Scott's clothes were ripped off and only a pair of white tennis shoes remained on the body," the *Tribune* reported. "The victim's body was swept almost ten miles from where the party was struck by the torrent, near the junction of Kolob Creek and the Virgin River." Perry told the *Salt Lake Tribune* that Scott had brought up the rear of the expedition to remain with some of the boys in the party who had trouble organizing their equipment after their night of camping.

Not far from the spot where Scott was found, the body of thirteen-year-old Steve Florence, a junior high school student from Park City, was discovered lodged in a pile of driftwood, about 4:00 p.m. on Monday. The remains of seventeen-year-old Ray Nichols came to light at about 2:00 p.m. Monday, lodged between two trees near the park's South Campground. Nichols was a student at East High School in Salt Lake City.

When the exhausted hikers arrived on Monday with four of their comrades still not in evidence, a search began for Alvin Nelson, Frank Johnson, Kenneth Webb, and Doug Childs. Waiting families and searchers were overjoyed when fifty-year-old Webb and Childs, a boy of thirteen, sloshed their way out of the Virgin River and turned up at the park headquarters at about 5:00 p.m., both alive and well. They had climbed onto an embankment to take a picture when they saw the flood coming at them, but they could not communicate with the people ahead of them. They stayed on the high ground as the flood overtook their position, watching the water come up all the way to their knees before it began to subside. Webb decided to wait until they were sure the entire storm was over before making their way out of the canyon.

The ordeal was not quite over for Doug Childs, however. It fell to him to identify the body of his friend Steve Florence. "The Childs youth looked at the human wreckage of what was once his friend, [and] whispered almost inaudibly, 'that's Steve,'" the *Tribune* said.

By Monday night there was still no sign of Nelson or Johnson. The park service sent a search party into the Narrows on Tuesday morning in hopes of finding the two young men alive, while jeep posses from Washington and Iron Counties searched along the Virgin River from the southern park boundary all the way to St. George.

The searchers soon discovered that the volume of water that had passed through the canyon brought with it massive quantities of silt, sand, rock, and other debris, a load as dangerous as the water itself. As the search wore on through the day Tuesday and broadened to include forty miles along the length of the Virgin River, the rescue teams surmised that the two missing seventeen-year-old Salt Lake City boys were buried under layers of newly arrived gravel and sand. The parents of the boys waited in the park as ground and air crews scoured the area for any clue that could lead searchers to the bodies. Cleanup crews, usually assigned to clearing driftwood and moving sand to restore the river's normal flow, had the grisly task of continuing the search as well.

Equally challenging, the river had not yet returned to its normally shallow level, making it difficult and even dangerous for the search to continue in some parts of the canyon. Sheriff Ray Renouf of Washington County finally called off the search Tuesday evening, promising the families of the two missing boys that the effort would continue at an intensive level once the waters had receded enough to allow crews to see the bottom of the river.

With less water and more debris visible over the next several days, searchers continued to try to locate the missing boys. "Searchers scoured a mile and a half stretch of the Virgin River from the southern edge of Zion Park through Springdale Thursday, but found no trace of the missing youths," the *Daily Herald* reported. The hunt beyond the Narrows continued on the theory that the boys' bodies may have been carried out of the park on the river's storm surge. The Washington County sheriff's department spent Friday, September 22, searching eight miles of the river with six hunting dogs, and park service searchers covered another eight miles within the park, scouring the riverbed and moving driftwood and rocks to attempt to uncover any trace of the bodies. Not so much as a scrap of clothing emerged.

On Sunday, September 24, two hundred volunteer searchers covered the length of the river, hoping to bring the final chapter of the Narrows tragedy to a close. Indeed, this became the last day of the search, but no sign of Johnson or Nelson came to light. Sheriff Renouf told the media that he believed the bodies were buried under debris left behind by the storm and flood, and that they were still somewhere at the bottom of the canyon. His statement brought the organized search to an inconclusive but necessary close.

Forty-five years later, in 2006, a man swimming in the Virgin River discovered a bone fragment, the top half of a human skull. He brought it to the Springdale Police, and Chief Kurt Wright thought immediately of the two boys lost in 1961. "That's the only thing that's never really been solved here," he told the Associated Press. "We've had numerous drownings since then in the Narrows, but we've always recovered the victims."

He brought it to the local medical examiner, but they decided not to "reopen old wounds" by contacting the families or testing the fragment, Wright said. At that point DNA testing would have been prohibitively expensive. The bone fragment was stored in a box in the evidence room until another investigator brought it up in 2012, when he learned that the University of North Texas offered free DNA testing to law enforcement—a boon that could clear up at least a portion of a mystery half a century old.

Wright found relatives of the two missing boys in Oregon and Alaska and acquired personal effects that might provide DNA samples. When the results came back from the lab, the skull fragment matched the DNA of Alvin Nelson. The boy's remains were returned to his sister, Doralee Freebairn, for burial in Salt Lake City.

"You'd think after all these years it would be put to rest, but all the stress and frustration just comes right back," said Freebairn. Still, she added, "I find this all very spiritual."

Two Men, Too Cold, Too Fast

On Wednesday or Thursday, April 21 or 22, 2010, Jesse Scaffidi and Daniel Chidester, two twenty-three-year-old men from Las Vegas, Nevada, began a trip into the Narrows that would test their skills as hikers, wilderness builders, and navigators of rushing water. They told their families that they planned to hike into the top of the Narrows from the Navajo Lake area, ford the Virgin River at its confluence with Deep Creek, and then build a log raft from materials they expected to find in the vicinity. With the raft constructed, they intended to float down the river a distance of fifty miles to Hurricane, Utah, where their journey would come to its triumphant end. They expected to arrive in Hurricane on Saturday, April 24.

It seemed like a great adventure, but none of it was sanctioned by the National Park Service, according to comments park spokesperson Ron Terry made to an Associated Press reporter a few days later. "The Park Service would not have issued a hiking permit in The Narrows because of the danger of high water, nor would officials have approved the plan to build a log raft," the report tells us.

Terry noted that the two men did not attempt to obtain permits or notify any rangers about their plans. Family members told the AP that despite the fact that water in the Narrows is usually very cold in April, the hiker-rafters did not bring cold-water gear or life vests for their journey down the river. "If they had [tried to get permits, they] would not have received a permit due to inappropriate planning and lack of personal safety equipment," a news release from the park informed the media. "At the time, the North Fork of the Virgin River was running about 250 cubic feet per second and the water temperature was around 40 degrees Fahrenheit."

The park's website notes that the Narrows closes when the flow rate is over 150 cubic feet per second (CFS), as well as during spring snowmelt. Swollen with meltwater from a particularly heavy winter snowfall in 2010, the Virgin River was closed to hikers when Scaffidi and Chidester began their trip—and rafting, should anyone have approached rangers with the idea, would have been strictly prohibited.

How fast and powerful is 250 CFS? The answer depends on the waterway itself. Imagine that a cubic foot of water is a box one foot high, one foot wide, and one foot deep, filled with water. Now, choose a spot anywhere on the river, and consider that a fixed point. The number "per second" is a measurement of the number of boxes that move past this fixed point in any given second. So at 250 CFS, 250 of these water-filled boxes move past your selected point in the time it takes to say "One Mississippi." This may be a calm flow in a mile-wide, open river, but in a tight space like the Narrows, where much of the canyon is only twenty to thirty feet wide, that's a lot of boxes of water rushing past a fixed point every second. To maintain that speed, the water must rise within the canyon walls and push through harder and faster than it would at, say, 10 CFS. For two young men riding a makeshift raft on this rushing river through a slim canyon with many twists and turns, 250 CFS would be a deadly speed.

At Zion Adventure Company in Springdale—one of the area's top outfitters and training companies for activities in the Narrows—a sign on the wall provides weather conditions updated daily by staff members. The bottom of the sign includes a "Virgin River Hiking Safety Continuum" chart that clearly indicates the relative danger the river poses at various measures of CFS. At 250 CFS the river is rated as "Very Difficult" for wading—that is, traveling upriver on foot. At 300 CFS the river becomes "Near Impossible" for foot travel. What would the rate be like in the downstream direction?

There is no way to know whether the two adventurers were aware of the dangerous conditions they would encounter, or if they skipped the permitting step because they knew their plan would not receive park approval. Given the risky nature of their intentions, however, it's entirely possible that they had no idea at all.

On Sunday, April 25, when Scaffidi and Chidester did not get in touch with their families to let them know they were safe, a family member contacted the park. The park launched a ground search and used a helicopter to try to locate the men, spending Sunday working their way up the Narrows from the Riverside Walk and down it from the top of the North Fork of the Virgin River.

The first body came to light on Monday morning, April 26, at about 9:00 a.m., near the Gateway to the Zion Narrows. Later that day, at 1:40 p.m., searchers found the body of a second man in the river, more than two miles downstream from the Narrows, near the park shuttle stop at Big Bend. Analysis by the Washington County medical examiner confirmed that these two young men were Scaffidi and Chidester. What exactly killed them—drowning, hypothermia, or a violent encounter with debris in the water—was not determined.

Searchers found no evidence that the men had succeeded in constructing a raft. Without some kind of floating craft, "they would have had to swim much of the Narrows in deep water that is around 40 degrees," Terry told the AP.

Reading the Warning Signs

When two men from Southern California began their hike up the Narrows on Saturday, September 27, 2014, at about 8:00 a.m., the river was flowing at 46 CFS at the Riverside Walk, and rangers had not yet hung signs warning of the potential for flash floods that day.

There were flash flood warnings already in effect, however, for the area surrounding the canyon. Beginning Friday evening, September 26, a storm dropped more than two inches of rain on much of Utah, breaking the day's rainfall records from the Salt Lake City airport all the way to Kodachrome Basin State Park. Roads within Zion National Park flooded with rainwater at various times over the weekend as long, pelting deluges fell and the river crested its banks.

As rain began to fall around 9:30 a.m., the two watched the weather and soon decided to turn back. They were just a quarter-mile from the paved walkway at 10:00 a.m. when floodwaters came barreling down the canyon corridor.

Scrambling for high ground, the two men found perches that kept them out of the water, but they were about two hundred feet apart on opposite sides of the canyon—and the roar of the rushing river made it impossible for them to communicate. They watched and waited for nearly six hours as the water pounded past them at a peak rate of 4,020 CFS, one hundred times harder than when they began their hike a few hours before.

By late afternoon, however, when the river had slowed only to about 1,000 CFS, one of the hikers (whose name was not released) concluded that he needed to move or risk death by hypothermia from sitting still in the chilly canyon. He leapt into the water around 4:00 p.m. and managed to swim out to safety, and he reached a ranger station by 6:30 p.m. to report that his friend, thirty-four-year-old Douglas Yoshi Vo, remained in the Narrows on high ground. He told them that Vo was not injured or in distress, but that he was stranded where he was.

Vo was no stranger to the challenges and unpredictability of the outdoors. His friends called him a Wilderness Explorer (in the spirit of the Disney movie *Up*), one who planned annual camping trips for family and friends. "He thrived on the opportunity to bring his close friends and family, not to his house in Westminster, but to his home in the tents, under the stars," says a tribute to him at YouCaring.com. "How can your sense of adventure not flourish when you have a real-life Wilderness Explorer as your campground leader?"

So Vo's hiking companion felt certain that his friend, who was not injured when last he saw him, would be safe for the short time it would take to bring a rescue party to his location. When the search team arrived at the Riverside Walk, however, they knew immediately that they could not attempt to retrieve Vo until the river's still-extreme pace slowed considerably.

"Rangers arrived at the Narrows, but the river was still flowing at approximately 1,000–1,500 CFS which is too high for them to safely enter the river from downstream," said a news release from the park the following day.

Based on Vo's friend's description of his location, they believed that the remaining hiker was in a relatively safe location, and they planned to hike into the canyon early Sunday morning to be sure he made it to safety.

In the early morning, however, when the other hiker returned to find him, Vo was not in the place his friend had described.

"The rescue effort then turned into a search," the news release noted. Rangers located Vo's body on the riverbank near the Riverside Walk at about 2:00 p.m., roughly a quarter-mile from his last position in the canyon.

"We don't know if he tried to swim as well or if he fell in," said David Eaker, National Park Service spokesperson, to the Associated Press.

Whether Vo fell asleep on his perch and tumbled into the river or attempted an escape and was overcome by the powerful floodwaters, the Narrows turned out to be the last wilderness he would see in his lifetime.

Six

Downed Pilot in the Jungles of Burma: A War Rescue

Lt. William Diebold

A GROUP OF EXCITED YOUNG PILOTS CROWDED AROUND THE DESK. I tapped one on the arm and asked what all the fuss was about.

"Here!" he said and handed me a sheet of worn, dirty paper. Laboriously written in a scrawling, unsteady hand were words beginning "Somewhere in Hell . . ."

With difficulty I read the remainder of the note: "I am the pilot who crashed. I need a pair of G.I. shoes, quinine, socks, sulfa for boils and infections rotting my limbs off. I would like to borrow a blanket if you could spare one. Cold. Cigarettes would be nice. I'm ashamed for asking for so much. Thanks for whatever you can do."

The note was signed "Lt. G. M. Collins."

I could see why everyone was so excited; the note packed more wallop than anything I'd ever seen. "That was brought into an airstrip in Burma two days ago by a native," a lieutenant explained. "The native said the pilot is in the Naga Hills, in a village we think is called Geda Ga."

It was the mission, I knew vaguely, of the 1352nd Search and Rescue Squadron to which I'd been temporarily assigned to find downed airmen along the Hump route and rescue them. That's all I did know, though, for I was just this morning reporting for duty. Having arrived the night before at this jumping-off place for China supplies, I was supposed to report immediately to the commanding officer, but given the lateness a sergeant at the airfield had directed me to a hut he called a *basha* and quartered me with fifty other men.

A basha is an American hay mound with doors. The army had gone native: straw roof over a bamboo frame with woven bamboo sides and windows with nothing in them. No glass, no frame, no nothing. They could better be called square holes for ventilation. The one modern touch, cement floors, added little to their attraction. Following a long flight across half of India, I slept well enough that night, though, if I'd known what was in the books for me this morning, there'd have been little sleep.

The inevitable began to kick in when I reported to Major Roland Hedrick, in civilian life a Salt Lake City lawyer.

The major was surrounded by pilots, all talking at once. He was the boss and brains of the outfit, and the pilots were discussing with him— "arguing about" would be more accurate—the note I'd just read. To say I received little attention when I walked into this melee of men puts it mildly; penetrating that circle of gesticulating arms would have been worth a black eye at least.

A pilot near the major made a mountain with one hand, while with the other he imitated an airplane in flight. He was trying to explain how difficult it was to fly around that mountain with the objective of coming low over a native village situated on the mountain's side, near the top. He'd had to come in low over the village, I gathered, to attract the attention of any airman that might be in it. Was the writer of the note in that particular village? Nobody seemed sure.

The major listened patiently enough, but eventually he started chasing off the crowd of officers, moving them gradually toward the door and out into the growing light. One by one they left, each being assured something would be done and that he'd let them know as soon as he knew himself. Figuring he was pretty busy, I turned to leave with them, but, catching my eye, the major indicated I should stay.

"You're Diebold," he said.

So much for a slow and gentle introduction to my new job. I would soon be donning a parachute and standing terrified in an airplane door over a forbidding jungle mountain top, preparing to jump—I hoped—to the downed Lt. G. M. Collins.

Eventually we came to the section of the country where our downed pilot was supposed to be. What a country! If a glacier made these mountains it must have been mad as hell at something. They were the biggest, highest hunks of earth I have ever seen piled in one place. When I thought of climbing around in them, they grew even larger and more formidable.

Anderson found the villages, then flew me from them to the Ledo Road, showing me the way out. It looked simple. There couldn't be more than two mountain ranges towering some two miles up apiece, or more than a hundred miles of solid jungle. Nothing to it! We buzzed the villages a couple of times, and it was some of the best flying I've ever seen done, thank God! First we dived down the side of one mountain, gaining excess air speed, and then shot up the side of an adjacent mountain. It would have been lots of fun if I didn't have to jump out of the ship on one of those shoots up the mountainside.

When I'd talked with the major, he said he hoped this second fly-over would give us an idea of which village the pilot was in, but no matter how close we came to the roofs of the houses—and the pilot came damned close—the only thing we saw were wildly waving natives. No parachute, no panel, no signal of any sort. I began to doubt if our pilot was in either of them, but the only way to find out was still the same as it was before: jump in and look.

Finally, as I knew it must, the time came to go. Pretty much at random we picked one of the villages, and Anderson described how the jump would work. He told me to stand at the rear door, and when the bell rang that was my signal to jump. The walk from the pilot's compartment to the rear of that ship was the longest I've ever made.

Sgt. Stanley Bloom from Boston, Massachusetts, helped me into my chute, showed me how to hook up to my static line, and I took my stand at the door. I could feel my heart thudding against my chest as I looked out. It was so far down to the rushing ground, and it was thick and rough. The village sat in a small clearing—very small from the airplane—but all around it was jungle. I could picture my chute being collapsed by one of the top branches of a tall tree, letting me freefall a hundred feet or so.

It seemed I stood there forever, scared to death! I was afraid even to think about it. I did think of my civilian insurance company and its directors, though. Wouldn't they be the happy lot if they could see me now? Once, back when I was a happy civilian, they insisted I stop flying because it was too great a risk for my insurance. Good God, how would they feel about this? Then the bell rang!

I had been waiting unconsciously for that sound, so it took no planned action on my part to get me out that door. I'd conquered my mind when I stepped up to it, and from then on leaping out was reaction to a sound. I'm sure of this, for I can't remember jumping. The bell rang, and the next thing I knew was the roaring of the slip-stream in my ears, the tumbling of the horizon, the tail of the ship passing overhead . . . and then the almighty jerk.

I'd learned to jump the hard way. Body position in the air was an unknown to me, so mine almost certainly was wrong. Also, my chute harness had been cinched too loose, so I got a terrific jerk. I blacked out for an instant, I guess, for the next thing I knew I was alone in the air, all was quiet and serene, and the airplane was gone.

The feeling of elation and exhilaration that came over me when I looked up and saw that big white canopy is indescribable. The chute had opened. Oh, happy day! I kicked my legs, waved my arms, and wiggled my body to make sure nothing had been broken. Nothing had.

I watched the big plane disappearing over the far mountain with definite misgivings. It made me lonely just to see it go. There I stood in the middle of a group of staring natives . . . and all I could think to do was stare back at them.

The women wore clothes, damn it. Wrapped around their middles were long pieces of varicolored cloth. Around their breasts they wore a plain piece of dirty white cloth or another piece matching the skirt. They all wore necklaces, made of anything from animal teeth on a string to old coins or pieces of metal. The men, most of them, wore nothing but a loincloth, and others had the same wrapping the women wore around their waists.

What surprised me most was their hair. Both men and women alike wore it up, piled on top of their heads. If it weren't for the very definite outline of women's bodies, I would have been bewildered as to which sex was which. As it was, nature provided the curves.

Well, we couldn't stand there staring at one another forever, so I took an important step: I smiled. There was one old geezer the others seemed to treat with respect who I had already guessed was the head man. On top of that, he had some sort of feather in his hair none of the others had. Either the others had lost theirs, or it meant something. I gave him the old try; I smiled directly at him.

He nodded his head a couple of times and gave me what I took to be a tentative smile in return. With that, I felt on more solid ground and decided to try to get things in hand. Scattered all over the clearing were the white para-packs. Some were even in the trees at the edge of the clearing. The kids of the village were beginning to poke experimental noses into their contents, and I could picture the results if they started opening them and spreading their contents all over the area. Best to get them gathered up and at least stacked in a pile where I could keep an eye on them.

I looked at the feather-headed village elder, smiled again, and gave him another cigarette from my last pack—there were more in the dropped supplies, I knew, which was another reason to get them secured. I pointed to the various para-packs and then to one of their houses. He must have understood what I meant because he barked out some orders, and in a flash the packs were being gathered up by the natives. The chief, if that's what he was, led me to one of the houses while this was going on.

What a place those houses were. Built on stilts about ten feet off the ground, they were long, bamboo-woven things with grass roofs. In front, they actually had a porch. *Very civilized*, I thought, but later I learned the hard way about the porches' uses.

The chief and I wallowed through the mud to his house. I called it mud, with a mental frown, for surrounding the house were two or three water buffalo and a dozen or so animals that slightly resembled pigs. *Ah, the beautiful odors of a Naga village* I thought as I followed the chief along. We entered his house via a fancy stairway made from a log with notches cut into it for steps. I wondered how my old Naga friend made it up that log on his night out; that is, if his wife gave him a night out.

The inside of the hut resembled a large communal basha, not unlike the one back at the base, though more worn with use. Several rooms ran to the rear of the shack, all connected to each other so that to go to the rearmost room, one had to walk through the sleeping quarters of everyone in the house. The front room looked like the natives' version of a living room or parlor. In the rear of the room a small fire flickered in the center of the floor on sand or something. But what stopped me cold were the decorations on the walls. On every wall hung a heterogeneous collection of dried heads. On some the skin had turned to a brown parchment-like covering. Others were nothing but the grinning, white skull. Though they were almost certainly animal skulls, one look at those and I wanted to move out of there in high gear.

Every kind of head imaginable hung in the shadows. The heads that were simply skulls really frightened me. The open holes that were once eyes, combined with the absence of any lower jaw, gave them a lurid expression. They looked as if they were smiling to me in an open invitation to join them in their vigil.

On one wall were the skulls of huge water buffalo, horns still intact. On another were the skulls of large birds, probably vultures. The long beaks protruded from the skull, and here and there I could see tufts of hairy fuzz.

What really made me gulp and thank Mr. Colt for inventing our .45 automatic were the monkey heads. I've been told since then, by men who should know, that they were monkey heads and not human. But from where I was standing they looked like the largest monkey heads I'd ever seen. They came awfully close to looking like what I thought mine probably looked like under the skin. I began to pick the spot where they'd probably put mine. At least I wanted a good spot, overlooking the porch.

The chief beckoned me over to the fire. I wasn't cold but I thought it a good idea, in view of the heads, to play ball with him. After all, I kept telling myself, I was his guest; morale and good relations, you know, are a lot of little things.

The chief sat cross-legged on the floor and motioned me to join him. He then pulled out a two-foot-long, two-inch-diameter pole made of bamboo, filled it with water, dropped in some brown stuff, put one end in the fire, and propped the other end against a forked stick. We were going to have tea, cooked in bamboo. It was almost too much. *The prisoner ate a hearty meal before . . .*

Our fire was very smoky, and there was no chimney. I watched the smoke curl up as the chief blew on the fire to make it hot. First the smoke filtered through a series of bamboo layers hanging from vines from the thatched roof. On some layers of bamboo lay meat; on others, nothing. The ones with nothing on them, I later learned, were drying and would be burned in the fire. On the others, the meat looked delicious.

I learned later that when bamboo was used in the fire, the meat was moved out of the smoke. My first lesson in jungle lore: There must be undesirable gases in bamboo smoke. After passing over the meat and helping dry extra bamboo for the fire, the smoke curled on up to the peak of the roof, followed the peak to the end of the house, and there dissipated into the outside air. As the smoke ran along the roof it blackened the straw, or whatever it was that covered the house. Every so often a big hunk of this soot would fall down on my head and the heads of the natives, which they casually brushed off.

The chief had poured water for the tea from fat bamboo logs racked in a row behind him. These were kept constantly full by the women. The nearest water being at the foot of the mountain, they had to make that hike a couple of times a day. Coming up with their backs loaded down with water-filled bamboo gave them a beautiful carriage, and strong legs—and, as I was to learn tomorrow, made them a lot tougher than they looked.

We had our tea from bamboo cups. That tea was so strong it snarled at me as I tried to swallow it. These natives, I decided, had galvanized stomachs. The stuff tasted like boiled tobacco. Nevertheless, I nodded, smiled, and smacked my lips in evident enjoyment. This pleased the chief, I was happy to see, and he, too, smiled, smacked his lips, and said something like "Kajaiee." I treasured the word as my first. It must mean good, although at the taste of the tea, I could hardly believe it.

By this time, the natives outside had piled up all the para-packs. I stood on the porch with the chief and looked at them in dismay. There were so many and all in the wrong village, and I wished Andy hadn't been so hasty in dumping them out of the plane. How I was ever going to get them from where they were over to the far mountain where they should be was beyond me.

It was now late afternoon and too late to try and make the trek to the other village. The jungle looked tough enough in the daytime, and it didn't take a lot of imagination to guess it could be deadly at night. I went down in the mud and lifted all the packs up on the porch. I was amazed to find that one of these native boys could carry one of those packs on his back, as they had done to get them in the pile, but it took three of them to lift one up. My hoisting them onto the porch caused no end of consternation among them. It gave them a mistaken estimate of my strength, which I was to become all too unhappy about the next day on the trail. Up on the porch again, I opened one of the packs and found a couple of cartons of cigarettes. I passed a few cigarettes around to the boys who had brought in the packs. They seemed tickled as hell. It made me think of the number of servants a man could have in that country for a buck a month.

My problem was to get as much of this stuff over to the next mountain as possible. I looked at the chief, pointed to one of the packs, then to the other mountain, and made a couple of motions as if I were carrying one of the packs and walking. Then I pointed to the handful of men below us. It seemed an impossible job. Those few men could never, even if they wanted, carry all this equipment.

Evidently the chief got the idea for he smiled, nodded, said, "Kajaiee," and called one of the older boys up on the porch. They held a lengthy conversation while I stood looking, wondering what the hell was going on. At the end of the conversation, the boy crawled off the porch and, with another companion, started down the trail. Was he being sent for more help? All I could do was to hope for the best.

We went back inside, for more tea I presumed, and sat down by the fire. They did pour more tea and then sat back contentedly smoking their cigarettes. I decided there would just have to be a stop to this tea drinking; I couldn't stand the gaff. Then I remembered what Andy had said about the bottle of medicinal liquor. After what I had been through that day I felt I wouldn't be cheating Uncle Sugar too much if I had a drink or two before dinner, so I found the bottle and did. It was damn good bourbon and was easier to swallow than the native's tea had been, but it also made me realize I was hungry.

I found some rations and started to cook a little dinner over the native's fire. I say dinner, but it consisted mostly of cereal because the rations consisted mostly of cereal. It wasn't what I would usually order for dinner, but, compared to what the Naga chief offered, the cereal looked delicious. His menu, deluxe style, consisted of monkey meat, which was cooked before my eyes. They tossed a dead monkey, whole and entire, into the fire.

The chief, after he had eaten, took out a long bamboo pipe. About a third of the way up the pipe from the bottom, an inch-thick piece of hard vine stuck out. He poured water into the mouth of the pipe, held it upright, and then lay down on the floor. In one hand he had a copper dish with a long handle. In this he put a brown pasty substance. He held this over the fire until the brown stuff came to a sizzle. At the same time he had shredded a green, folded leaf with his knife. He browned the shreds in front of the fire. When they were good and brown, he mixed the sizzling stuff into it. All these elaborate troubles were for what? Was he going to smoke the stuff or eat it?

When the mixture was cooked to his satisfaction, he put it in the vine sticking out of the bamboo. Now I was really puzzled! I've watched a lot of people smoke pipes, but this was the damnedest conglomeration of tobacco or anything else I'd ever seen. I didn't really know that he was smoking opium, but I soon guessed when I saw the beatific look on his face, the utter relaxation of his body, and the "out of this world" look in his eyes. I was surprised, but I wasn't shocked, not after these many years in the Army. Everyone had their own way of getting tight—even if this one was a bit unusual. It certainly seemed to agree with him; he looked so happy, so self-satisfied that I almost envied him. And he wasn't alone, for on all sides of me, the boys were reaching with bamboo tongs for embers out of the fire to light their own pipes. This was going to be quite a party.

I had my choice: either go to bed or have a couple more drinks of medicinal liquor. (The chief had his vice; I had mine.) This opium den held quite a bit of interest, though, so I decided I'd stay up and see how it ended. Anyway, it was darn good liquor. After a few more, the party seemed to be getting dull. Then a song, for no reason I could think of, came out of nowhere into my head, "Old McDonald Had a Farm." It seemed lively enough for the occasion, anyway, so I sang a couple of verses, and it wasn't long until a few natives began chiming in "E-I-E-I-O." Soon they were all doing it, with real gusto, and we had ourselves a chorus.

But after a couple thousand "Old McDonald"s I figured we'd disturbed the jungle enough, and I decided to go to bed. The bourbon had been so good I'd completely forgotten it was at all unusual to be singing in a shack on a mountain in the middle of the Burmese jungle with a bunch of opium-drunk natives. But at the time it all seemed rather natural.

I walked out to the porch and to the para-packs. One of those fool bags had my bed in it, but which one? I tried the one on top, and my luck was good. In it was a jungle hammock, which I'd never used, but it came with directions. The directions went something like this: "Find two trees, ten to fifteen feet apart . . ." etc. In the dark I had little desire to go wandering in the jungle looking for two trees ten to fifteen feet apart, but in the hut there was nothing even remotely resembling two trees. Then I remembered the uprights supporting the porch. *Just the spot*, I thought. As I fell down the niched log stairway and picked myself out of the mud, I decided Charlie King had been right, there had to be a better way to make a living.

With a flashlight in one hand, directions in the other, and the hammock between my legs, I tried to figure out how it should be put up. Two of these poles under the porch should do it.

The two end ropes I tied to the poles. Then there was the little matter of the mosquito netting that surrounded the hammock and attached to it. At each of the four corners the manufacturers had put a small cord. I tied these to the lattice-work the natives had covering their porch. The whole thing, as I stood back and surveyed my work, made quite a nest.

But when I tried to get into it, it wouldn't stop swinging. A zipper ran the entire height of the mosquito netting with another joining it that ran half the length of the hammock. I tried to crawl through the hole made by the two zippers and somehow made it, but when I was in, I found I'd forgotten to remove my boots. With the type of mud surrounding that hut, removing them was a necessity. I slowly reached down to get them off—a move I shouldn't have tried because I became tangled in the blankets. I guess I was twisting and turning more than the manufacturers of the hammock had foreseen, and I capsized, ending up lying on the part that should have been over my head.

It looked to me like the best thing I could do was get out and start all over, but how? The hammock was swinging furiously back and forth, tossing me around inside like a squirrel in a bag. I'll never know how I got my body out of the torture chamber, but eventually I stood in the mud and looked at the twisted, impossible mess that was supposed to be my bed.

So I started again. I had to sleep somewhere. But how was I to get my boots off and get through the hole without putting my stocking feet in the mud? I tried sitting on the edge and removing them, but it was like sitting on a swing and trying to remove one's shoes. Naturally I ended up standing in the mud in my stocking feet. By this time I was so angry I didn't care how I got into it or where I slept, on the sides, bottom, or top of the hammock. I was sweating, breathing hard, and covered with mud.

The solution turned out to be simple: I dived at the hammock's opening and made it, though it took a second to stop revolving, but eventually the hammock and I ended our struggle right side up. Even so, the blankets were wound around my body so tightly I could hardly move, the mosquito netting was in my mouth, and my feet were wet and muddy. I had also forgotten to take off my web belt so my canteen was jabbing me in the back and my .45 was making a poor impression on my ribs. To top it off, I wanted a cigarette.

Slowly, so as not to upset my precarious equilibrium, I stalked the cigarette pocket with one hand, clutching the side of the hammock with the other. Somehow I got the pack out of my pocket without upsetting the whole works, got the cigarette lit without setting fire to the hammock, and settled back, exhaling a cloud of smoke and listening to the jabbering of the natives in front of their fire. It occurred to me that the bourbon (together with some of the wayward opium smoke) might possibly have contributed to my struggles with the bedding, but I dismissed the idea as unlikely.

It seemed a beautiful night now that I had stability. Surrounding our mountain were other giants of this country, each outlined in cloaks of mist and moonlight. It would have been eerie had it not been for the billion stars surrounding a huge yellow moon. It was so peaceful I almost forgave the man who had invented the jungle hammock.

On a far mountainside, a jackal raised its voice; a nearer one answered. The sound drifted to my ears out of the mist. With the flicker of the fire inside the hut and the voices of the natives, the jackal didn't scare me much. When I became convinced the animal wasn't under my bed, I relaxed again. It was still a beautiful night.

The natives continued to talk, and it wasn't long until I could recognize the different voices. The words were impossible to understand except for one which sounded like they might be trying to say, "American." I didn't care much for that; it seemed to me little good could come out of their becoming too curious about me. One voice rose above the others, and every third word seemed to be "American," and I worried a little more. The less I entered into their conversation, the better I liked it, since I could still close my eyes and picture those heads on their wall. The hair on the back of my neck crawled at the thought. I grabbed my .45 and with a trembling hand took a firm grip on it. Of course the natives were never safer than when I had that gun, but I was hoping they wouldn't know that.

As the conversation increased almost to shouting, one of the natives walked out on the porch and looked down at me. With what I hoped was a forceful voice, but was probably little more than a squeak, I asked, "Wonderful night for murder, isn't it?" The character didn't answer. He just stood there in the moonlight looking at me, the fire lighting up one side of his face.

He stared for what seemed like forever; then to my surprise came the sound of running water. I couldn't believe it, but in the moonlight I could see it was true: I was sleeping in the Naga's bathroom and this guy was using it. After the first Naga, came a long procession, all relieving themselves over my bed. I thanked the manufacturer of the jungle hammock for the tarpaulin he had put over the top; otherwise it would have been a very damp night.

During the night, dozens of natives entered the village. The two men the chief had sent out earlier evidently had been emissaries to other Naga villages, though God knows where they were in the jungle. The men had done their job well, though. There seemed to be an ample number to carry our equipment the next day.

One thing that interested me no end, and scared me more than a little when I first saw it down the trail, was their version of a flashlight. Having decided I was in no danger from the natives—other than getting peed on—I was lying there relaxed and smoking. As I looked out into the darkness, I saw a small red ball bobbing and weaving in the air. The medicinal liquor had been good, perhaps even better than that, but I hadn't drunk enough to be seeing things that weren't there. But red balls don't appear for no reason. All I could do was sit up in the hammock—as much as I could sit up—and watch them approach. It wasn't really fear that made me shake, I told myself, it was only nervousness. Then, from the faint glow of the balls I glimpsed the human forms behind them. I lay back relieved, for the balls were only the glowing tips on the end of bamboo poles.

Finally I went to sleep. It was a fitful, disturbed sleep filled with little brown men looking down at me through their front porch, peeing into the night, and waving red balls in the air. I seemed to be stuck knee-deep in mud and unable to miss the man-made dew that was falling so heavily. It was not a comfortable night.

If the Naga ever went to bed that night I don't know, but at 4:30 in the morning, while it was still dark, the women were up and pounding something I correctly guessed to be rice. The muffled thud, thud, continuous and without rhythm, would wake a hibernating bear. Shortly thereafter I heard the voices of the men and could see the brightening reflection of their fire. Wearily, I swung my feet out of the hammock, wiggled my mud-caked toes, and eased into my boots.

As I climbed the notched ladder, my eyes met a sight I won't easily forget: The big front room of the chief's house was filled to overflowing with brown-skinned Nagas, all of them staring at me. The fire behind them framed their squatting bodies, their piled up hair, with a flickering, weird background. All I could see was the glint of white teeth and the glitter of eyes. The leering, naked skulls on the wall framed them, and the air was heavy with tobacco smoke, sweaty bodies, and effluvium. Standing at the entrance of that room, I tried to smile and said my one Naga word, "Kajaiee." It worked. They actually laughed. The tension was broken. The old chief unfolded himself and came forward, took me by the hand, and led me to the fire.

My God, I thought, *not tea, not at this hour!* But tea is what the good and venerable chief had in mind. Holding up both hands to him in a negative gesture, I went to the food sack for some good old American coffee. I didn't know how it would taste cooked in a bamboo tube, but it couldn't be worse than their tea.

Taking a bamboo tube from the rack behind the chief, I poured in some coffee and water, stuck the end of it in the fire, and propped up the other end with a forked stick. At first the chief looked puzzled, then slightly annoyed until I poured him a bamboo cupful and he tasted it. His face lit up in evident enjoyment and he passed the cup around the circle of men. A few were missed, so I put another tube-full on to boil. That was a mistake. In the next half-hour, I did nothing but make coffee for the Nagas. They drank it as fast as I could brew it.

Finally calling a halt to the coffee making, I put water on to boil for cereal. The brightly colored box, proclaiming it the finest cereal in the world, was cause in itself for a murmur of assent from my friends. I cooked more than I could possibly eat since I had a feeling this was going to be a repetition of the coffee incident. It was, but I underestimated the food capacity of a Naga.

Batch after batch of cereal went down those hungry gullets. I wondered what they would have done for food if I hadn't been there to cook breakfast for them. When I finally called a halt to this noise, I sat back and contemplated them with a lifted eyebrow. I looked at my burnt fingers and reflected on the peculiarities of life. *Once was*, I thought, *the wife* . . . but, hell, that was too long ago to remember.

Still, the Naga were very appreciative and smiled their thanks. In a way, I was rather proud of having pleased and filled them, much like the hostess who has spent hours in the kitchen appreciates guests who enjoy the dinner. I leaned against the wall, lit a cigarette, and gazed with warmth upon the recipients of my labors.

But having finished his cereal and understanding I wasn't going to make any more, the chief moved to the fire and began boiling rice—and in huge quantities. It couldn't be! These people were so small and yet had eaten more per capita than is ordinarily consumed by a food-loving American soldier. The shock, so early in the morning, was almost too much. I sat there and watched with awe as those damn natives ate all that rice—and there wasn't a potbelly in the crowd.

By then the dawn was beginning to lighten up the jungle. Red beams poured down the green mountainsides and probed the interior of our hut. In the valleys, a few trees reached through the mist they'd slept under. In the forest, the animals began to stir and yawn. The strange early morning cries of birds mingled with the dog-like bark of deer. *Soon we'll be on our way*, I thought, which proved how little I knew yet about the Nagas.

Fooling around with this and that in preparation for the day's hike, I didn't pay much attention to the chief and his men. I presumed, though, that they, too, were getting ready. But when I finally looked over at them, they were all stretched out around the fire smoking their pipes again. I went over to the chief and made signs like walking and hurry-up and pointed to the mountain he'd indicated yesterday as the one where my flyer was. To my gesticulations the old chief just nodded and smiled in a sapient sort of way . . . and continued smoking his pipe. It was most exasperating. Generations of American habit were ahead of me, which included getting a job done when it needed to be done, but like it or not I would have to wait until they were good and ready to go.

Soon, though, my friends began to stir a little. They'd started opening the para-packs, oohing and aahing at each article they uncovered, from cans of beans to a tube of shaving cream, the latter an item I could have done without. Each of the natives had a little basket which would hold, I imagined, about thirty pounds. The baskets were of a peculiar construction. The top of the baskets had two shoulder straps of woven bamboo, with another strap looping from the top of the basket through a wooden yoke. It looked a little puzzling, until they put them on their backs; then it became a sensible arrangement. They put their arms through the two loops attached to the basket and the yoke fitted on the backs of their necks against their shoulders. The end of the other loop went onto their foreheads. It looked so solid and balanced that they probably could have done somersaults without the baskets falling off.

Gradually their work grew efficient: the men formed a circle, baskets in hand, and the chief loaded them. Evidently they had union rules, though, for each man was loaded according to his size. The larger a man was, the larger his load. The chief was the big cheese, and there was little or no argument from the men in the circle.

When all of his men had their baskets full, a considerable number of things remained in the packs. The old chief went out and recruited all the youngsters, male and female, plus a number of young ladies. To all of these he gave lighter loads, but it emptied the para-packs completely.

It was a long and colorful line of porters that started down the trail. Interesting, I thought, that a complete stranger could drop out of the sky with enough equipment to fill a large truck and, merely by asking, get so much help and cooperation. So far there had been no question of payment. Either they didn't expect any or I, somehow, was supposed to know what to give them for their work.

Going downhill was fine as far as I was concerned, no effort at all. The jungle was thick, though, with brush close in on all sides and in many places overhead as well. We went through a field of grass that was at least ten feet high. I gawked so much at everything around me that I kept tripping over rocks and roots in the trail. The chief cut me a bamboo stick and, like a blind child, I felt my way along.

But if downhill was O.K., the jungle nearly smothered me, and I could seldom see more than a few feet off the trail. The jungle was a solid mass of vines, trees, and brush all interlaced, forming a solid, almost impenetrable wall.

Then there were the leeches. As I walked down the trail I could see them sitting up, half their bodies waving around in the air, waiting for me to brush them with my foot or leg. When I did, they attached with such tenacity that pulling them off was a terrific job. In the first place, their bodies are covered with slime; to get a grip with my fingernails was next to impossible. Those fool slugs could crawl through the eye of a shoe or between the belt of my trousers and shirt—which some did. When they hit flesh, they sank in their jaws, excreting a fluid that frees blood of its usual ability to coagulate. Then they grew larger and larger as they drank my blood.

If, after they'd sunk their jaws, I tried to pull them off, their jaws remained, poisoning the wound and causing infection. One leech wouldn't have been hard to deal with, but the jungle was full of them, and they attached themselves by the dozens. They hung from trees, they were on the brush that whipped by bare arms on the trail, they lay in wait in the mud. If a man should lie down on the grass for very long without taking precautions, the leeches would certainly have him.

But I only began to be aware of the leeches gradually and especially after I noticed that after about ten minutes of walking the Naga would stop and pick something off their bodies. Though I couldn't feel anything biting me, I began to look myself over. *My God*, I thought as I saw them on my legs. *I'm establishing a leech-head in Burma.* They were all over me. I tried to flick a few of the crowd off, but they'd catch onto my fingers and hang on. It was like trying to throw away chewing gum.

As I struggled, more climbed up my legs from the ground. I was being swamped with leeches. It made me almost panic-stricken; I wanted to run, to do anything to escape these weird, disgusting organisms. They turned what looked like a tropical walk in the woods into a nightmare. From there on, I, too, stopped every few minutes and pulled leeches. The natives in their bare feet and loincloths could see all the leeches that landed on them. Earlier I had thought of the Naga as nearly naked; now I thought of myself as over-clothed. With all my clothing, I was at a disadvantage, and it worried me to think about the ones I couldn't see that were drinking away.

At the foot of the mountain we came to a river, a roaring torrent of water, all the more surprising because the thick growth had muffled its sound until we were almost upon it. The mountainside swept straight down to the stream, and at first it seemed impassable. But the trail had been chosen with care. Behind a huge boulder in the stream was a comparatively quiet pool, and in a second the men had stripped and were in it. The women, too, showed no hesitation as they joined in the swim.

The bath had a two-fold purpose: It was fun, and it washed off the leeches. Slightly abashed, I stripped and joined them. Women or no, the leeches had to go. When I took off my trousers I saw my legs were covered with the fat and blood-swollen creatures. The Nagas stopped their splashing and helped me pick them off my naked body. My crimson face, I guess they thought, must be getting sunburned.

By now the early coolness had passed. The sun was hot, and the cold water tumbling down out of some high place was refreshing. It was fun to stand there and watch these primitive people, unaffected by civilization, relax and enjoy themselves. But it was clear we had to move on. If the poor guy in the village we were making for was in serious shape, minutes might count. This time, though, I took a hint from these "primitives" and started out in nothing more than my shorts and boots. After all, this was their country, and being nearly naked had obvious advantages.

So out of the water and up the mountain we started, and with each step uphill—and each new leech—it became hotter and hotter. The Naga are hill people, and hills are their business, but with me . . . well, hills are wonderful when you're flying over them or walking down them, but the Naga build their trails straight up and down a mountain. The trail went up in front of my face. If I stuck out my tongue, I could have picked up a leech or two on it; and why not? They were everywhere else! I began using both hands and feet to make the grade.

For a while we followed the bed of a small secondary stream tumbling down the hill. The water rushing against my unsteady feet on the slippery rocks made walking not only difficult but hazardous. Where the bank of the stream was steepest was where the Naga, naturally, chose to climb out. We clambered along a slippery mud path for a while, sliding back half a step for every one we moved forward. Then we came to a fallen tree slanted upward across what looked like a shallow depression in the ground. Though the log's surface was covered with slippery moss, the Naga with their bare feet walked along it with ease. Then I tried it. It didn't look too bad: even if I did slide off, the ground below me was covered with foliage, or so I thought. About halfway up the log, my feet started slipping, and off I went, right through the foliage under which I expected to find the ground—but the ground was another ten feet down. The log had covered an over-grown ravine.

I landed stunned and bruised and a little shaken. My friend the chief threw me a vine and hauled me out, a somewhat embarrassed jungle novice. None of the Naga who were watching the performance laughed; I would have felt far better if they had. To the contrary, they seemed upset about the whole thing, which puzzled me. The next log we came to like that one, they all stopped, lay down their packs and built a bamboo railing for me. I felt rather silly but a hell of a lot safer, and I began to realize they were concerned that this big dumb American might hurt himself and ruin the whole trip.

On and on we chugged up the mountain, the hill people keeping up a running conversation as they climbed. I was thankful I was still able to breathe. Every cigarette I ever smoked came back to haunt me. The chief in front of me actually stopped once, lit an old pipe, and continued up the hill. How he did it I'll never know. The odor of that foul tobacco whipping past my nose cut down considerably on my oxygen supply.

It seemed forever, but we finally hit the top. And perched up there was a village, if I may call one house a village. I looked around for the lost pilot, but of course this wasn't the right village; we still had another mountain to climb.

By now it was around noon, and the sun was really pouring it on. The water in my canteen was about to boil—so was my blood, what blood the leeches had left me. All the Nagas jabbered to each other, and I staggered under the shade of the house. When I finally got the sweat out of my eyes enough to see, I lit a cigarette and looked around.

As soon as I did that, though, I had to pass cigarettes out to all the party. There went another pack. *The money I could make as a cigarette salesman out here after the war*, I thought as I passed them around to eager hands. Everyone quietly sat down for a smoke except one woman who stood in front of me holding a baby in her arms.

The baby was a cute little thing, except where there should have been hair there was nothing but a mass of scabs and running sores. Some of the scabs were dry and puckered and must have hurt the baby like hell. It was almost unimaginable to me, raised in America, that there should be a place where babies were raised without proper medical attention. I felt for the child and, though no doctor, thought there must be something I could do to help.

The mother handed me the baby, and, showing him a small bandage I carried that had a red cross on it, I asked the chief for the medical kit. He got the idea, unpacked a couple of baskets, and found it. First I washed the child's head with warm water and then smoothed the whole thing with boric acid ointment. I remembered that a doc had once used boric acid in my eyes, so I knew it probably wouldn't be too strong for the baby's tender skin. The salve I knew was needed to soften the scabs and relieve the pain, but that's about all I knew. I gave the mother a can of it and, through signs, was able to make her understand to put some on twice a day and to keep the child out of the sun.

All this treatment, though, must have given the Naga the impression I was a medicine man, for they all crowded around, each with a complaint. Here, I guess they thought, was a man who could help them with their aches and pains at last. My presence took on a new meaning for them, and they began clamoring for attention. Being human, I couldn't resist the temptation; also, I figured I could at least help them more than if they had no treatment at all. Naga after Naga came forward, many with the same trouble, infected leech bites. They were rather vicious-looking things in their later stages. Some of the holes looked like volcanoes and bore down to the bone. I opened each one with a sterilized knife, swabbed it clean, applied sulfa powder, and wrapped it with a bandage. I was doubtful about how much good I was doing, but it was at least an effort in the right direction. They all seemed satisfied with my treatment, though, for they went away smiling.

So far, I had been the great white savior, that is until a case appeared that stopped me cold. A woman made her way over to me. She tapped her chest below the breast and grimaced. She was older than some of the girls and rather heavy, and her trouble might have been any number of things. But so as not to lose face with my new crowd of patients, I put on my best professional air: I thumped her chest with one hand tapping the other, put my head down as I had seen doctors do, and listened with an intent expression. Actually I couldn't hear a thing except one hand tapping the other, but I could see the Naga watching in wonderment.

After three or four thumps, I raised my head as if I had found the solution, a smile of assurance playing around my mouth. But the solution I'd found was to my trouble, not hers, for my eye had caught the caption on one of the bottles in the medical kit. It said "bicarbonate of soda, peppermint flavored." I solemnly unscrewed the top, handed her a couple of tablets, and told her to chew them by putting an imaginary pill in my mouth and chewing vigorously. The old gal put the two I'd handed her into her mouth and chewed. The effect was immediate: After rice all her life, the peppermint must have tasted swell. Her face lit up with evident enjoyment. From there on, after she told the rest, I had a dozen cases of chest pains, and my bottle was soon empty.

Other cases came forward as well—various infected cuts, punctures, and sores, and I fixed them all up, one after another. I was making friends by the dozen, and, frankly, I felt sorry for them. And, curiously, I began feeling friendship toward them as well; the fact is, I was learning to like these people. I liked them for their toughness and their willingness to help, for their friendliness and enthusiasm and quickness to smile, and for the way they trusted this oversized American stranger who had entered their lives by dropping out of the sky.

Eventually we started out again. Though I still felt the urgency of getting to the pilot, by now I wasn't in so much of a hurry. My muscles ached, and my head swam. The thought of another grueling climb like that last mountain nauseated me. But off we went.

What goes up must go down, thank the Lord, because for us it was now down, but so steep and muddy that I spent most of my time sliding on what was left of my undershorts. The stones didn't bother my posterior much; it was the sharp roots that did it. Still, we made good time and soon reached another river. This one wasn't as large as the last one, but it was just as welcome. To the natives, who obviously knew this stream was coming, the trip down didn't seem so bad, but to me, who could see another half a day ahead with nothing but leech bites and the sweltering heat, it seemed longer than it was.

We shed our clothing again, and in we went. I took a moment to look at my feet, though, and they seemed like bloody stumps. Blisters everywhere. Then, when I jumped into the pool, damned if I didn't get almost swept downstream with the current. Going under, I grabbed the nearest hand. When I got back onto my feet and blew the water out of my lungs, I was able to mutter a meek "kajaiee." I looked at the person whose hand I had grabbed and who was now holding me up, and my face turned crimson; the big strong hero had been saved by a gal half his size . . . and she wasn't hard on the eyes either. Mumbling at the vagaries of fate, I felt like a country bumpkin, but she smiled at me as if she saved stupid Americans every day. I smiled back . . . and we began to pick leeches off each other. It was fascinating, too, to see where a quick-eyed girl with nimble fingers could think of to look for leeches. I was becoming accustomed to this primitive way of life and began to think it an inviting way to live.

The stream, of course, was at the bottom of the mountain we'd just descended, but to me it had been the top of the day. But from here on it was up, up, forever up. I was so slow that even the women, burdened as they were with packs, pulled away from me. I just couldn't keep up. No longer was I walking: Stumbling and struggling were more the words for it. Climb a hill for an hour, most of us can do, but when it comes to climbing them all day—give me a streetcar. Two hours after we left that stream, I was about finished. I kept thinking of Rudyard Kipling's poem "If." The line kept running through my head—"And so hold on when there is nothing in you . . . you'll be a man, my son!" Hell, I didn't have anything in me now, and I didn't care if I ever was a man. All I wanted at that point was to lie down and die.

I thought I was beginning to imagine things when I heard the sound of airplane motors, but I wasn't. I grabbed the little radio and lay down on the ground and started calling. An opportunity to rest my weary bones is about all it meant to me; I was so exhausted I'd almost forgotten why I was in this hell. I was so hot, so tired, so wet from sweat it had become a battle just to keep moving.

The cool, firm voice that came out of the set brought me around a little. It was Andy. "Where the hell are you, boy?"

"You've got me," I answered. "But where I am is hell sure enough, though I haven't been introduced to Satan yet."

"Well, get on the ball, Diebold. You haven't got all day, you know."

The injustice of it, I thought. He sits up there in a nice cool cockpit in a blue sky I can barely make out through the foliage, turning a wheel and telling me to get to work. I counted to ten and then answered him. "Give us four more hours, and I should be with the body, I think."

"Four hours. O.K., we'll be back then, but hurry up."

I was so mad at the absurdity of it that I beat the hot, steaming jungle floor with my fists while the chief, who had come back down the trail to find out what the fuss was about, clucked his disapproval. Andy had only been riding me, but it was tough to take at that point. It was just as well that I didn't speak the chief's language, for I'm certain if I had I would have been in for a fatherly lecture on temperament.

Wearily we ploughed ahead. My throat was raw from the quick gasps of hot air. Somewhere this God-awful churning of the legs and sweat in the eyes must end, I thought.

It was unexpected when it happened. Around the corner of some heavy brush, they came into view, the most beautiful sight I'd ever seen—two Naga houses. To me, instead of being surrounded by mud and filth, those two huts seemed made of ice cream and peppermint candy. There's no describing reaching the ultimate goal when everything inside you tells you you'll never make it. It's like a gambler raking in an unbelievable pile of winnings. Home never looked better.

I staggered to the nearest log, slumped down on it, and simply stared at those huts. They were only a hundred yards away, but I didn't think I'd make it even that far. Tomorrow, the day after, a thousand days after that, I didn't think I'd be able to move again.

But when I'd regained my breath I thought better of it and made my way up to the largest of the two huts. On the porch stood a wrinkled old man, a welcoming committee of one. My native friends were standing below the porch looking at the old man, and all were talking at once.

As I approached, the jabbering ceased. I stood with the crowd and looked at the old man, too. "We're in the wrong village again," I moaned. "Not that. I simply can't go any farther." The old man spoke a few words to me, none of which, of course, I could understand, and then he motioned me up on the porch. I climbed the notched log and entered the house after him. As tired as I was, I was getting excited. Was he there?

I peered into the dimly lit front room. Over by the fire I could see the outline of a form stretched out on the floor. I walked over to it, afraid of what I might find, but he was there, lying by the fire, the back of his head toward me. But was he alive?

He twisted around, and I saw his face, and tears were running down his cheeks. Neither of us said a word. I knelt beside him, and we gripped hands. It was impossible to say anything; I was too choked with emotion. I tried an experimental smile, but it was forced, for even though he was alive I thought even now we might be too late. He looked to me as if he were on his way out of this lovely world of ours as he lay there softly sobbing.

He was covered with dirty pieces of cloth, so all I could see of him was his face, but that was enough. It told a horrible story of suffering and starvation and exposure. His beard was long and tangled, his hair spread like a woman's on the log he was using as a pillow. The bones of his cheeks stood out in ugly relief below yellowing, bulging eyes. He spoke, through cracked, fever-ridden lips. "Thank the Almighty. You've come."

I spoke with all the unfelt confidence I could muster. "Right you are, lad, and a couple of doctors will be here in a minute. We'll have you running as good as new in no time and out of this fire trap in a jiffy."

He smiled at my slang, and I realized it must have been a long time since he'd heard any language but Naga. He closed his eyes and gave a long sigh. I was afraid this was it, but then he opened them again. "Have you any food?"

"Coming right up," I answered. "Would some nice warm cereal fit the bill?"

"Of course," he said and closed his eyes. I have never made cereal faster. As I cooked, I could see his hands; they were nothing but bones covered with a layer of skin. He was a human skeleton.

When the food was ready, I fed him. All he was able to take were a few spoonfuls and a couple of sips of tea; he was exhausted from the effort. He seemed to go to sleep or he was in a coma, I couldn't tell. I lifted the dirty burlap the natives had covered him with for an examination. He opened his eyes again when I did this. I hoped my face remained normal when I looked, but my stomach turned inside-out. He was all bones, and his legs and body were covered with huge, ulcerous sores. He was looking at me hard, and I had to say something, so I smiled and said, "Prickly heat, eh?" It was a poor attempt at humor, but he managed a feeble grin.

This boy needed a doctor in the worst way. I began praying for the rescue ship to come. This was too much for my first-aid knowledge of medicine. I replaced the sacking and started talking to him, anything to make him feel better. It seemed to help. As I talked, I could see him improve . . . or at least to become more alert. It made him feel safer. Another American was there, he was rescued.

He told me, in a weak voice, that his name was Greenlaw W. Collins (he actually gave his middle initial) and that he was from New Orleans. I took up the conversation and talked about New Orleans since, luckily, I had been there. He liked to hear me talk of his home, it was easy to see. He mumbled in the middle of one of my sentences that it had been his first Hump trip and his last, he hoped. I assured him he was on his way back to New Orleans as of right now.

"I was flying a pea shooter"—a fighter—"and had engine trouble," he said. "The plane went into a spin, so I had to bail out. I landed in a tree and lost my jungle kit, so I had no food. I followed a river I found. How long I don't know, but it was over three weeks."

Out in this country for more than three weeks without a knife, a compass, food, or anything. This boy was tough, and then some.

"The natives found me going down the river and brought me on a litter up here. Don't know how long that was, I lost track of the days. On the way down that river, I slept on rocks in the middle of the water to get away from the leeches and the animals. My shoes wore out, and the rocks cut my feet to ribbons. It was tough going at times. The natives here have been trying to feed me. It's pretty awful stuff, monkey meat and rice and then rice and monkey meat. I just sorta lost my appetite, I guess."

No wonder, I thought, remembering the smell of burning hair before the meal at the other village. A piece of soot fell from the roof onto his face. He raised a shaking hand and brushed it off.

"Did you get my note?" he asked.

"Yep, that's why I'm here."

"Never thought you would. I thought sure I was a goner. You know, it took me a whole day to write it."

Talking was an effort, and he rested a bit. He closed his eyes, but in a moment he spoke again.

"Didja see those sores on my legs?"

"Yes."

"Well, once they got me here I kept 'em open with a native knife. I thought I had better keep them running. That was right, wasn't it?"

"Perfect. You'll be up and running in a week."

"Thanks," he said with a wry smile. I wasn't fooling him, I could see that.

He told me a little more, and I learned other details later, like his eating bamboo shoots, bitter berries, and even leeches! He talked about the soaking rains, using his socks as gloves and wrapping up his head at night to escape the mosquitoes and crawling pests. In that fetid, humid jungle, his boots rotted and started to fall apart. And most of all he mentioned the cold, how awful cold the nights got, and the terrible, solitary loneliness of that sea of green.

But mostly he seemed to drift in and out of focus. There was no doubt his had been a close thing. What I was worried about was that it was a close thing still, that if we didn't get help there soon, he might not make it.

Then I heard it—the search plane approaching the village. It was faint at first, but in less than a minute it sounded as if the pilot had brought the plane right down in the hut with us. Collins heard it, too, and looked at me.

"Here come your doctors."

I went out on the porch and turned on the radio. Andy's voice came over the ear-phone. "Air rescue calling gravel shuffler. Air rescue calling gravel shuffler."

I was in no mood for jokes right then. "Yeah, this is gravel shuffler, and we need medical help down here as soon as you can get it."

"Stand by Diebold," he answered. "I've got the docs on board, and they'll be right down. How bad is he?"

"He's not too good. Tell them to bring the works as far as equipment goes. And may they be young and strong, for this is no country for the feeble."

"Will do," Andy answered. "And they look pretty big and strong to me."

The plane circled around, and I knew just how those two medicos felt as the big C-47 skimmed down the side of the far mountain. It shot up the side of our mountain and over the village and then a parachute blossomed from the rear. It was exciting to watch from the ground and not a little satisfying. But then the wind caught the falling chute, and it disappeared over the far side of the mountain. I wished the boy luck and then turned to the chief and pointed in the direction the chute had gone. He immediately sent two of his men on the run in that direction.

"Pretty lousy aim," I radioed Andy. "It shouldn't take more than two days to find him out there." He deserved that dig after the gravel shuffler guff he'd been handing me.

Andy didn't answer. Around again came the plane, and the sprawling, tumbling figure of a man flew out of the cargo door of the ship. The figure tumbled and fell straight down, but the chute didn't open. It was free fall, no paratrooper chute! I could see the doctor's arms flailing in the air as his hand grasped for the ripcord and missed. My knees turned to water as I stood there holding my breath. I didn't want to look, but I couldn't tear my eyes away. The sensation of helplessness was awful.

It seemed almost too late when he finally found the ripcord and the chute opened. The canopy streamed out and snapped open above his head, and a split second later he hit the ground. As I ran to where he hit, I hoped and prayed it had opened in time to break his fall. I expected to find him with his hips driven up between his eyebrows. As the natives and I approached on a dead run, he slowly sat up and shook his head.

"My God," he said to no one in particular, "I thought I'd had it."

The doc had landed in soft mud at least six inches deep, the chute slowing his fall and the mud cushioning his landing. That was all that saved him from being seriously injured. He was a big man, over six feet with wide, husky shoulders. After I helped him to his feet, he stuck out his hand, and we shook. His fingers were long and narrow but strong. He had a grip like a vise. This must be the surgeon, and did we need him! "My name's Spruell," he said, "although it was damn near mud." We both laughed in relief. "Bill to my friends. I'll look after the patient. You had better try and find our friend. He's somewhere over in that . . ." He waved his hand in the general direction the other chute had fallen.

"The natives have already gone after him," I said. "Don't worry, they'll get him. They've been a big help. Come on, I'll take you to see Lieutenant Collins. He needs you fast, and I'm not foolin'."

Suddenly I remembered the radio. Andy's voice squawked out at me, "Get on the air, gravel shuffler, get on the air, will ya' before I have to bail out and find out what's goin' on."

"Everything's going to be all right, Andy," I said as the major and I walked toward the hut. As I spoke, I saw the figure of a white man with some natives come limping out of the jungle above the village. "Everything *is* all right," I corrected. "Everyone accounted for and unhurt as far as I can tell."

"Whew! I'm sure happy as hell about that. They had me plenty worried."

"Don't think for a minute they weren't worried, too."

"Right," he said. "Is there anything else you want?"

"Better stick around for a few minutes until the doc takes a look at Collins. He may need more supplies than we have here, although I can't see what it'd be except a kitchen sink or something."

"If he wants one, tell him we'll drop it."

Around us the natives had gone wild. This was too much for them, a big noisy airplane swooping over the mountain, men dropping from the skies all over the place.

Inside the hut, the major took a quick look at Collins while I laid out the medical supplies dropped to me the day before. The major rummaged through them. "Tell them all I need is some glycerin."

I told Andy who radioed back, "O.K., I'll be back with it in the morning. Good luck, old top."

Up the notched log came the other parachutist. We shook hands, and he introduced himself as Captain "Sandy" Morrissey from Milwaukee, Wisconsin.

The two doctors went immediately to work on Collins. I watched them start to give him blood plasma, and though I wanted to help they didn't seem to need me. Then I thought I'd better be paying off the natives who had helped bring the stuff over from the other village; they might want to go home again. I opened the pack I'd carried and took out my bag of silver rupees. I went down the ladder and tried to hand each of the natives a couple, but they wouldn't take them from me. Instead, they pointed to the chief, so I turned to him and gave him a handful. He took them, went around to each of the natives, and handed them one apiece, then he handed the remainder back to me, keeping one himself.

One rupee, about thirty cents American for all that work. I handed the chief back the extra rupees, enough for another round, and motioned that he give them to the others. Everyone looked highly pleased. Sixty cents for all that mountain climbing burdened down with heavy packs, and they considered it high wages. *What a place to retire*, I thought.

SEVEN

The Mysterious Disappearance of Dennis Martin

Michael Bradley

SPENCE FIELD IN MID-JUNE IS ONE OF THE LOVELIEST SPOTS IN GREAT Smoky Mountains National Park. The skies are clear most of the time with only a few cumulus clouds dotted here and there. Wide vistas stretch away in all directions; flame azalea, rhododendron, and mountain laurel display their blossoms along with numerous wildflowers. The high elevation, forty-five hundred feet, makes for pleasant daytime temperatures and provides just enough coolness at night to encourage a camper to snuggle into a sleeping bag. Spence Field is a popular hiking destination and backcountry camping spot, but huge crowds do not gather there. A backcountry shelter and a spring are the only accommodations. Spence Field is atop the high crest of the Smokies and is reached by hiking uphill for three and a half miles on the Anthony Ridge Trail and then following the Bote Mountain Trail for a little over a mile to reach the "bald" known as Spence Ridge. According to an often told story, a group of Cherokee road builders in the 1850s were asked to choose the route to follow up the mountains. The "v" sound is not part of the speech pattern of native Cherokee speakers, so the decision was reached by a "bote" instead of a "vote."

In the Smoky Mountains a "bald" is a mountaintop largely devoid of trees but covered by grass and shrubs. How and why an area becomes a bald is an ecological mystery, but it is agreed that grazing livestock on these meadows in pioneer times helped keep them open. Today the balds provide the best viewpoints of the surrounding mountains because of the absence of trees.

Considering the natural beauty of the location, it is no wonder that the Martin family of Knoxville, Tennessee, made an annual camping trip to Spence Field a Father's Day tradition. Indeed, this was part of a family tradition dating back to a time before the founding of the park.

Early in the twentieth century, John and Jim Martin were operators of a sawmill in the Anthony Creek area. The family owned a farm in the Little River area and drove their cattle up the Bote Mountain road every summer to allow the livestock to graze on the bald at Spence Field. There was no need to keep a daily check on the cattle, and they were left to fend for themselves except for a visit in mid-June when salt blocks were carried to the pasture.

After the park was established, the Martin family continued to hold something of an open-air family reunion at Spence Field each June. A dozen or more members of the Martin family—men, women, and children—would make the hike and enjoy the outdoors as well as each other's company.

The trip to Spence Field for 1969 was a special time because Clyde Martin, a Knoxville schoolteacher, would be accompanied not only by his adult son, Bill Clyde, but by Bill's two children, Doug and Dennis. Doug was nine years old and had made the trip before, but this would be the first time grandfather Clyde had enjoyed the company of six-year-old Dennis on the annual expedition. Dennis was a special education student, but he was healthy, strong, and had been on many day hikes with the family. In addition, Clyde's three brothers and a sister would be joining the party along with members of their families.

Clyde led his party up the Anthony Creek Trail to its junction with the Russell Field Trail and then on to the shelter at Russell Field to spend their first night in the mountains, and the next day the group made the short hike on to Spence Field where the rest of the group had been camping for a day or so. Not much was seen of wildlife as the group hiked along, although they did see one young black bear and, later, a sow bear with two cubs. Some of the hikers thought these bears were acting too familiar, as if they had come to associate people with food. This was, and is, one of the most serious problems in the park when it comes to managing wildlife and people. Wildlife usually shy away from people, but if the animals are fed by humans they begin to lose their fear of people and may become aggressive. This is particularly a problem with bears, which are quite fond of human food. Feeding bears always causes problems, sometimes for the person doing it, always for the bear, and often for both!

But, except for swatting gnats, there was no problem with wildlife and the hikers reached Spence Field and united with the rest of the Martin group. After lunch Dennis helped his grandfather clean up the dishes and square away the campsite, and then the group relaxed and the children began to play. After some time had passed one of the adults noticed the children gathered in a huddle, sneaking glances toward the group relaxing and dozing on the grass. Then the children began to spread out and approach the adult group from all sides. It seemed their plan was to sneak up on the adults and scare them. Doug and two other boys circled along the North Carolina side of the ridge while Dennis headed west on the Appalachian Trail by himself. Dennis stepped behind a bush and the adults thought he was using this as cover to make his approach.

In just a couple of minutes the "ambush" was sprung as Doug and his companions rushed into the open, yelling like demons. Dennis did not appear. Since he was the youngest, it was thought, perhaps he was just a little slower than the others. But when Dennis did not appear in two or three minutes all the members of the party began to call for him. Grandfather Clyde and father, Bill Clyde, walked out the trail in the direction Dennis had taken and the rest of the party continued to call his name, but Dennis was nowhere to be found. He has not been found to this day.

The Martins were experienced outdoorsmen, so they quickly set up a search with adults taking each of the trails that led away from their campsite. There was plenty of light since June brings the longest day of the year, although in the hollows and under the heavy tree canopy shadows would lengthen in an hour or so. One by one the searchers returned with no news. They had seen no footprints matching the shoes Dennis was wearing, and hikers they met said they had not seen a lone boy on the trail. Grandfather Clyde knew more help was needed, so he hiked back down the Bote Mountain and Anthony Creek Trails to reach the ranger station in Cades Cove. Then Clyde hiked through the now dark woods back to Spence Field. As the evening wore on a thunderstorm rolled over the mountains, deafening searchers with thunder and drenching them with cold rain.

The response by the Park Service was immediate. As Bill Clyde, Dennis's father, had been searching for his son he had met the park naturalist, Terry Chilcote. The naturalist had used his jeep to take Bill Clyde down the mountain to meet a ranger coming from the Cades Cove Ranger Station. Bill and the ranger then drove up the Bote Mountain route to within a short distance of Spence Field. The father and a ranger had thus thoroughly covered one possible route Dennis might have taken. When Dennis's grandfather reached Cades Cove, another ranger was sent up the trail leading from the west to reach Spence Field. Within a few hours of Dennis disappearing, the main trails east and west of Spence Field had been gone over by family members and by park rangers.

On the mind of the rangers was the risk hypothermia posed to Dennis. A dangerous medical condition, hypothermia occurs when the body loses heat faster than it can produce heat. A normal body temperature is about 98.6 degrees and hypothermia begins to occur when the body temperature falls below 95 degrees. Getting wet causes the body to lose heat, and if there is a wind the loss of heat is more rapid. Small people, with less body mass, will lose heat quickly. Dennis was about four feet tall and weighed fifty-five pounds. He was wearing only shorts and a T-shirt when he disappeared. During the night 2.5 inches of rain fell, and there were gusts of wind while the air temperature fell to near 50 degrees.

In addition to the danger of hypothermia, the rain presented searchers with treacherous footing on muddy trails and the loss of any footprints Dennis might have left. Dennis disappeared on Saturday, June 14. Even as they searched the trails in the Spence Field area for the first time, the Park Service was making calls to park employees and to area rescue squads asking them to assemble at the Bote Mountain trailhead early on Sunday morning. By Sunday the news of Dennis's disappearance was being broadcast over area TV stations, and that caused two problems. One was curiosity seekers who wanted to get a look at the search operations and who only made a nuisance of themselves by clogging the roads. The park superintendent reacted to this by simply closing the road into the area. The second problem was too many volunteers. Rangers found themselves swamped with offers of help from people who were not qualified or physically fit to go into the backcountry. These volunteers had to be carefully screened to make sure some of the would-be rescuers did not have to be rescued! During the day on Sunday about 250 qualified searchers were out looking for Dennis.

By Monday the story of Dennis Martin was on the national news. The Red Cross was included in the search effort to provide food for the searchers, and helicopters were brought in to transport searchers from Cades Cove to the various balds on the high crest of the mountains. Tracking dogs with their handlers were brought to the area, although continued heavy rains made slim the likelihood of finding a scent trail.

Two flashes of hope came during the week, one when a radio call from a ranger saying "the little boy has been found," was heard, but this proved to be another child who had briefly wandered away from his family. Another surge of hope occurred when a boy wearing a red T-shirt and green shorts was spotted in the Cades Cove campground. This young fellow was camping with his family and by chance had worn the same color combination of clothes as Dennis had on when he went missing.

Members of the Special Forces, also known as the Green Berets, came to assist in the search as did members of the National Guard. Billy Clyde Martin felt his son might have been kidnapped, so the FBI sent a team to assist. If a kidnapping had occurred, it had taken place on federal property. Also, Spence Field straddles the state line between Tennessee and North Carolina so there was sufficient basis for federal involvement. The national attention to the story led to psychics and clairvoyants offering their services and, in many cases, their "leads" were followed up. Not surprisingly, some of these types wanted money for their information and they were ignored. Still, numbers of well-meaning people poured into the park to help in the search with the number rising to as many as fourteen hundred on the weekend. Sadly, Friday, June 21, was Dennis's seventh birthday. By this time hope was waning that the lost boy would be found alive.

Exposure was considered the greatest danger for Dennis, but there was some concern over wild animals, especially bears and wild hogs. The mast, or nut crop, on which bears depend for much of their food, had been poor and more bears than usual were on the move looking for food. At that time there had never been a fatal bear attack in the park, but the possibility could not be ruled out. This suspicion was reinforced by the experience some of the family had with the somewhat aggressive bears during their hike into Spence Field. While no shreds of clothing had been found, orders were given that all bear feces be examined to determine if human remains were present in them. None was found.

A less likely suspect for a fatal attack was wild hogs. There is a population of wild hogs in the Smokies, dating back to the early twentieth century when Russian boars were imported to a private hunting preserve. Some of these escaped and have bred with local pigs to produce feral animals. These animals are quite destructive to flora in the park and can be dangerous to humans, although there were no known incidents, then or now, of attacks on people. An examination of hog feces showed no evidence of an attack on a human.

As an example of the thoroughness of the search, all the pit toilets at nearby backcountry campsites were examined. A ranger wearing chest-high waders was lowered into the pit of each toilet and felt with his feet to determine if a body was hidden in the vault of the toilet.

As the second week of the search began, the weather continued to be uncooperative. Frequent heavy thunderstorms drenched the mountains and on some occasions rain fell for most of the day.

Very little effective searching could be done under such circumstances. Then a report was received from Harold Key, who had been visiting the park on the day Dennis disappeared, taking photos of wildlife in the Sea Branch area. Mr. Key reported hearing a child scream and then seeing a dirty, unkempt man getting into a white car and driving away. He did not see a child. The place where Mr. Key heard and saw these things was about five miles from Spence Field. To go from the point where Dennis was last seen to Sea Branch, it would have been necessary to go for some distance across country since no trail links the two spots. From the time Dennis disappeared until the time Mr. Key saw the unkempt man did not seem long enough for anyone to cover that distance. For this reason this report was not followed up to a great extent.

On June 29 a decision was made to end the mass search for Dennis Martin. The searchers and their equipment were brought down from the mountains and the volunteers went home. After two full weeks of searching with no results, the chances of Dennis being found alive were nil. All along the searchers had been told by family members that Dennis was a shy child who probably would not call out to help them find him; he would likely respond to his name. This had made the search more difficult. Many people who get lost experience a psychological reaction that makes them afraid of people, so they hide from searchers who are very close to them. In the rhododendron and laurel thickets of the Smokies, a small person such as Dennis could hide himself from a careful searcher who was only a few feet away. However, three of the most expert trackers in the employ of the park were assigned to keep going over the area where Dennis was last seen. Arthur Whitehead, Grady Whitehead, and J. R. Buchanan would continue the hunt for the rest of the summer. No trace of Dennis was found. Clyde Martin, Dennis's grandfather, would spend weeks and days on the mountains searching for the little boy. False leads would continue to surface for another fifteen years, but none of them were productive.

The lush foliage of the Great Smoky Mountains National Park produces from one to four inches of leaf litter and debris every year. If Dennis did meet his end in the park, his remains are now buried deep in the soil of a place he and his family loved.

Dennis was gone but not forgotten. In 2009 Dennis's cousin Hayley Martin wrote about the fortieth anniversary of his disappearance. The family still grieved the loss of such a young life, and she noted that the event had forever changed the way they viewed the mountains, a place with which they have been connected for a century.

The loss of Dennis Martin's life did produce changes that have helped save other lives. The Park Service did a thorough assessment of the way in which the search was handled and, as a result, changed some of its policies to make the process more efficient. It was learned that there can be too many searchers, especially untrained ones. The current policy is to limit the number of searchers to those who have the needed skills and training. These smaller groups are more effective because they cover the ground properly and eliminate the need for repeated searches of the same area.

The large number of participants in the Dennis Martin search may have accidentally destroyed clues as to his route and whereabouts. Hundreds of people hiked the trails and woods looking for Dennis, and their very numbers may have obliterated footprints or other signs of his passing. Currently one of the first steps taken is to block off the trails leading to the point where the lost person was last seen. Hikers already on the trail are allowed to exit the area and are interviewed as to what they may have seen of the lost person, but no new hikers are allowed into the area. This preserves whatever clues there may be until the tracking dogs and expert rangers can look over the scene. A smaller number of searchers also means there is less need for logistical support to supply food and transportation. In searching, less may be more.

A good deal of study has been done into the psychology of lost persons in an effort to understand their emotions and to predict their actions. Depending on psychological factors a lost person may stay in a very limited area or they may try to cover as much distance as possible. Knowing as much as can be known about the emotional state of the lost person helps determine how large an area should be included in the initial search.

Since a lost person becomes regional news in less than twenty-four hours and national news within two days, it is now the practice to appoint one person to deal with the press. In addition to the simple news that someone is lost, the park works to let the public know what they can do to help, such as keeping an eye out for anyone fitting the description or matching a photograph of the lost person, and what they need to avoid in order not to hinder the search, for example, staying out of the area and not getting in the way.

Technological advances have made search efforts more effective. Helicopters are much improved over the models used in 1969 and more of them are available for use in search missions. The dense tree cover of most of the Smokies means that searches from the air are not particularly effective, but during the seasons when leaves are on the trees helicopters can transport search teams and supplies into remote areas of the park quickly, saving hours if not days of travel by foot or horseback.

The advent of small, lightweight Global Positioning System (GPS) devices makes it much easier for the person coordinating a search to know precisely where search teams have been and where they still need to go. An increasing number of hikers carry a variation of the GPS device, which they can turn on if they become lost to broadcast their precise location to aircraft flying over the area.

The tragic disappearance of Dennis Martin continues to affect the lives of those who knew and loved him. But the lessons learned from the search for him have been true life-savers for others. To this extent, the sad events surrounding Dennis have not been in vain.

EIGHT

Experience Is No Guarantee

Tracy Salcedo

There are old climbers, and there are bold climbers, but there are no old bold climbers.

—A CLIMBER'S ADAGE

AS MOUNTAINEERS GET SMARTER, TECHNIQUES ARE REFINED, AND GEAR gets better, the long-lived truism paraphrased above has lost some of its relevance. While climbers like Alex Honnold, who scaled Yosemite's three-thousand-foot El Capitan without a rope, and Kilian Jornet, who reached the summit of Mount Everest twice in one week, continue to test the limits, even the neophyte, if properly outfitted, guided, and willing, has a good shot at reaching the summit of a mountain like Rainier and living to tell the tale.

A generation of mountaineers who cut their teeth on Mount Rainier—and then went on to climb other coveted, deadly peaks—have lived to tell their stories into their golden years. Jim and Lou Whittaker, as well as mountaineer Dee Molenaar, another sage of the volcano, are among the most well-known and respected of these elder summit statesmen.

But even the best and most experienced sometimes tragically fail.

Many Rainier summiters have logged impressive ascents elsewhere on the planet. The stories that follow chronicle the deaths of several climbers with international résumés whose careers ended on the volcano. Their passages also highlight another backcountry truism: You don't have to be on the steepest, or the highest, or the coldest, to meet your maker in the wild.

THE TEACHER AND THE STUDENT

Willi Unsoeld was an alpinist of the finest pedigree. Over his long career, he climbed peaks in the Cascades, the Tetons, and the Sierra Nevada. He summited Everest in 1963 via the difficult and then-unclimbed West Ridge, and claimed the first ascent of Masherburn, another Himalayan peak.

He was also a father, husband, smokejumper, philosopher, theologian, teacher . . . "Willi was a very complex, wonderful human being," recalled Tom Hornbeim, one of his Everest teammates, in an *Outside* magazine interview about the 1963 expedition. As an experiential educator—Unsoeld was a faculty member at Evergreen State College, with a focus on outdoor education—Hornbeim noted that his friend had "inspired many young lives."

His daughter Nanda Devi was one of those inspired by her father's passion and experience. She was named for a Himalayan peak that had enchanted Willi (and, later, would enchant her). In 1976 the twenty-two-year-old Devi succumbed to illness on an attempted ascent of her name-sake mountain with her father by her side. "We are not in charge in the face of reality and nature," Unsoeld said in the wake of Devi's death, "and in the final analysis, I wouldn't have it any other way."

Reality and nature, in the form of Mount Rainier, were in charge in 1979, when it unleashed an avalanche on the thoughtful mountaineer and his students near Cadaver Gap.

Unsoeld and his party, composed of twenty-one outdoor education students from Evergreen State, had been on the mountain for several days attempting to make the summit. Bad weather and hostile conditions kept them low on the peak at first, but one weather window allowed them to ascend to Camp Muir, and a second allowed them to climb to 11,800 feet, where they established a high camp.

But that was as close to the crest as they would get. Unsoeld and some of the party made an aborted summit attempt before a storm forced them to hunker down in tents near Gibraltar Rock on the Ingraham Glacier.

In the face of worsening weather, Unsoeld made the decision to return to Camp Muir. The group was on the retreat when, according to the *American Alpine Journal* accident report, the first rope team triggered a slab avalanche with a "fracture line [that] measured the entire width of Cadaver Gap and had a depth of three feet in the center."

The slide swept the four climbers on the lead rope, including Unsoeld, five hundred feet down the mountain. The leader was buried under three feet of compacted snow and ice, and one of his students, twenty-one-year-old Janie Diepenbrock, of Sacramento, California, was also completely buried. Another member of the rope team, Frank Kaplan, was only partially buried, and upon extricating himself was able to free the fourth climber, Peter Miller, who had managed to punch an arm to the surface.

The rest of the team, which was above the fracture line and not caught in the slide, acted quickly to resuscitate Miller.

But it took longer to locate, and then to uncover, Unsoeld and Diepenbrock, with one of the rescuers following the rope that had hitched them together from climber to climber. Miller survived, but despite earnest efforts at CPR, Unsoeld and Diepenbrock did not.

The *AAJ* analysis of the incident reflects not only on the decisions that played into the outcome of the climb, but also on the skills that Unsoeld's outdoor program sought to instill in students. "The foundation upon which The Evergreen State College Outdoor Education Program is built is the belief that individuals need to engage in demanding physical and mental activities in order to acquire the strength and energy it takes to accomplish something worthwhile in life," the report states. "Climbers in general believe that the risks involved in climbing lead to the benefits. It is only a question, then, of whether the risks are entered into responsibly." In the end, the report concludes, "Unsoeld made reasonable judgments under the circumstances."

The annals of the *AAJ* also include a rebuttal to this view, authored by Jeremy Bernstein in a review of *Fatal Mountaineer: The High-Altitude Life and Death of Willi Unsoeld, American Himalayan Legend*. This is included not to disrespect Unsoeld, but to highlight how individuals may view and react to the same set of inputs in different ways, for better or worse. "The conditions were so bad that [noted climber] Yvon Chouinard was leaving the mountain because of his perception of the avalanche dangers," Bernstein wrote in 2003. "This did not stop Unsoeld. Nor did the potentially bad weather. The whole thing seems to me like sheer irresponsibility—almost suicidal. In France, where guides are sanctioned by the government, this sort of performance would have led to a trial and a probable jail sentence. As it was, it led to Unsoeld's death in avalanche along with that of a young woman whom he was guiding. That anyone survived was something of a miracle."

Regardless of whether blame can be laid, the passing of Unsoeld and Diepenbrock left a profound hole. "The empty space which has been left in our lives, as in so many others, often feels as deep as the crevasses Willi used to leap and as vast as the mountainous regions of the world that used to echo his joyous yodels," Unsoeld's widow, Jolene, wrote in the wake of his death. "Yet through our tears breaks an understanding smile, a shared recognition that here went two remarkable people doing what they chose to do, knowing that in the mountains they would find wondrous beauty along with risk and the lesson of each other."

Almost Old and Bold

An accomplished Norwegian climber, Arvid Lahti had not only reached the top of the world—twice in a single year—but had also logged a number of attempts and successful climbs of Himalayan peaks, as well as topped Aconcagua in Argentina and Mount Kilimanjaro in Tanzania.

But on March 26, 2016, Lahti succumbed to hypothermia on the Gibraltar Ledges route near the Beehive.

Lahti, 58, had reached the summit with partner and fellow alpinist Monique Richard, 41. Then a winter storm swept in, with high winds and temperatures dropping into the single digits. That night, according to the park record, a Mountaineers group at Camp Muir became concerned when the two climbers, who had left gear at the camp, didn't return. They contacted rangers to report the missing summiters. The park was also aware of a snowshoer in trouble on the Muir Snowfield; he had activated his SPOT device, a satellite GPS locator that can be homed in on by rescuers in backcountry emergencies. But rescue teams would not be able to begin their ascent to Camp Muir until daylight.

On the mountain, according to Richard, she and Lahti sought shelter from the wind and cold among the rocks on the route. But they had planned to be up and off within the day; they weren't prepared to spend the night on the peak. Richard wrote that though she was sure she would be the one to die of hypothermia in that long night, it was Lahti who was unable to survive the cold, and who perished in her arms.

In the morning, according to the park service, "the climbers at Camp Muir reported that a female climber had been heard screaming from above the Camp Muir area. They were able to assist her in getting to the shelter at Camp Muir." The snowshoer also made it back to Camp Muir, and both were airlifted off the mountain and to an area hospital.

A Chinook helicopter was dispatched and Lahti's body was spotted at about 10,600 feet, "about 400 vertical feet away from Camp Muir," the park reported. A couple of days later, on March 30, "the high winds abated" and four rangers were able to bring Lahti down off the mountain.

The park service notes, rightly, that climbers like Lahti and Richard, as well as snowshoers, skiers, and others who venture high onto Rainier, should be diligent about following weather forecasts and be prepared for an emergency bivouac. Exactly what Lahti and Richard—or the unnamed snowshoer, for the matter—carried is not described. Though the storm was, in Richard's words, "unexpected by all," the lesson is clear: Carry the gear whether you think you'll need it or not.

A picture posted by Richard on Facebook following the tragedy shows her companion on descent from Rainier's summit, drenched in sunshine. Richard's tribute to her climbing partner, a montage of images from expeditions and adventures shared with Lahti over the years following their meeting on Mount Everest in 2012, is punctuated with smiles and mountain vistas. "I will carry your human legend," she pledged, and it's easy to imagine her keeping that promise on every mountain she's climbed since Lahti's passing.

A Calculated Risk

Fifty-one-year-old Donald McIntyre of Reno, Nevada, an experienced mountaineer and climbing guide, died on descent after reaching Rainier's summit via its challenging north face in July 1997. He and teammate Joel

Koury, 37, another experienced climber from California, were on their way down to Camp Schurman when the accident occurred. A storm had enveloped the mountain, creating challenging conditions and depositing wet, new, slick snow. Koury was attempting to clean snow off his crampons when he lost purchase, and when he slipped, he took his partner with him. The two men fell 25 to 30 feet into a crevasse on the Emmons Glacier at about 13,500 feet. McIntyre's aortic artery was ruptured in the fall; he perished several hours later. Koury was injured, but with the help of rangers who arrived to assist in search and rescue he was able to descend to Camp Schurman. McIntyre's body was eventually airlifted off the glacier.

In a memorial in the *American Alpine Journal*, McIntyre's business partner in Sierra Mountain Guides, John Cleary, noted that McIntyre's twenty-year career as a mountaineer included expeditions around the world, and that he had "reached the summits of Changtse, the north peak of Mt. Everest, Denali in Alaska, the Matterhorn and the Eiger in Switzerland, and Peak Communism in the Soviet Union, among many others." McIntyre was also a veteran of the US Air Force, having served a tour of duty in Vietnam, and made a career as an investigator with the US Department of Energy.

"It's like a lot of things. There's calculated risk," Cleary told the *Seattle Times* after the accident. "High-altitude mountaineering is the most dangerous, followed by mountaineering in glacial terrain as in Mount Rainier. More people are seriously injured per capita mowing their lawns."

POWER AND LOSS IN EXPERIENCE AND PARTNERSHIP

In May 2004 Peter Cooley, an experienced mountaineer with summits including Rainier and Denali notched on his ice ax, suffered a fall near the Black Pyramid on the Liberty Ridge route. According to friend and partner Scott Richards, who recounted the story to *News Tribune* reporter Craig Hill in 2009, the tragedy began to unfold when Cooley caught his crampon in a gaiter, then slid and fell over a twelve-foot cliff, sustaining a serious blow to the head. Richards knew they needed to get off the mountain to seek medical help, but a storm was building. He hacked a platform into the snow and set up a tent in the shelter of a "rock outcropping he hoped would protect them from the Volkswagen-size chunks of ice that regularly tumble down the mountain."

Richards then used his cell phone to call for help, initiating what Hill calls "one of the most intensive rescue attempts the park has ever seen." The gears were engaged, but bad weather pinned down the rescuers and the stranded climbers for an excruciating two days. During that time, Richards did everything in his power to keep Cooley comfortable and alive. One report describes how he kept the head wound clean and his friend warm. Richards even dripped water into Cooley's mouth when the stricken man could no longer drink. Meanwhile, the park service was able to airlift supplies to the stranded climbers, but the storm precluded a formal rescue.

A pair of rangers were finally able to climb to the aid of the two mountaineers, but with aircraft still grounded by storms, the only option for Cooley's evacuation appeared to be a long, roped descent over dangerous terrain. The rescuers got a break before the overland descent started, however: A weather window allowed a Chinook helicopter to pluck Cooley off the mountain and carry him to a local hospital. Unfortunately, Cooley died on the flight.

Hill's *News Tribune* story vividly exposes the rawness of such a loss, for the surviving climber, for the dead man's family, and for the rescuers. Climbing ranger Mike Gauthier describes the letdown the rescuers felt on learning of Cooley's death as "devastating." Cooley left behind a wife and three children. His parents, who had traveled to the mountain during the rescue attempts, were en route to the hospital when they got the news. For Richards, even years after the event, the accident and loss are "still vivid. I'm still sad."

NINE

A Decade of Heroism: Rescues in the 1970s

Charles R. "Butch" Farabee, Jr.

WHAT FOLLOWS ARE ONLY A LIMITED NUMBER OF EXAMPLES OF THE immense workload in our national parks. There are tens of thousands of stories left to be told.

"WE DROPPED HIM!"

"A terrible scream rang up out of the void, and Bridwell's shocked voice thundered from the radio." Everyone froze. Jim Bridwell, a legend among the world's great rock climbers, was in the middle of one of the "hairiest," most technically demanding cliff rescues ever performed anywhere.

To the ancients of Yosemite, the 1,400-foot long "Lost Arrow" was frozen in stone. Aimed skyward, its 300-foot tip splits 75 feet away from the main wall and then tapers to a V notch hundreds of feet down. The vertical face then continues plunging to a jumbled, brush-covered base more than 1,000 feet below.

Twenty-year-old Roy Naasz and Andy Embick, 19, were a rope-length from the top of the "Arrow Direct," their goal for the past three tough days. Devoid of cracks, the face of glaringly white granite was one of the most challenging climbs in the country; it had been conquered for the first time only two years before.

Naasz studied his next move intently. Hammering his third pin in, a 2-inch-wide piton called a "bong," he cautiously shifted his weight onto the thin nylon loop that dangled off it.

As if on a triggered trapdoor, he dropped into 1,200 feet of nothing. Rock climbers call this "getting air time," but the former high school gymnast got more than a quick thrill. His rope soon snapped taut as he skidded down the rough, crystal-studded cliff face. Smashing into the tiny ledge 25 feet below, aptly called "Second Terror," Naasz hung limply at the end of the thin life line, his femur and ankle shattered. Embick climbed out for help.

Wayne Merry, former park ranger and director of the Yosemite Mountaineering School, and Lloyd Price, his chief climbing guide, flew by park helicopter to the rim above the Lost Arrow.

Lloyd and I roped into the notch real fast and climbed to Salathe ledge with sleeping bags and medication, getting there pretty close to dark. It was cold as hell—seems like it was about 17 degrees or so. Roy was straight down, 90 feet below Salathe. It was so steep you couldn't see him from the ledge.

We tossed a rope down into the gloom and I went down to Roy, who looked very tiny and very exposed on that wall, with a real white face and big eyes . . . sitting tied-in on a little ledge just about the size of his hips and legs.

The ledge was so small that there was no way I could stand on it, so I just stood in the slings with my shoulders level with him. I got out the Demerol. There was a little wind, and so darn cold I was afraid the drug might freeze in the needle, but it didn't. I gave it in the shoulder. It hit him fast, and almost immediately he leaned over and barfed on my boots.

Yosemite Falls roared; frigid winds blew . . .

By midnight, Price was so cold he needed to go to the rim to warm up; he actually tied his hands to the ascenders to do so. His replacement out on the Arrow, Herb Swedlund, became "desperately entangled" in the nine ropes running from the rim. Swedlund would later describe the confusion of lines as resembling a "direct hit on a spaghetti factory." Eventually, over 3,500 feet of nylon rope were "tied" to this rescue operation.

At sunrise the gray-shadowed rock wall started humming with action and color; Merry and Swedlund welcomed the six other climbers. Place anchors. Rig pulleys. Play ropes out. Take the stretcher down to the victim. They knew what to do, and they did it well.

Getting Naasz into the Stokes basket "was quite a feat, as the bad leg was on the side against the cliff . . . and they just had to dangle on the ropes while loading him in."

On the rim, Yosemite Rescue Ranger Pete Thompson directed the placement of more anchors and ropes. Price designed an elaborate hoisting system. Eventually, through a sophisticated combination of ropes and pulleys, Naasz would be pulled from the outside of the base of Lost Arrow and then lifted 400 feet vertically while simultaneously being hauled 200 feet sideways. This seldom-done, elaborate maneuver would require the ropes and stretcher to turn a 90-degree corner while suspended over 1,000 feet above the rocky slabs below. Few rescue techniques require greater skill, coordination, effort, and luck.

Now, at midmorning and with more than 25 people involved on the cliff, the delicate operation began. Again, Bridwell's voice came over the two-way radio, this time hastily clarifying his earlier announcement. They hadn't really dropped him, but only toppled him a foot onto a ledge. Everyone relaxed a little.

By sunset, 30 hours after he probably should have died, Roy Naasz was in the Yosemite Hospital. He would climb again.

Even years later, Wayne Merry would remember: "While we were working we heard radio talk that Governor Ronald Reagan and his entourage were in the Valley and were watching us through binoculars. Instantly and simultaneously, five arms shot up with an internationally recognized hand signal." Someone later swore, "Damn . . . we shoulda mooned him!"

Gas, Heat Stops Rescue Attempt for Two Marines

Winterhaven (UPI)—High temperatures and poisonous gas Sunday stalled efforts to rescue two marines missing and presumed dead in a maze of tunnels in an abandoned gold mine near this community.

Officials said the missing men and two other marines, all stationed at the nearby Yuma Marine Corps Air Station in Arizona, climbed down into the mine Saturday.

Imperial and Los Angeles County Sheriff's deputies said temperatures at the bottom of the 600-foot shaft the men entered reached more than 150 degrees Sunday. The surface temperature stood at 115. Deputies said the mine was full of carbon monoxide gas from a fire in the shaft last week.

"They were taking me to a level where they had been before" (survivor) Fontana said. "We started getting dizzy and all messed up. Lopez passed out on us."

—*LAS VEGAS REVIEW-JOURNAL*, 7-13-70
(REPRINTED BY PERMISSION OF
UNITED PRESS INTERNATIONAL, INC.)

Leaving his three companions to explore deeper into the Senator Mine, the 19-year-old marine was quickly overcome by fumes in a lateral tunnel. His friends, climbing out to summon help, returned with two deputies. Because their air packs lasted only 35 minutes, however, the officers were unable to reach the victim.

One of the marines then "fought his way by the deputies" and worked his way back to his downed comrade. Deputies tried to drop an air pack through a crevice to the second ill-fated marine but were forced to retreat before they were successful.

When Lake Mead Rangers Don Chase, Rick Gale, and Jerry Phillips—summoned because they had favorably impressed the nearby Mohave County (Arizona) sheriff on a recent "simple mine shaft recovery"—arrived at the scene, they joined 14 other rescue organizations trying to reach the two downed men.

Phillips worked on the Incident Command Team, bringing order to a chaotic operation while Chase and Gale were lowered into the "hell hole." The two rangers, unable to use standard rescue breathing tanks because of insufficient air, wore larger scuba tanks designed for diving but not for the many noxious gases they encountered.

At one point, Gale vividly remembered, "[I had] to take my tank off over my head, wiggle it through a narrow crack and then crawl through sideways behind it." Chase recalled "a lot of rope and cable work to reach the victims and a very long and arduous haulout."

On July 15, 1970, Imperial County Sheriff-Coroner Raymond B. Rowe awarded the three rangers a Certificate of Appreciation "in recognition of outstanding service and accomplishment."

"THEY WERE TEN DAYS OVERDUE AND HAD 1,600 FEET TO GO!"

Truly an epic, the first ascent of the 2,200-foot Wall of the Early Morning Light—one of the most demanding and intimidating rock faces in the world—was a testimony to endurance and talent.

At 47, Warren Harding was the undisputed "hard man" of Yosemite Big Walls. Along with his partner, 27-year-old Dean Caldwell, the super-climber wrote on their registration card that they were going to haul 300 pounds of gear, including food for 12 days "and some emergency supplies"; they expected to be off El Capitan by October 31. On November 9, with Harding and Caldwell only halfway up, the park's rescue ranger, Pete Thompson, began to get nervous.

They had been up for many days longer than anyone had ever been on a wall before, their rations should have been critically short, they reported that their feet were numb, their gear got wet when it rained and that they were suffering from open sores brought on through lying in wet bags during the first big storm. They were ten days overdue and had 1,600 feet to go!

Two days later, faced with six massive, unseasonable wet-weather fronts rolling in from the Pacific, the climbers were asked if they could rappel off if needed. Impossible! Caldwell's last comment that night, heard through the park's sophisticated electronic listening device, was, "We know that our asses are in a sling." Appreciating the double entendre from a thousand feet above, Thompson knew Caldwell could have been "merely referring to his belay seat, or that they were in trouble." That night, nearly an inch of rain soaked the valley—but up above, snow soaked the two climbers.

Caldwell and Harding were still 1,800 feet from the top, having made only 400 feet in the last six days. In fact, they averaged a mere 85 feet each day of the climb. Ranger Thompson, charged with protecting "life and limb," knew that a rescue had to be mounted now or it might be too late. "Feeling that it would be better to have the equipment poised on the top prior to the advent of a major storm which might preclude the possibility of flying equipment to the top, I carried forward arrangements." It was a very difficult decision for Thompson, one that would later be loudly—and unfairly—criticized by the "victims."

With the U.S. Army graciously volunteering six hours of helicopter time, 19 men and 1,900 pounds of rescue equipment were lifted to the top. "Of course, by that time the weather had stabilized nicely and our two friends on the wall . . . were beginning to move nicely." On November 18, 27 days after starting up and without ultimately needing a rescue, Harding and Caldwell "peered over the top to find some seventy newsmen peering back."

DIVING BELL IN THE DESERT

When Chuck Rowland came to, he was already totally underwater. Fumbling with his seatbelt, the pilot somehow forced a door open and swam upward, where he was quickly rescued by the tour boat "Echo." The crew vainly looked for his passengers. And for the next 13 days, one of the most unusual searches in NPS history took place.

NPS Patrol Plane N-736 was only a few hundred feet up when it left the west end of Boulder Canyon. Those aboard were observing terrain likely to be affected by underground nuclear explosions at the nearby Nevada Test Site. The small Cessna 206, catching a sudden and violent desert downdraft, crashed and quickly sank 390 feet; Rowland escaped— the three others didn't.

The Atomic Energy Commission was sure that Theos Thompson, one of its three commissioners, and two of his key staff were at the bottom of the lake. Fearful of losing another scientist to China, and of the ever-mounting international antagonism toward nuclear testing, the AEC needed to be certain.

Near one of Lake Mead's deepest spots twists the steep-sided and submerged bed of the Colorado River. Somewhere among these drowned hills and dead cliffs lay a small plane. Were there still three men strapped inside, or had they somehow escaped only to quickly sink and drown?

Park Dive Officer Weir and Clark County Sheriff's Sergeant Leemon met with Harry Wham. Wham, a member of the World War II famed Underwater Demolition Team and an advisor for Lloyd Bridges's Sea Hunt TV series, knew this was far beyond their combined capabilities. The Department of Defense volunteered.

Crude but intricate preparations were hastily made for Ocean Systems, a Navy contractor, and acknowledged deep-diving experts. Buoys, moorings, and thousands of feet of cable were placed as anchors against the unpredictable desert winds. A flat barge, large enough to cradle a portable decompression chamber, with a crane sturdy enough to lift a ton of diving bell—or an airplane—was built from scratch. The Florida-based, mixed-gas, deep-sea divers would have to manage with the makeshift rig.

Through the use of state-of-the-art electronics such as side-scanning sonar, radar, and underwater TV cameras, as well as old-fashioned common-sense, intuition, and hard work, a tiny bottom "blip" was swiftly found. That was the easy part.

Six days, almost exactly to the minute, after the crash, a military C-141 set down at nearby Nellis Air Force Base. Onboard, along with the rest of the crack team of underwater professionals, was a collection of unique underwater search "hardware" never before seen in the desert.

N-736, even though located electronically, now needed to be pinpointed to the foot by the small, two-person diving bell. Working from it at a depth of 400 feet, divers had only 20 minutes before they would need to be brought back to the surface and decompressed. They worked in the cold darkness, surrounded by thousands of pounds of water pressure, attaching heavy, steel hoisting lines. If the plane dropped . . .

After the bell's six round-trips and the divers' numerous decompressions, a cable was finally secured to a strut and the plane's small lifting eye. Gently encouraged off the lake bottom, it then took nearly three hours before the red and white tail of N-736 broke the surface. Uttering something about national security to the numerous rangers who were providing logistical support, the AEC "clamped the [publicity] lid on," including confiscation of all their film.

Commissioner Thompson and his special assistant, Lieutenant Colonel Jack Rosen (U.S. Army Retired), were still inside. Bill A. Smith, a private contractor assigned to the AEC, was not.

Park Ranger Gene F. Gatzke was the National Park Service team leader on this unique mission.

"Probably the Worst Single Accident"

"Probably the worst single accident in the history of the park" is how Chief Park Ranger Frank Betts described the bizarre deaths of the three skilled mountaineers.

Several parties had signed out to climb 10,500-foot Symmetry Spire. After reaching the top, they all were in various stages of descending the steep, snow-filled gully by glissading—a quick way of "skiing" downward on the feet while dragging an ice axe along behind to serve as a brake.

Robert Deal was the first to lose control. After sliding down and around a prominent rock outcropping, the 28-year-old disappeared from the view of teammate Richard DaBell. A 19-year-old college student, DaBell quickly determined that Deal had tumbled into a partially hidden, water-carved snow cavern.

Roping up, DaBell lowered himself through a near-freezing waterfall only to see his partner tightly wedged between rocks. Unable to reach Deal, the would-be rescuer swiftly grew numb from the icy water showering down. Team leader William Radtke joined DaBell and was able to reach the still form of his friend Deal. Knowing it was too late, the two violently shivering men scrambled from the crevasse and learned that help had been sent for.

The second party, including 30-year-old Minneapolis policeman Ron Ottoson, halted above the rock ledge and yelled to the third party to stop. Despite the frantic warning, however, 36-year-old Wayne Creek could not slow down and he, too, slid into darkness. Then, his father looked on in sheer terror as nine-year-old Luis Y. Barrando plunged into the hole.

Ottoson, believing he had heard a faint reply to his shouts, threw a coil of rope into the crevasse. Feeling no tugs on this lifeline, he then rappelled the 20 gloomy feet only to find the two climbers tightly buried up to their necks in white. The falls had created a small avalanche and the wet snow was compacted around the three; their arms were pinned tightly to their sides.

"The unfortunate thing about this avalanche," Chief Ranger Betts later explained, "was that it also dammed up the stream so that the water level rose over their heads and both drowned."

Horrified at watching the two die in front of him, Ottoson desperately grabbed for nine-year-old Luis's helmet, but the strap broke. Frantically the policeman then tried lifting the boy up by his nylon jacket, but it slowly peeled off the small body.

Led by Ranger Bob Irvine, the park's seasoned rescue team reached the now-quiet scene at 6:30 that night. Having been dispatched for one victim, they were shocked to learn of the other two. Irvine, a veteran of hundreds of rescues, rappelled in but could no longer see anyone—snow and water covered all three.

A recovery team of 12 arrived the next morning. Donning a wet suit, District Ranger Tom Milligan dropped into the narrow, slushy moat. The dammed-up water had drained overnight, such that two of the dead climbers were clearly visible. Despite harrowing conditions, including the icy torrent falling from above, the seasoned Milligan was able to attach a nylon sling to one victim. Other rescuers, working together like the veterans they were, engineered a rope system to pull the body from its watery grave. This took most of the day, and the rangers elected not to try for the remaining two until the following day.

Eight of the team started down the second night with one victim, while the remaining four rangers made the watery trap safer by removing a large, snowy overhang from its edge. On the third day, Ranger Milligan again went into the hole. By noon the second body was removed. Milligan thought he could see the last body but could not quite reach it.

Rather than drop into the watery grave to use the same dangerous technique a third time, they tried to reach the remaining climber by "drilling." Using an 85-foot fire hose and the force of falling water from the same stream that had originally drowned the three, they dug to the creek below. They ended successfully only a few feet from Robert Deal.

In a July 12 letter to Secretary of the Interior Rogers C. B. Morton, Ron Ottoson and his teammate, James Hovoda, wrote:

It is a credit to yourself and to our National Parks system that such high caliber personnel staff these areas. We wish to express our sincere appreciation for being able to witness their very inspiring team while operating on a mountain rescue mission.

DaBell, Radtke, and Ottoson received Carnegie Hero Commission Bronze Medals for trying to save the three mountaineers.

The 12 members of the Grand Teton Mountain Rescue Team received DOI Special Achievement Awards of $150, except for Rangers Irvine and Milligan, who received $250.

CREWS PLUCK INJURED CLIMBER FROM MOUNTAIN
Park Ranger Griffiths described the accident scene like this.

The ledge is located on the Northwest Face of Silver Run Peak (12,500 ft.) which . . . has not been ascended. This face is characterized by large towers, a maze of steep ridges, inundated by steep talus couloirs . . . interrupted periodically by cliffs of 150 to 300 feet high. The rock appeared to be . . . weathered granite which was friable in nature. . . . The face dropped approximately 3000 feet from the summit . . . 0.8 of a mile . . . and the slope averaged about 60 degrees.

The *Salt Lake Tribune* described the rescue like this.

Red Lodge, Mont.—Gayle Zachary, a 22-year-old Girl Scout counselor who spent 79 harrowing hours on a 12,610-foot Montana mountain, was reported in good condition Monday after a dramatic rescue.

The Boise counselor was stranded Thursday evening when she tumbled and slid down a rocky embankment to a nearly inaccessible spot on a cliff.

Miss Zachary and a fellow counselor, Leslie Appling, 18, Hillsborough, Calif., had set out on a four-hour hike from a scout base camp at 11 a.m. Thursday. They were last seen by their hiking party at 1 p.m., waving from the top of a steep rocky slope on Silver Run Peak. The girls had climbed to above the 10,000-foot level by 6 p.m. when Miss Zachary fell.

The first report that the hikers were missing came in the middle of the night Thursday and search efforts by horseback and air began early Friday.

Efforts were fruitless, however, simply because the searchers were looking well below the 10,000-foot level. "We didn't believe they would be as high as they were," said district ranger Gary Wetzsteon. "There was no rhyme or reason why they should be there."

Wetzsteon said the searchers were finally made aware of Miss Zachary's location when Miss Appling walked into base camp at 1 p.m. Friday.

She boarded a helicopter with Carbon County Sheriff James Echler and Wetzsteon directed them to the spot where the injured Miss Zachary had been since late the day before, without food or water.

Wetzsteon described the section of the mountain as quite treacherous and said no one could figure out how the women got there.

"The climbers all said it was impossible," he said.

The first to reach the injured hiker were two climbers from the National Park Service, stationed at nearby Yellowstone National Park. They were helicoptered to near the summit of the mountain and then climbed down.

The two—Tom Griffiths and Dick Goss—said they found the young woman weak, dehydrated, and badly bruised but said she perked up when they "poured some lemonade down her."

The men put the woman in a large sleeping bag to ward off the near-freezing nighttime temperatures and the next morning began the harrowing descent down the sometimes vertical mountainside.

Several other climbers had joined the party by then, including Billings, Mont., physician, Dr. Warren Bowman.

The rescue workers said in the course of bringing her down they made three drops of 300 feet and four of about 150 feet, sometimes carrying the girl piggy-back.

One of the most dramatic events of the rescue operation came at the bottom of the precipice when Vietnam veteran pilot Jim Sanchez of Steamboat Springs, Colo., brought his helicopter dangerously near the rocks and lifted the woman to safety.

Rescue worker Joe Regan of Billings said Sanchez landed "on a nubbin, with the roters [sic] nearly touching rock." He added, "I could hardly believe it."

Regan said if the pilot had not landed, Miss Zachary would have had to have been carried across a long series of treacherous boulder fields.

When the helicopter finally landed here at 8:15 p.m., all the battered hiker could say was, "I've never felt so dirty. I've never been so happy to be alive."

—*Salt Lake Tribune*, 7-20-71
(reprinted by permission)

14-Year-Old Lowered 850 Feet on Ranger's Back

Rescuing the daring young climber—injured at 13,000 feet—required a spectacular 850-foot lowering off an overhanging cliff; a bold, extremely perilous nighttime climb of 1,500 feet; use of the Secretary of the Interior's helicopter; and the "Longs Peak Navy."

Chris Chidsey badly fractured his right leg while scaling the difficult east face of Longs Peak. The injured youth, assisted to the relative security of a large ledge by his doctor-father, now needed the herculean efforts of a crack rescue team to be moved any further.

By 7 that night, veteran rangers were ready to roll. Luckily for them and for Chidsey, Interior Secretary Morton was in the park when word of the young man's plight reached headquarters. It would be dark before a chopper from Denver or Ft. Collins could get there so Secretary Morton quickly volunteered his B-1 helicopter and pilot and then closely monitored the night's unfolding drama through a borrowed park radio.

Airlifted to a tiny rock shelf by fading light, Rangers Larry Van Slyke and Walt Fricke were forced to finish climbing the icy 900-foot Lamb's Slide after dark. "I wanted to rope up on the traverse but Walt just laughed and started off. Where it is about a foot wide with 800-foot exposure, I remember telling Walt that if I fell that I would come back and haunt his ass until he died." Reaching the boy after some difficulty, the two rangers spent a cold night preparing for the most dangerous part of their mission.

By first light, the rest of the team climbed into position and skillfully rigged a lowering system 1,000 feet long. Then, using a "tragsitz"—a leather and buckle device designed for one person to ride piggyback on another—Fricke, with Chidsey tightly strapped to his back, slowly scrambled onto the lip of the overhanging cliff and gently eased into space.

In a nearly picture-perfect operation led by Steve Hickman, the well-drilled rescue team on top lowered the two to the snowfield below. So sheer was the rock wall that Fricke touched only twice during their 850-foot descent. Once safely down, Chidsey was piggybacked to Chasm Lake where a rubber raft—the Longs Peak Navy—ferried him across. Chidsey's painfully long odyssey to the waiting ambulance finally ended after a torturous 5-mile horseback ride.

Walt Fricke received the Department of the Interior Valor Award, and he, Paul Anderson, Mike Donahue, Steve Hickman, Bob Pederson, Charles Post, Clarence Serfoss, and Larry Van Slyke were named in a DOI Unit Award for Excellence of Service.

Icicles Hung from Frozen Beards

Doomed before they left the road, the two Colorado State University students were dead before they were missed . . .

They were prepared more for a gala than for a gale; stuffed in Joan's small daypack were a dress, nightgown, cosmetics, and extra lingerie, but no sleeping bag, extra warm clothing, or survival necessities. Fred carried steaks, eggs, and two sleeping bags, but no stove, fuel, or water. They failed to register with anyone.

Their goal was Chasm Lake Cabin, a stoveless, barren rock shelter built above treeline in the frigid shadow of Longs Peak. There at 11,590 feet, hurricane winds are winter's rule—a cruel trial for raw beginners on recently rented skis.

Searchers performed "far beyond the call." Numbering more than 125 at one time, they included rangers, deputies, and mountain rescue groups from around the state. Green Berets from the Army National Guard and search-dog teams from Washington volunteered. Armed with skis and snowshoes, helicopters and snowmobiles, rescuers spent days battling the mountain. Windblown snow covered ski tracks within minutes and swept them clean the next day. Statewide front-page news pictured bone-weary volunteers with icicles hanging from their frozen beards.

Exactly what had happened to the two young people, who were just out to play, will never be known. The thin air and the brush-studded uphill slog probably proved overwhelming. Four miles from where they started, they abandoned their frustrating skinny cross-country skis, a practice common among novice skiers. With storm clouds and darkness closing in, they fought their way upward toward the bleak rock refuge on foot. Crossing the steep snowfield below the cabin, Fred probably hurt himself when he slid into the large boulders below. Then, it was up to Joan.

After helping her friend into his sleeping bag—one not designed for snow and wind—the nearly exhausted young woman probably went for help. Without skis and blinded and confused by wind and storm, she plunged downhill through the waist-deep snow. Shortly afterward, Fred left his crude shelter and followed. Desperate to escape the storm's fury, Joan nestled in the lee of a boulder.

On the fifth day of the search and less than a half mile from the road, her frozen body was found still huddled against the huge rock. Eight months later, Fred's remains were discovered a mile upstream from his girlfriend's.

Grizzly Meal

The bear that ate Harry Walker weighed just 232 pounds. The 25-year-old, jobless construction worker from Alabama ignominiously became the first person known to have been killed by a Yellowstone grizzly since 1942—the fourth in the park's 100-year history.

From the moment Walker and his high school buddy hitchhiked into the park, the two did everything wrong. They unlawfully pitched their tent in a restricted area after disregarding advice from a concession employee; they ignored fresh bear scat near camp; they littered the site with smelly scraps and dirty cooking utensils; and they left open food when they went hiking.

Shortly past midnight, the two campers were talking as they returned to their isolated hideaway, 600 yards beyond the huge summer crowds of the world-famous Old Faithful geyser.

We stopped and I heard something in front of us. Just as he shined the light [we] could see . . . a bear, coming at us. Approximately 5 feet away. And I immediately dove to my left and sorta rolled down the embankment. I got back on my feet and was running and then I stopped and paused for a second and I could hear a lot of commotion and I heard Harry hollering "help me, Crow help me." And I hollered back, "Is there a bear there?" And that's all—he didn't respond anymore.

"Crow" collapsed when he stumbled into the Old Faithful Inn; within minutes the search for hapless Walker was in high gear. Ranger Gerry Tays will never forget that very long night.

We gathered along the boardwalk in the geyser basin and split up into 3-person parties. One ranger in the middle with a light was accompanied by rangers on either side with rifles/shotguns. . . . Our first obstacle was to leave the safety of the boardwalk and in the blackness of the night make our way through the geyser basin.

Needless to say, it was probably the scariest assignment I have ever been on, because unlike most other rescue activities that require specific skills that you can count on, this exercise required no particular technical skills and success was largely left up to fate. It was difficult to hear any movement in the woods over the sound of your own heart beating and the deep breathing of your two partners.

At one point during the wee hours Tom and I found ourselves walking side by side along the boardwalk having just returned from an unsuccessful search of the hillside. Tom, walking on my left, had a shotgun in his right hand, the barrel pointing down. Without warning the gun went off, blowing a large hole in the boards right next to my left foot. Tom, reacting to an array of mind-scrambling feelings, was through for the night. We put him in a Stokes litter, covered him with a blanket, and told nurse Kathy Loux to keep an eye on him. He was literally a basket case.

At first light Harry Walker was found 50 yards below camp—everything between his pelvis and heart was gone. Hoping to catch the killer bear, rangers anchored three wire snares to lodgepole pines. Within 24 hours, a 20-year-old female grizzly—left ear tag no. 1792—was caught and quickly dispatched. An autopsy confirmed that she had eaten on Walker.

Although Walker had done almost everything illegally, his family sued the federal government.

Over the years there have been legal challenges involving bear attacks in national parks: *Rubenstein v. U.S., Claypool v. U.S., Johnson v. U.S.,* and *Martin v. U.S.* Under the Federal Tort Claims Act, private citizens have the right to sue the United States; liability generally depends upon the law where the alleged negligence occurred. In Montana, where natives seem to relish an occasional brush with a grizzly, the case might easily have gone in favor of the National Park Service. Walker's family, recognizing this frontier mentality, however, asked for and received a change of venue—to a more "civilized" San Francisco.

The man who heard this case, Judge A. Andrew Hauk of the District Court for the Central District of California, ruled that technology such as radio collars readily existed for keeping minute-by-minute track of wild animals, as seemingly evidenced on numerous *Wild Kingdom*-type television shows. Judge Hauk found in favor of Walker and awarded $87,417.67, saying the "Park Service willfully failed to warn decedent of a dangerous condition." The government appealed.

On December 3, 1976, Judges Barnes, Ely, and Van Pelt of the U.S. Court of Appeals for the Ninth Circuit declared that a "mistake has been committed" and that the original verdict "should be reversed and dismissed." Case closed.

In the spring of 1977, Alabama's influential Senator Allen introduced a private relief bill into Congress to award the Walker estate $87,000 for the loss of Harry. These special measures are seldom challenged; congresspeople defer to the good intentions of their peers and pass them without seeking public input. There is neither testimony nor the normal review process that accompanies a routine money authorization. If enacted, this bill would still have inferred that the United States was liable for Walker's death!

Once Wyoming's conservative Senator Wallop was apprised of Walker's flagrant misdeeds, the private relief bill never came to the Senate floor for a vote.

DOUBLE SUICIDE OR SUICIDE-HOMICIDE

Yosemite park rangers truly believe that California is the "land of weirdos and wackos"; Bruce Norris simply validated their belief. Rescuers never did learn, however, if his pretty girlfriend willingly joined in when the young student physicist hurled himself over the third highest waterfall in the world.

At the base of 1,623-foot Yosemite Falls, an inverted "snow cone" grows almost every year. The steep, often 100-foot-high mini-glacier springs from the wind-driven spray of the world-class waterfall plunging from far above. This same freezing mist also coats the surrounding ledges and brush with treacherous, clear ice.

After struggling up the 4 miles of trail to the top of the waterfall, several visitors found two sets of clothing neatly folded just beyond the guardrail of the falls overlook. After carefully retrieving the strange find, which included high-top lace boots, the anxious hikers started down to report their discovery.

Simultaneously, but 2,000 feet lower, another couple could make out a nude body on the far side of the impassable, water-choked gorge between the falls. Scanning upstream, they then spotted a second flesh-colored splotch, stark against the "snowcone." After bushwhacking their way back up to the path, they accidentally met the first party on their way to the ranger station.

Officials, realizing no lives were to be saved even if they hurried, knew caution was paramount for retrieving Norris and his dead companion from one of the most dangerous spots in the Sierras.

Before first light, a team of 12 rangers wound their way up the trail to clean up after the grim ritual. Some, dispatched to the crime scene above, dangled off the lip of the 1,600-foot cliff to inspect the wall below with binoculars. Investigators spotted Norris's body now partially obscured by frozen mist, but could find no further clues to what had happened.

Other rangers, many donning scuba wet suits to work under the cascade tumbling from far above, dealt with headaches of their own. Three of the recovery team, roped together to climb on the huge "snow cone," dodged large sheets of falling ice. So dangerous were these frozen, sail-like chunks that it became one ranger's sole duty to scan the cliffs above, hoping to give ample warning before they struck somebody below.

The body recovery team, in black neoprene wet suits and orange plastic helmets, swinging metal ice axes and trailing brightly colored climbing ropes, somehow looked obscene against the white and gray. For two days this ranger force endured freezing spray and near-gale-force winds, ducked large hunks of ice peeling from far above and dodged death over ice-covered cliffs—all for Norris.

Two Rangers Killed in Plane Wreck

Rangers Ron Trussell and Jake Metherell, en route in Jake's single-engine Mooney to a conference in Boise, were an hour west of southern Utah's Cedar City when they vanished from radar. Trussell, 34, was a supervisor at Bryce Canyon, and Metherell, 45, was a resource specialist at nearby Curecanti National Recreation Area.

Faced with darkness and worsening weather, Metherell told the Salt Lake Flight Service Station that he was dropping from 14,500 to 12,500 feet just before 6 p.m. When the little plane disappeared 10 minutes later, it was somewhere southwest of Elko, Nevada.

The Civil Air Patrol promptly began routine airport checks while querying for other helpful information. Based on data and the best guesses available, the search focused on the rugged, highly remote Ruby Mountains of northern Nevada. Because of poor weather, Civil Air Patrol and local pilots conducted a limited air probe over the next two days. Snowstorms kept everyone grounded the following 48 hours, but on the 12th and 13th, six pilots were up and at it again.

With conditions improved by late on the 14th, Grand Teton Chief Ranger Frank Betts launched in his private plane, as did Glen Canyon's Warren Adams in the National Park Service patrol plane.

In addition to the intensive air effort, a skilled mountain climbing team was flown in that evening: Grand Teton Rangers Tom Milligan (leader), Pete Hart, and Ralph Tingey, as well as Rocky Mountain National Park's Walt Fricke, Bob Haines, and Steve Hickman. Driven to 9,000 feet by Snow Cat, the group spent three days skiing the most probable search area. A wreck was actually found, although it soon proved to be a plane located six years before.

On February 17 and 18, more than 15 search craft crisscrossed above the high desert. They stretched to the north of Elko in case Metherell had managed to skim below the radar and between the peaks of the isolated area. After 12 days and no further clues, the mission was scaled down on the 19th.

On April 3, the two rangers were found; they had been hidden by deep snows in a remote canyon in the Rubies for nearly two months.

While on duty 100 days after this accident, a pilot and three more NPS employees would die in another plane wreck in the West on May 19. Studying bighorn sheep in Canyonlands National Park, pilot and Moab-based owner-operator Dick Smith (25), Utah State graduate student John C. Ebersole (26), Capitol Reef National Park biologist William D. Cooper (30), and Las Vegas–based NPS Research Biologist Chuck Hanson (52) were killed when their Cessna 185 smashed into a remote canyon 23 miles southwest of the airport. Why Smith, a veteran of the redrock of southern Utah with 6,668 hours of flight time, crashed will never be known.

THREE DIE IN AVALANCHE

Triggered by the two lead skiers, the snow slab that swept three unseasoned young men to their deaths was some 250 yards wide and 3 feet deep. According to veteran Winter Ranger Pete Hart, "the party ascended the wrong slope at the wrong time."

Skiing up from Amphitheater Lake, the 11 trainees had already crossed the most demanding obstacle of their route: the delicate traverse below the north face of Disappointment Peak. They and their leader were members of the National Outdoor Leadership School (NOLS) Teton Winter Mountaineering Expedition. NOLS, a developmental program focusing on motivation through fun in the wilderness, has a long history of caution and good judgment on such trips.

They started onto the moraine below Teton Glacier. When the avalanche cut loose, Wes was leading, followed closely by Mike Moseley. Both were pulled 500 feet downhill by the wave of white. Wes survived, miraculously "swimming" on top; firmly entombed, however, 24-year-old Moseley had perished by the time he was dug out some 20 minutes later. Tom, the expedition's leader, was carried 50 feet; buried to his waist upright on a large boulder, he watched the others disappear below.

Bart Brodsky was alone in the middle of the moderately steep slope when struck by the huge slab. Although he was pulled only 50 feet, the 18-year-old was dead when he was freed 25 minutes later. Peter, Donald, and David were within two steps of the slide's edge when they were engulfed. The first two were just under the surface and were dug out immediately—alive; 20-year-old David Silha was uncovered within eight minutes—dead.

Even with CPR, as well as other heroic measures used for more than an hour that frozen afternoon, the three young men could not be revived. Tom and Wes skied out for help, and the following morning, the shocked, numb climbers bore their lifeless comrades to Delta Lake, where they were soon lifted out by helicopter.

Predictably, avalanches are always unpredictable. Contributing to the mishap was the subzero cold spell of the preceding week, along with high winds and recent heavy snowfall. A highly unstable wind-slab condition developed on this steep, southeast slope at the 10,000-foot level. After examining the situation carefully, Grand Teton National Park's Board of Inquiry could make "no determination as to fault of leadership in this accident."

C-141 "Starlifter" Crash

With its 10-man crew and six Navy passengers, the huge, 110-ton "Star-lifter" neared the end of a routine cargo flight from the Philippines. At 37,000 feet for most of its 16-hour journey, MAC 40641 descended to 10,000 feet and was then given a heading of 150 degrees to skirt the populous Seattle area, inbound for McChord Air Force Base, headquarters of the 8th Military Airlift Squadron. Reaching his new altitude, the aircraft commander, 28-year-old First Lieutenant Earl Evans, was quickly cleared down to 5,000 feet.

With only 10 minutes until touchdown, the instructions were clearly acknowledged: "40641 is out of ten at 0556Z." This was the plane's last recorded transmission before crashing into the snow-covered, 7,300-foot-high ridge of Inner Constance two minutes later. When the 145-foot aircraft hit the wall at nearly 250 knots, it triggered a massive avalanche. There were no survivors—men and metal cascaded to the frozen valley below.

Just before midnight, less than 47 minutes after the giant plane vanished from radar, a Coast Guard chopper from Port Angeles was in the air; it was promptly beaten back by thick clouds and heavy snows down to the 500-foot level. Far overhead, above the storm, an HC-130 "Hercules" soon began listening for signals from its ill-fated big brother. As day broke, the search intensified.

Army, Navy, and more Coast Guard helicopters arrived, as did McChord's disaster response team of 25 doctors, radio operators, truck drivers, and other support personnel. Forty skilled mountain rescue volunteers and park rangers mobilized at the Coast Guard station. Everyone waited for better weather and word from the search crew circling high above the storm. Finally, just before dark, the wreck was sighted through the broken clouds.

Debris and bodies were scattered down the length of the steep 1,900-foot-high slope, from the flight deck to the large vertical T of the tail section. The plane's navigator, still strapped in his seat, was recovered first, but because of colossal avalanche hazards as well as the specialized climbing skills needed on the rugged peaks, it was another two months before the second body would be found. The plane's flight recorder—and its last victim—weren't located until late the following June.

On September 1, more than five months after the crash and after approximately 200 people representing numerous federal, state, and local groups had spent nearly 30,000 hours on this mission, the Upper Dungeness River Drainage was reopened to the public.

DEATH OF AN ANGEL

Scrambling off a short climb on El Capitan, Peter Barton slipped and fell 150 feet. His stunned companion wanted to believe that there were still faint signs of life in the broken body of his friend.

Launching quickly to the alarm, Gordon Sibel, hovering just above Barton and the jumbled base of the 3,000-foot, sheer wall, was unable to land the park helicopter. From inside the ship, Ranger Dan Sholly, looking at hundreds of feet of treacherous cliffs over which a stretcher would need to be lowered, called for an "Angel."

Godsends to rescue agencies in California, the fleet of twin-engine UH-1 "Huey" helicopters—"Angels"—from the San Joaquin Valley's Lemoore Naval Air Station had flown hundreds of park rescues since 1961. Angel 6, with its 270-foot cable hoist and 1,100-hp engine, was only 45 minutes away.

Sholly, clambering up through an 800-yard maze of truck-sized boulders and a jungle of gnarly oaks, found Barton dead. Twelve other rescuers soon reached the scene. They zipped the well-liked, young redhead into the black body bag, moved to a nearby level spot for the Angel's easy cable pickup, and waited.

Lieutenant Tom Stout commanded Angel 6; built like his name, the red-bearded, young lieutenant had performed numerous rescues for the park. Joined at the controls by John Sullivan, Stout had the mission and ship well in hand. In the back, Ranger Paul Henry and the three crewmen prepared to lift the body aboard.

On his second slow pass over the scene, Stout pulled a "hover check"; after rising 300 feet to guarantee sufficient power for the operation, he slowly lowered Angel 6 to within 20 feet of the dead climber. After swiftly hooking the thin wire cable to the stretcher, Sholly gave a thumbs-up to the crew chief above.

> *Just as the litter was being secured to the ship, R/R (Reporting Ranger Sholly) heard a sudden change in engine sound as if the ship was shutting down after landing. At this same time R/R observed the ship tilt back and forth and drop a few feet in altitude, causing the rotor blades to come close to the ledge. At this point the helicopter tilted strongly to its port side, and "rolled" into a spiral descent down the cliff making what appeared to be at least two full 360-degree turns before it went into the trees, approximately 500–600 vertical feet below R/R's position and then out of sight. The victim was still secured outside the helicopter when last seen.*

Peter Barton and the $1.2 million Angel were burned to ash, but miraculously nobody onboard was seriously hurt. Barton's was the second of three climbing deaths in Yosemite in three days.

WANDERED FOR 20 DAYS IN CANYON

Linda only wanted to hike down to Supai Village. Now, with 7 miles behind her and less than one relatively easy mile to go, she came to a fork in the broad, sandy trail. Unfortunately, the 25-year-old nurse took the wrong path. "I never got to the village.... It just started getting very dark. I laid down . . . but I was too scared to sleep."

Rugged and remote, the area is a stunning collection of orange-toned sandstone cliffs and gorges. In 1880 the Army Corps of Engineers found the new, 60-square-mile reservation too rough to survey accurately. Home today to 350 Supais, the tiny community at the bottom of the Grand Canyon is isolated from the outside world except for one telephone and an 8-mile trail.

In a postcard mailed to her parents the day before her hike, Linda had written of her proposed trip to the secluded village. Lost that first day and not due back to Pittsburgh for two more weeks, more than 17 long days—and longer nights—would pass before anyone would even miss her.

Three days after veering the wrong way, she finally found a tiny trickle of water in a crack in the rocks; "it took her 45 minutes to fill her eyeglasses case." Without those precious drops, she would have been dead in a few short days. "I just kept wandering and wandering. . . . Being without water is truly frightening."

"For the first four days I tried screaming, but that didn't help. Your voice doesn't carry that far."

Daydreams blurred to nightmares. The 100-degree, ovenlike heat drove her to seek lifesaving shade. She felt the bone-chilling nights the most frightening, however. "There was always a continuous buzz or hum at night."

Linda was finally reported missing by her anxious parents. Her dust-covered car was promptly identified at the trailhead. A day into the search, Hardy Jones, a local Supai, reported to mission leader Dick McLaren that footprints were spotted "where nobody should be." All that day and into the evening, the faint tracks of the woman's crepe-soled shoes were skillfully followed. At sunrise "they heard her hollering."

Now 21 pounds lighter, Linda had been lost for 20 days.

Two Killed by Tidal Wave

Within seconds of the earthquake, the sea quietly, subtly rose. Without warning, a monstrous wave sired by this seismic belch raced inland. The tsunami that swallowed the 32 terror-stricken campers just before dawn was 30 feet high.

Some 100,000 quakes rattle Hawaii each year; most are never felt. At 3:36 a.m. a sharp roller shot beneath the Big Island; the tremor registered a magnitude of 5.7. Seventy minutes later, residents were once again rudely jarred from a fitful sleep. This jolt began with violent ground pitching, but instead of subsiding after a few seconds, the intensity swelled to 7.2. The earthquake that struck from deep within the molten core of Kilauea Crater that Saturday morning was the Islands' most powerful shock of this century.

Out of the darkness rose the deafening roar of rocks crashing off the nearby volcanic cliffs, and then the campground simply vanished beneath the foaming, dark waters. The sea approached faster than the startled campers could escape. A huge, rolling wave sucked up people, horses, boulders, and trees and blended them into a churning, doomed mass. The energy carried the highest swells a quarter of a mile inland. At least two more large waves battered the Halape coast before the disaster was over, scant minutes after it had begun.

Of the campers caught on the beach that morning, 30 survived; one was killed outright and one was never found.

Death of Some Rescuers

High on a cliff, two ill-prepared young rock climbers, saddled with inexperience and trapped by recklessness, cried out in the dark.

It was 3 in the morning when the six rescuers started up the Yosemite Falls Trail. All accomplished Big Wall climbers, their mood was relaxed and confident. Just how hard could a rescue on the "YPB," a beginner's climb, be? Zig-zagging up the broad path, they moved easily, their headlamps bobbing eerily in the mist that swirled around them. Light rain added to the air of excitement as they moved higher, wind and trickling water mingling with the fading sounds of an occasional car from below.

Jack Dorn, like everyone else in Camp Four—the climber's campground—lived for the challenge of the Yosemite walls. A veteran of the valley's demanding granite, Dorn was also on the park's semivolunteer rescue team. In exchange for a free camp spot and his expertise on the rocks, the 30-year-old was to be available for plucking wimpy kids from cliffs.

Perhaps he got lost listening to tunes on his portable tape cassette, had partied too long, climbed too hard or, just maybe, he didn't notice the winding trail turn to the left.

Why Jack Dorn, responding to pleas for help in the middle of the night, walked off the well-worn path and plunged 600 feet to an instant death, no one will ever know . . .

Dorn, one of the 110 rescues the park handled that year, was rumored to be one of the many Yosemite Valley entrepreneurs who "struck it rich" from the marijuana aboard the ill-fated twin-engine plane lost in Lower Merced Pass Lake on December 9, 1976. There are some who think his death was more than accidental.

Beginning with Herb Sortland, who died on January 25, 1925, Jack Dorn was the 14th person to be killed while involved in an NPS SAR. Nine more would sacrifice their lives for their fellow-man before pilot Clayton Reed and observer James Matthews ran out of fuel over an extremely isolated section of the Everglades on October 2, 1991.

The two Civil Air Patrolmen were searching for a small fishing boat reported to be in distress. The two 70-year-old volunteers were concentrating on a nightmarish maze of shallow bays and mangrove-covered keys near Everglades City. Reed and Matthews crashed only 3 miles and two minutes away from the stranded fishing guide and his two customers. Killed on impact, the two men in their tiny Cessna 172 were not found for 15 days. Despite the involvement of at least four ships, 15 aircraft, and numerous agencies, the downed CAP plane had nearly succeeded in disappearing into the Everglades.

Ten

Arctic Rescue

A. W. Greely

AFTER A LONG AND DANGEROUS BESETMENT IN THE POLAR ICE TO THE north of Bering Strait, the American whaling-ship *Navrach* was abandoned August 14, 1897. Twenty-one of her seamen perished on the moving ice-pack of the Arctic Ocean in their efforts to reach land across the drifting ice. Captain Whitesides with his brave wife and six of the crew intrusted their fortunes to the sea, and almost miraculously escaped by using a canvas boat, which was alternately hauled across the floes and launched where open water was reached. On landing at Copper Island, off the coast of Asia, the party was in danger of death through starvation when rescued by the United States revenue-cutter *Bear*, which chanced to touch at that point. The news of the loss of the *Navrach* and the reports of very bad ice conditions in the Arctic Ocean created great alarm in the United States, owing to the fact that no less than eight whale-ships with crews of two hundred and sixty-five men were missing that autumn.

Appeals for prompt aid were made to the President of the United States by the members of the chamber of commerce of San Francisco and by other interested persons. Refitting in three weeks' time, the United States revenue-cutter *Bear*, manned by volunteers under Captain Francis Tuttle, R.C.S., sailed from Seattle on November 27, 1897, and wintered at Unalaska. The story of the relief of the whalers, happily and heroically accomplished by this expedition, forms the substance of this sketch.

From the character of the duties of the revenue-cutter service its officers and men are not favored with such frequent opportunities for adventurous deeds as are those of the army and of the navy, but whenever occasion has arisen they have ever shown those qualities of courage, self-sacrifice, and devotion which go far to inspire heroic action.

As the period of navigation had already passed for the northern seas, the *Bear* was to winter at Dutch Harbor, Unalaska, communicating with the distressed seamen by an overland expedition, which should aid and encourage them until the spring navigation should make their rescue possible. If practicable the land party was to be set ashore on the north side of Norton Sound, near Cape Nome, which would require some eight hundred miles of sledge travel at the least.

From the eager volunteers for this arduous and novel service, Captain Tuttle approved of Lieutenant D. H. Jarvis, commanding, Lieutenant E. P. Bertholf, and Dr. S. J. McCall, with a reindeer driver, Koltchoff.

With dauntless courage and skill Captain Tuttle skirted the growing ice-fields of Bering Sea, seeking in vain a lead through which he could reach Norton Sound, but it was finally clear that the ship could not be put north of Nunavak Island without danger of her loss as well as sealing the fate of the whalers. The winter darkness, storm conditions, an uncharted coast, and drifting ice forced him to land the party as far north of Kuskowim Bay as could be safely reached.

Fortunately, on December 16, a wild, stormy day, the shore ice drifted far enough seaward to enable a hasty landing to be made near Cape Vancouver. There were forebodings of evil in attempting this winter journey now stretched out to fifteen hundred miles, under conditions which increased its perils. But with the splendid confidence and magnificent vitality of youth, the fearless revenue-officers hailed with satisfaction the beginning of their arduous journey of mercy and relief.

South of the landing was a deserted village, but fortunately a few miles to the north, near Cape Vancouver, was the still occupied Eskimo settlement of Tunanak. Ashore, Jarvis found himself in difficulty, for the snow-free rocky beach was impassable for his sledges, while he was without boats. Here, as elsewhere on this journey, the native aid was obtained on which he had counted from the knowledge of the kindly feelings of these children of the ice that he had gained in his past cruises in the Bering Sea region. As there was now an ice-free channel along the coast, the Eskimo sea-hunters deftly lashed together in pairs their kayaks (skin canoes), catamaran fashion, and piled thereon helter-skelter the various supplies.

Jarvis and Bertholf watched this cargo-stowing with great anxiety, not unmingled with doubt as to the outcome of the voyage. Following the progress of the kayaks and shouting advice and encouragement from the sea-shore they were dismayed to see now and then a breaking wave threaten to overwhelm the boats and to find that the short sea trip had ruined much of the precious flour and indispensable hard bread.

Overhauling his cumbersome, heavy sledges and inspecting his few unsuitable dogs, he knew that they could never do all the work required. Fortunately he found a half-breed trader, Alexis, who agreed to furnish dogs, sledges, and serve as a guide to the party as far as the army post at Saint Michael. As the half-breed knew the short shore route and was familiar with the location and supplies of the succession of native villages, this enabled them to drop much of their heavy baggage and travel light. Their outfit was carefully selected, consisting of sleeping-bags, changes of clothing, camp-stoves, rifles, ammunition, axes, and a small supply of food.

Their three native sledges were open box-frames, ten feet by two in size and eighteen inches high, resting on wooden runners a foot high. Tough, pliant lashings of walrus hide bound together with the utmost tightness the frame and the runners. This method of construction, in which not a bit of iron enters, avoids rigidity and thus gives a flexibility and life to the sledge which enables it to withstand shocks and endure hard usage, which would soon break a solid frame into pieces. A cargo-cover of light canvas not only closely fits the bottom and sides of the box-frame but overlaps the top. When the cargo-cover is neatly hauled taut and is properly lashed to the sides of the sledge the load, if it has been snugly packed, is secure from accidents. Its compact mass is equally safe from thievish dogs, from the penetrating drift of the fierce blizzards, and from dangers of loss through jolts or capsizings.

Of a single piece for each dog, the harness used by the natives is of seal-skin; the half-breeds often make it of light canvas, not only as better suited to the work but especially for its quality of non-eatableness which is a vital factor during days of dog-famine on long journeys. The harness is collar-shaped with three long bands; the collar slips over the dog's head and one band extends to the rear over the animal's back. The other bands pass downward between the dog's legs and, triced up on each side, are fastened permanently to the back-band, where there is also attached a drag-thong or pulling-trace about two feet long. In harnessing, the three loops described are slipped respectively over the head and legs of the dog.

The animals are secured in pairs to the long draught-rope of the sledge by the Alaskan pioneers, who much prefer this method to the old plan of the natives whereby the dogs were strung out in single file. With the dogs in couples the draught-line is shorter, so that the better-controlled animals will haul a larger load.

In the first day's journey they crossed a mountain range two thousand feet high, and in making the descent of the precipitous northern slope Jarvis records a sledging expedient almost unique in sledge travel. The four Eskimo drivers detached the dogs from the sledge, and winding around the runners small chains so as to sink in the deep snow and impede their progress, prepared to coast down the mountain. Two men secured themselves firmly on each sledge, and when once started the descent was so steep that the sledges attained a fearful speed, which brought them almost breathless to the bottom of the range in ten minutes.

Jarvis describes in graphic language the trying task of feeding the always famished, wolf-like dogs: "They are ever hungry, and when one appears with an armful of dried fish, in their eagerness to get a stray mouthful the dogs crowd around in a fighting, jumping mass, which makes it difficult to keep one's balance. After throwing a fish to each dog, it takes all of us with clubs to keep off the larger fellows and to see that the weaker ones keep and eat their share. When being fed they are like wild animals—snarl, bite, and fight continually until everything is eaten."

As the dogs, worn-out by the hard journey, could not be replaced by fresh ones at the Eskimo colony of Ki-yi-lieng, Bertholf and Koltchoff waited there to bring them up later, while Jarvis and McCall pushed on, marching across the Yukon delta in temperatures below zero daily. They found the natives of this alluvial region wretchedly poor and illy protected against the bitter cold. To the eye they were a motley crowd, as they had levied tribute for clothing on the birds of the air, the beasts of the tundra, the fish of the river, and the game of the sea. There were trousers and heavy boots from the seal, inner jackets of the breasts of the wild geese, fur ornamentation of the arctic fox, and the poorer Eskimos even made boots, when seal were lacking, from the tanned skin of the Yukon salmon.

With all their dire poverty they were not unmindful of their duty to strangers and always offered the shelter of the *khazeem* (a hut built for general use by the unmarried men, from which women are rigidly excluded). His sense of fastidiousness had not yet left Jarvis, who surprised the Eskimos by tenting in the midwinter cold rather than endure the tortures of the stifling *khazeem*, which to the natives was a place of comfort and pleasure. Of this half-underground hut Jarvis says in part: "The sides are of drift-wood, filled in with brush. The roof is ingeniously made by laying logs along the sides and lashing them thereto with walrus thongs. Two logs notched on the ends to fit securely are then laid across the first logs on opposite sides, but a little farther in toward the centre. This method is repeated until a sort of arch is formed, which is filled in with earth-covered brush leaving a small hole in the centre of the roof. Other drift-wood, split in rough slabs, forms the floor, leaving an entrance space about two feet square. From this hole in the floor, which is always several feet below the level of the surrounding ground, an entrance passage has been dug out large enough for a man to crawl through it into the main earth-floored room. Over the entrance opening is hung a skin to keep out the air, while the roof opening is covered with the thin, translucent, dried intestines of the seal or walrus, which gives faint light during the day.

"In the *khazeem* the animal heat from the bodies of the natives, with that from seal-oil lamps, raises the temperature so high that the men sit around with the upper part of the body entirely naked. The only ventilation is through a small hole in the roof, invariably closed at night in cold weather. The condition of the air can be better imagined than described, with fifteen or twenty natives sleeping inside the small room."

The culmination of danger and suffering on the march in the delta journey was at Pikmiktellik, when they strayed from the trail and nearly perished in a violent storm. Almost as by miracle they staggered by chance into the village long after dark, so exhausted that without strength to put up their tent they gladly occupied the dreaded *khazeem*.

Twelve days brought them to Saint Michael, where they were given cordial and humane aid from Colonel (now General) George M. Randall, United States Army, and the agents of the Alaska Commercial and North American Trading Companies. Without such help Jarvis must have failed. The feet of his dogs were worn bare by rapid, rough travel of three hundred and seventy-five miles, the rubber-covered, goat-skin sleeping-bags were cold and heavy, which in bitterer weather would be actually dangerous. Deerskin clothing and fresh dogs were necessary for rapid travel with light loads on which final success depended.

Leaving orders for Bertholf, yet far behind, to bring up relief supplies from Unalaklik to Cape Blossom, by crossing the divide at the head of Norton Bay, Jarvis and McCall pushed ahead on January 1, 1898. The third day out they met a native woman travelling south on snowshoes, who told them that she was with her husband and Mate Tilton of the *Belvedere*; the two parties had passed each other, unseen, on trails three hundred feet apart. Tilton brought news even worse than had been expected. Three ships had been crushed by the ice-pack, two losing all their provisions, while five other ships were frozen up in the ocean ice. As the worn-out mate went south, Jarvis pushed on with new energy, realizing the great need ahead.

Severe storms and deep snow made travel very slow, and at times the runners sank so deep that the body of the sledge dragged, while the dogs were almost buried in their efforts to struggle on. They soon realized that actual arctic travel is far from being like the usual pictures of dog-sledging. Instead of frisky dogs with tails curled over their backs, with drivers comfortably seated on the sledge cracking a whip at the flying team, snarling dogs and worn-out men tramped slowly and silently through the unbroken snow.

It very rarely occurs that there is either a beaten or a marked trail, so the lead is taken by a man who keeps in advance, picking out the best road, while his comrades are hard at work lifting the sledge over bad places or keeping it from capsizing. The king dogs, who lead the way and set the pace, never stray from the broken path save in rare instances of sighting tempting game, but follow exactly the trail-breaker. One day Jarvis came to fresh, deep snow, where it took all four men to break a way for the sledge, and when they themselves were worn out they had the misery of seeing their utterly exhausted dogs lie down on the trail, indifferent equally to the urging voice or the cutting whip. That wretched night the party had to make its camp in the open instead of at one of the native huts which were always in view.

The dog teams were sent back from the Swedish mission, Golovin Bay, where reindeer were available. Of this new and unusual method of travel, Jarvis, who drove a single-deer sledge, says: "All hands must be ready at the same time when starting a deer-train. As soon as the other animals see the head team start they are off with a jump, and for a short time they keep up a very high rate of speed. If one is not quick in jumping and in holding on to his sledge, he is likely either to lose his team or be dragged bodily along.

"The deer is harnessed with a well-fitting collar of two flat pieces of wood from which short traces go back to a breastplate or single-tree under the body. From this a single trace, protected by soft fur to prevent chafing, runs back to the sledge. A single line made fast to the halter is used for guiding, and, kept slack, is only pulled to guide or stop the deer. A hard pull brings the weight of the sledge on the head of the deer and generally brings him to a stop. No whip is used, for the timid deer becomes easily frightened and then is hard to control and quiet down. The low, wide sledges with broad runners are hard to pack so as to secure and protect the load." As the dogs naturally attack the deer, it was henceforth necessary to stop outside the Eskimo villages, unharness the animals, and send them to pasture on the nearest beds of reindeer moss.

Jarvis thus relates his straying during a violent blizzard: "Soon after dark my deer wandered from the trail, became entangled in drift-wood on the beach, and finally wound up by running the sledge full speed against a stump, breaking the harness, dragging the line from my hand, and disappearing in the darkness and flying snow. It was impossible to see ten yards ahead, and it would be reckless to start off alone, for the others were in advance, and I might wander about all night, become exhausted, and perhaps freeze. I had nothing to eat, but righting the sledge I got out my sleeping-bag in its lee and made myself as comfortable as possible." His comrades were greatly alarmed as a reindeer dashed by them, and fearing disaster hastened back on the trail, which, although followed with difficulty on account of the blinding snow, brought them to the lieutenant still unharmed.

If the relief expedition was to be of use to the shipwrecked men it was important that food should be carried north. As this was impossible by sledge, it was evident that the sole method was to carry meat on the hoof. The sole sources of supply consisted of two herds of reindeer, at Teller and at Cape Prince of Wales. If these herds could be purchased, and if the services of skilled herders could be obtained and the herd could be driven such a long distance then the whalers could be saved. To these three problems Jarvis now bent his powers of persuasion and of administrative ability, feeling that lives depended on the outcome and that he must not fail.

The reindeer belonged in part to an Eskimo, Artisarlook, and in part to the American Missionary Society, under the control and management of Mr. H. W. Lopp. Without the assent and active aid of these two men the proposed action would be impossible. Would he be able to persuade these men to give him their entire plant and leave themselves destitute for men whom they had never seen and knew of only to hold them in fear? Would they consider the plan practicable, and would they leave their families and go on the arctic trail in the midst of an Alaskan winter? If they thought it a bounden duty, what was to happen to their families during their absence? Day after day these questions rose in the lieutenant's mind to his great disquietude.

With Jarvis and Bertholf there was the stimulus of the *esprit de corps*, the honor of the service, always acting as a spur to their heroic labors, while in the case of Dr. McCall there was also that sense of personal devotion to the relief of suffering that inspires the medical profession as a whole.

On January 19 Jarvis reached the house of Artisarlook, when he "almost shrank from the task." From this untaught, semi-civilized native, wrestling for a bare subsistence with harsh, forbidding nature, what favor could be expected? The starving men were of an alien race, and of that class from which too often his own people had reaped degradation, suffered outrage, and endured wrongs too grievous to be ignored or forgotten. To relieve these men Artisarlook must voluntarily loan his entire herd of reindeer without certainty of replacement. He must leave behind him his wife, unprotected and subject to the vicissitudes of an arctic environment. He must also endure the hardships and sufferings incident to a midwinter drive, in the coldest month of the year, of reindeer across a country unknown to him—a desperate venture that might cost him his life. Altruistic souls of the civilized world might make such sacrifices, but would this Alaskan Eskimo?

Of the crisis Jarvis writes: "I almost shrank from the task. He and his wife were old friends, but how to induce them to give up their deer—their absolute property—and how to convince them that the government would return an equal number at some future time was quite another matter. Besides, he and the natives gathered about him were dependent on the herd for food and clothing. If I took the deer and Artisarlook away these people were likely to starve unless some other arrangements were made for their living.

"I explained carefully what the deer were wanted for; that he must let me have the deer of his own free will, and trust to the government for an ample reward and the return of an equal number of deer.

"Artisarlook and his wife Mary held a long and solemn consultation and finally explained their situation. They were sorry for the white men at Point Barrow and they were glad to be able to help them. They would let me have their deer, one hundred and thirty-three in number, which represented their all, if I would be directly responsible for them.

"I had dreaded this interview for fear that Artisarlook might refuse, but his nobility of character could have no better exposition than the fact that he was willing to give up his property, leave his family, and go eight hundred miles to help white men in distress, under a simple promise that his property should be returned to him."

Has there ever been a finer instance of the full faith of man in brother man than is shown in this simple pact, by word of mouth, under the dark, gloomy sky of an Alaskan midwinter? Far from the business marts of crowded cities, in the free open of broad expanses of country, there are often similar instances of man's trusting generosity and of personal self-sacrifice, but more often between those of kindred race than between the civilized man and the aborigine.

Giving written orders on the traders to tide over the winter for the natives, Jarvis pushed on, leaving Artisarlook and his herders to follow with the deer. Meantime the lieutenant had adopted the native garb, saying: "I had determined to do as the people who lived in the country did—to dress, travel, and live as they did, and if necessary to eat the same food. I found the only way to get along was to conform to the customs of those who had solved many of the problems of existence in the arctic climate." His clothing consisted of close-fitting deerskin trousers and socks, with hair next to the skin; deerskin boots, hair out, with heavy seal-skin soles; two deerskin shirts, one with hair out and the other with hair toward the skin; close hoods, with fringing wolfskin, and mittens, the whole weighing only about ten pounds. In stormy weather he wore an outer shirt and overalls of drilling, which kept the drifting snow from filling up and freezing in a mass the hair of the deerskins.

The five days' travel to the Teller reindeer station, near Cape Prince of Wales, were filled with most bitter experiences. The temperature fell to seventy-two degrees below freezing; the sea ice over which they travelled became of almost incredible roughness; while fearful blizzards sprang up. With increasing northing the days became shorter and the exhausted reindeer had to be replaced by dogs. Much of the travel was in darkness, with resultant capsizings of sledges, frequent falls, and many bodily bruises. Of one critical situation he reports: "The heavy sledge was continually capsizing in the rough ice. About eight o'clock at night I was completely played out and quite willing to camp. But Artisarlook said *No!* that it was too cold to camp without wood (they depended on drift-wood for their fires), and that the ice-foot along the land was in danger of breaking off the shore at any minute. In the darkness I stepped through an ice-crack, and my leg to the knee was immediately one mass of ice. Urging the dogs, we dragged along till midnight to a hut that Artisarlook had before mentioned. A horrible place, no palace could have been more welcome. Fifteen people were already sleeping in the hut, the most filthy I saw in Alaska, only ten by twelve feet in size and five feet high. Too tired to care for the filth, too tired even to eat, I was satisfied to take off my wet clothing, crawl into my bag, and to sleep." Failure to find the house and to have his frozen clothing dried would have cost the lieutenant his life.

On arriving at Teller station he had a new problem to solve—to win over the agent. He had high hopes, for although this representative of a missionary society was living on the outer edge of the world, yet he had become familiar with the vicissitudes of the frontier, and from vocation and through his associations was readily moved to acts of humanity. Jarvis set forth the situation to Mr. W. T. Lopp, the superintendent, adding that he considered Lopp's personal services to be indispensable, as he knew the country, was familiar with the customs and characteristics of the natives, and was expert in handling deer. Lopp replied that "the reindeer had been built on by his people as their wealth and support, and to lose them would make a break in the work that could not be repaired. Still, in the interests of humanity he would give them all, explain the case to the Eskimos, and induce them to give their deer also [aggregating about three hundred]." Lopp also gave his own knowledge, influence, and personal service, his wife, with a noble disregard for her own comfort and safety at being left alone with the natives, "urging him to go, believing it to be his duty."

It is needless to recite in detail the trials and troubles that daily arose in driving across trackless tundras (the swampy, moss-covered plains), in the darkness of midwinter, this great herd of more than four hundred timid, intractable reindeer. Throughout the eight hundred miles of travel the reindeer drivers had to carefully avoid the immediate neighborhood of Eskimo villages for fear of the ravenous, attacking dogs, who, however, on one occasion succeeded in stampeding the whole herd. For days at a time the herders were at their wits' ends to guard the deer against gaunt packs of ravenous wolves, who kept on their trail and, despite their utmost vigilance, succeeded in killing and maiming several deer. A triumphal but venturesome feat of Lopp's was the driving of the herd across the sea-floes of the broad expanse of Kotzebue Sound, thus saving one hundred and fifty miles of land travel and two weeks of valuable time.

While there were eight skilled herders, Lapps and Eskimos, the most effective work was that done by a little Lapp deer-dog, who circled around the herd when on the march to prevent the deer from straying. If a deer started from the main herd the dog was at once on his trail, snapping at his heels and turning him toward the others. Very few deer strayed or were lost, and three hundred and sixty-two were brought to Barrow in good condition.

Travelling in advance, following the shore line by dog-sledge, Jarvis and McCall were welcomed with warm generosity even by the most forlorn and wretched Eskimos, who asked them into their huts, cared for their dogs, dried their clothes, and did all possible for their safety and comfort. The relief party, however, suffered much from the begging demands of almost starving natives, from the loss of straying dogs, and the desertion of several unreliable native employees. They were quite at the end of their food when they reached, at Cape Krusenstern, their depot. This had been brought up across country from Unalaklik through the great energy and indomitable courage of Bertholf, whose journey and sufferings were no less striking than those of his comrades.

Inexpressible was the joy of the party when, fifty miles south of Point Barrow, the masts of the *Belvedere*, a whale-ship fast in the ice, were sighted. Four days later they were at the point, their marvellous journey of eighteen hundred miles ended and their coming welcomed as a providential relief.

They found conditions frightful as regards the shelter, health, and sanitation of the shipwrecked whalers. Three ships had been lost and another was ice-beset beyond power of saving. The captains of the wrecked ships had abandoned the care and control of their men as to quarters, clothing, food, and general welfare. Provisions were very short, and the seamen were depending on their safety through successful hunting among the caribou herds in the neighborhood of Point Barrow, which were rapidly disappearing.

Jarvis at once took charge of the situation. Dr. McCall found the seamen's quarters in a most horrible condition, its single window giving but a feeble glimmer of light at midday, and its ventilation confined to the few air draughts through cracks in the walls. Eighty seamen occupied for sleeping, shelter, and cooking a single room twenty by fifty feet in size, wherein they were so badly crowded that there was scarcely room for all to stand when out of their bunks together. Moisture was continually dropping from the inner ceiling and walls, which were covered with frost. Their bedding was never dry, sooty grease was coated over all things, and no place was free from great accumulations of filth and its accompaniments. The whalers were "scarcely recognizable as white men," and large numbers of them would without doubt have perished of disease but for the opportune arrival of the relief party.

Order, cleanliness, decency, and discipline were instituted, the men were distributed in light, airy rooms, their clothing was washed and renovated, and intercourse with the natives prohibited. By inspection, precept, and command the general health greatly improved. At every opportunity individual men were sent south by occasional sledge parties. Hunting was systematized, but it failed to produce enough food for the suffering whalers. Recourse was then had to the herds driven north by Lopp and Artisarlook, and with the slaughter of nearly two hundred reindeer suitable quantities of fresh meat were issued. Out of two hundred and seventy-five whalers only one died of disease. Captain Tuttle by daring seamanship reached Icy Cape July 22, 1898, and took on board the *Bear* about a hundred men whose ships were lost.

With generous feeling Jarvis gives credit in his report to the whaling agent, A. C. Brower, and to "the goodness and help of the natives [Eskimos], who denied themselves to save the white people," subordinating with true heroic modesty his work to all others.

Gold and commerce have peopled the barren Alaskan wastes which were the scenes of this adventurous journey with its unique equipment and its cosmopolitan personnel of Eskimo, Lapp, and American.

While these men worked not for fame but for the lives of brother men, yet in Alaskan annals should stand forever recorded the heroic deeds and unselfish acts of Jarvis and McCall, of Bertholf and Lopp, and of that man among men—Eskimo Artisarlook.

Eleven

Katahdin

Eric Wight

You may well wonder what place Mount Katahdin has in a book about Maine game wardens. Well, it is a good question—and I have some good answers.

According to several sources, on a clear day there is more land mass visible from Katahdin than from any other mountain in the United States. Although only a mile high, it sticks out like the proverbial sore thumb, and can be seen for miles and miles. It breaks an otherwise more or less flat terrain that covers all of central and northern Maine.

Katahdin's uniqueness has been discussed and written about many times by many people, with good reason. It is undoubtedly the most striking piece of real estate in all of Maine—but it will never again be for sale, since Percival P. Baxter's purchase and gift of Katahdin and the surrounding wilderness territory included provision that it remain "forever wild" for the people of Maine. The most awesome feature of Mount Katahdin, in my opinion, is the weather. New Hampshire's Mount Washington reportedly attracts the worst weather known on Earth. Because of similar characteristics, including latitude, comparisons between Mount Washington and Mount Katahdin indicate that both peaks share pretty much the same weather conditions.

The Indians held Katahdin in awe and fear. It was their belief that the evil god Pamola dwelt on the mountain, and they feared his wrath should they venture into his domain. Many superstitions had their beginnings in some incident that through years of telling became distorted, and I can easily believe that a group of Indians may have ventured onto the mountain one nice fall day years ago in quest of the caribou that were moving up to their winter range on the Tableland. Without warning, a tremendous storm must have engulfed them and they perished, leaving others to speculate, and thus adding fuel to their belief in Pamola. In modern times, unfortunately, Pamola has swung his mighty club several times—and believe me, he can hammer you without much in the way of warning.

October 28, 1963, was a most typical Indian summer day on Mount Katahdin. Although Baxter State Park was officially closed, Mrs. Helen Mower and Mrs. Margaret Ivusic, both from Massachusetts, had received permission to hike to the summit. They left Chimney Pond around seven a.m., and spent the day enjoying the scenery and basking in the warm sun as they made their way up Cathedral Trail to the summit. After having lunch on Baxter Peak, they began to cross the Knife Edge to Pamola Peak.

Margaret Ivusic was some distance ahead when Helen Mower heard her call from below her, "Come this way—it's a shortcut." It did not appear to be a shortcut to Helen Mower. She was apprehensive about leaving the trail, so continued to Pamola and down Dudley Trail to Chimney Pond. When she arrived back at the campsite at around 6:30 p.m., no one was there. She built a fire and waited. Around 8:15 p.m., Ranger Ralph Heath returned to his camp at Chimney Pond, and Helen related the story to him. Heath went to a place where he could, by hollering, communicate in the still night air with Mrs. Ivusic. She told him she was on a wall and could not go up or down. Heath left Chimney Pond again at around eleven p.m. to try to reach the stranded woman. Around four a.m. he returned, saying he had again been unable to reach Mrs. Ivusic.

Heath rested and had breakfast. The wind had begun to blow and snow to fall. Ralph radioed Supervisor Helon Taylor around six a.m., stating that if the woman was going to be saved, it would have to be now. Again he left, with his gear and warm clothing for Mrs. Ivusic. Mrs. Mower watched him disappear into clouds of swirling wind and snow for the last time. Ralph Heath gave his life in the finest tradition, attempting to save another.

By the time rescuers were able to reach Chimney Pond, a full-fledged arctic blizzard was raging and wiped out any trace of the two. Warden Elmer Knowlton and Ranger Rodney Sargent made a tremendous effort to reach the spot, but were turned back by the weather. Elmer suffered a badly wrenched knee from which he never completely recovered. Then began the long winter's wait until spring, when the snows would melt and the full story could be pieced together.

During that winter, wardens Donald Gray and Roger Spaulding were sent to New York State to receive some training in ice climbing, in anticipation of the chore that lay ahead come spring. Later that winter, they were on the mountain instructing other wardens in the techniques they had learned. The nucleus of our eventual rescue team had taken shape.

In late April, the snows began to melt, and it was time. Wardens Elmer Knowlton and Charlie Merrill made the long trek onto Pamola and began to scan below for any sign of the missing ranger and woman. Finally, with binoculars, Elmer spotted a rope hanging over an outcropping of rock far below.

The team of wardens was contacted. Then began the arduous task of locating the bodies, freeing them from their icy tombs, and transporting them off the mountain. Margaret Ivusic's body was located near the rope. It was apparent that Heath had in fact reached her and had placed her with warm clothing in a more sheltered spot. It took several days to remove the woman's body from the ice, each day making the strenuous trip up and down the mountain. Finally, she was freed. Then came the backbreaking task of transporting the body back up to the Knife Edge, across to Baxter Peak, then down to Thoreau Spring. It was here that a large helicopter was able to pick up the body and remove it from the mountain.

Ralph Heath's body was not found until sometime later, when the ice and snow had receded further. The procedure was repeated once more. This whole evacuation took place during the most hazardous time of all—during the spring, when ice and snow are melting, and there is ever-present danger of ice and rock fall. The higher the angle involved, the greater the danger to those below. These rock and ice falls, along with snow slides, have been the death of many a climber throughout the world.

What would have to be called a bruising, exhausting job was pulled off in terrific fashion by game wardens and park rangers. But this incident appeared to trigger a series of incidents around and on the mountain. The following year, two men slept one night in their vehicle at Roaring Brook. Before daylight, one of them left on foot, telling his companion he was climbing the mountain to watch the sun rise. The next time anyone saw him, his bones were discovered behind a log on the back side of Basin Pond. The year after that saw us involved in the search for the Mott brothers. Was there no end to Pamola's wrath?

One evening in July 1966, I received a call from my supervisor, Dave Priest, reporting an injured climber on Katahdin. I gathered my gear and left Grindstone to meet team member Glenn Speed from Haynesville. We met and struck off for Katahdin. Forty-five minutes later we were at Roaring Brook, then headed for Chimney Pond. I always dreaded that 3.3-mile hike to Chimney Pond, but it went quickly this night, and we arrived about 9:30 p.m. There was a strange tenseness about the place, as there usually is when you have what is known as "a situation."

Sixteen-year-old Jim Ludwig told us of the day's climb he and his father, Charlie, had made. Partway across the Knife Edge, his father had wanted to take what had appeared to be a shortcut to Chimney Pond. They had descended quite some distance, when, while trying to descend a waterfall, his father had slipped and fallen. Jim had been able to reach his father and determine that he was badly injured and unable to move. He then returned to the Knife Edge and down to report the incident. The boy was very calm, but due to his unfamiliarity with the mountain, could not pinpoint the exact location for us.

At that point, we received word via radio that the rest of our team would arrive early in the morning. Shortly afterward, Glenn and I left for Pamola Peak. As we climbed in the dark, I began to understand why the Indians dreaded this place; I was beginning to dread it, too. We arrived on Pamola at 12:45 a.m. Winds were fairly still, but we got into our sleeping bags behind a rock windbreak to await daylight. As dawn came, the air became very still. The whole world as far as you could see looked as though someone had packed it in cotton batting and left just the tops of a few hills poking up through. It was a tremendous sight.

Very soon we began to work our way across the Knife Edge, hollering for Charlie as we went. Almost immediately, we could hear his voice from far below trailing upward in the still air. The problem was, it sounded like it was coming from several different places. The echoes would not let us pinpoint his location. We continued across until we both agreed that he was directly below us somewhere, then started down. At five a.m., guided by his yells, we had reached a point where we could see him. He had slipped and fallen about twenty-five feet straight down, and was lying on his back in a shallow pool of water. At his back was the cliff he had fallen from; a short distance in front of him was another vertical drop of an unknown distance.

We immediately rigged up and rappelled down to the injured man. I have observed people who were glad to see someone, but I believe he had to take first place. We were greatly relieved to learn that he was all right. Aside from being extremely cold, he was in good spirits. It appeared that he had suffered a broken leg and shoulder in the fall; fortunately, the cold water had kept the pain to a minimum. It did not take long to assess the situation and know that it was going to take a lot of help to extricate Charlie Ludwig from his predicament, 1,500 feet below the Knife Edge.

Glenn decided that the quickest way to get back to Chimney and report the seriousness of the situation would be to continue down from this point. We would need more help than we knew was coming up the mountain. After placing an anchor pin, he took my rope along with his and dropped off in front of me on a long rappel. Eventually, he called for the rope. I unclipped it, and it, too, disappeared from view.

I quickly went to work, trying to make Charlie more comfortable. There was nowhere to put him other than where he was, in the water; the sides were too sloping. After splinting his leg and trying to make his shoulder more comfortable, there was not much to do but wait. (I did have some pain tablets, which he took; but after the ordeal was over, he wrote me and acknowledged that it was my "vocal anesthesia" that did the most good.)

Anyway, we began to get acquainted as the hours passed. Several times, I helped him change his position in an attempt to make him more comfortable. We wrapped his leg in my raincoat and propped it up under my rolled-up sleeping bag to keep it out of the water. The hours dragged by. By ten o'clock, I began to listen and watch anxiously for the rescue team. Our conversation ran primarily as to how we would get him out of the chasm. I kept telling him we would get him out that day, but I was beginning to be not so sure. Concerns about the possibility of Glenn's having fallen began to tug on my mind.

Around noon, clouds began to roll in and the wind began to blow and the sky grew black. My hopes of pulling off the evacuation that day vanished.

Suddenly, it was raining harder than I ever thought possible. Lightning and thunder seemed to come all at once and were striking every several seconds. It was ear-shattering at times. In less than five minutes, the previously innocent little trickle of water at our backs had become a roaring waterfall. It was cascading onto Charlie, and there was no place to relocate him. Small rocks were bouncing around everywhere as if flung by an unseen hand. I heard several strike my hard hat, which I had placed on Charlie's head. I watched the brink of the falls, expecting a large rock at any moment, but it never came. The storm, instead of passing, only grew worse. It was extremely cold, and by now Charlie's shivering resembled convulsions.

The wind was curling the water from the falls in front of us back into our faces. The noise from the wind, lightning, and thunder was unbelievable. The mountain seemed to literally tremble with each lightning strike. Charlie was praying out loud and asked me to do the same. By now, I knew we were in grave danger. I recognized the signs of advancing hypothermia in myself. The most startling thing I recall in that regard is that, as I watched for the rescuers, I several times saw bushes move and thought they were people. It was then that I knew I must leave if I could. Charlie had pleaded with me several times to leave and save myself. I had studied the left-hand wall for a long time even before the storm struck, and knew it could be used to escape if one had to. That was before standing on a rock for eight hours and shivering.

Suddenly Charlie hollered. The water had risen enough, and the flow had started him toward the brink in front of us. Quickly I braced him with my knee. That damned storm had apparently found a home and was not about to leave. Several times Charlie begged me to go. At one point, he asked the Lord to take him. It was a tremendously hard thing to see a man go through. If I left, or tried to, I knew the water would move him.

Finally, at three o'clock, I knew I had to leave, or possibly two people would die instead of one. The rock on which I had been standing was not large, so I was able to roll it through the water to where Charlie was. By maneuvering around, he was able to brace his good leg against it and hold his position. I told him I was leaving and would be back, if possible, with help. I told him to hang on with all he had. As I turned to leave, he thanked me, and said, "If I don't make it, Eric, tell my wife and son I prayed for them."

Moving up and out around the edge of the crevice we were in, I looked back just before the next move would take me out of sight. He waved back; then I rounded the corner. In my heart, I guess I felt we would not see him again, alive. He had been through so much, and he knew he could end it by simply relaxing.

By good fortune, I was able to get back around, and began working back up toward the Knife Edge. Although it seemed impossible, the weather began to worsen even more. Once I had left the protection of the gorge, the wind was brutal. It had gotten colder and was now sleeting. The sleet was being driven at a great velocity, and it felt like the flesh was being sandblasted from my face. By sheltering my eyes with one hand, however, I could make my way. It was really crazy. Lightning was striking every few seconds somewhere, and quite often too close for comfort. I can remember looking ahead at rocks and wondering whether I would get to them or be struck. The lightning danced about everywhere.

After a while, I approached the Knife Edge, and wondered what I would do when I got there. Traveling across it would be impossible. Suddenly, I saw something move. For some damned reason that I cannot explain, it appeared to be a monkey in a yellow rain suit. Donald Gray's wife has gotten a big laugh over the years about this. Anyway, that is who it was, along with the rest of the rescue team. There were also several wardens. Everyone had been pinned down, unable to move for several hours. Glenn had returned with them to show them where we'd descended.

The storm continued with fury for some time longer, and we waited in the relative calm just over the lip of the Knife Edge. Lightning continued its random walking about, blasting funny, jagged places in the rock here and there. Occasionally, a fat little blue spark would work its way up a portable radio antenna. One fiberglass rock helmet simply cracked. It was not a good place to be.

Eventually, the sleet and lightning abated, leaving only the wind. When I say wind, I am talking about the kind where you have to hang on to someone to keep from being blown over and landing in the rocks. Team members Don Walker and Don Gray and several volunteers made their way down over the side around five p.m. Charlie was still there. They lowered down to him, then put dry clothes on him and got him into a Stokes litter. Using a piton, they raised the litter up out of the water. They gave him some food, and secured a poncho over him. There were not enough people, equipment, or remaining daylight to effect a rescue before dark. Glenn and I left for Chimney Pond.

The following morning we were back on the mountain in force with ropes and volunteer rescuers, including wardens and park rangers. The wind was fairly gusty, but at least the sun shone. We were packaging Charlie for his evacuation by eight o'clock. The first hurdle, the 25-foot vertical pitch behind him, went fairly smoothly. Then came the backbreaking 1,500-foot lift to the Knife Edge. We had given him some strong painkilling medicine before we began, and had to give him some more on several rest stops. A 180-pound man is not the easiest thing in the world to carry, especially in conditions such as those. Despite attempts not to, we jostled him several times; it was obvious that it hurt, but he remained silent each time.

Taking turns being clipped into the litter, we were a little over four hours getting back to the Knife Edge with our cargo. It was then by no means over. In another four hours, we were across the Knife Edge to Baxter Peak. From there it was a relatively easy carry to Thoreau Spring, where a large military helicopter airlifted him to the Millinocket Hospital. Even though the walk to Chimney Pond and down to Roaring Brook was a long one, it was made easier knowing that despite everything Pamola could muster, we had pulled it off safely.

In addition to his injuries, Charlie Ludwig suffered a mild case of pneumonia from his ordeal. He made a full recovery and returned later to climb Katahdin again. This time, there were no shortcuts.

Wardens have gone to Katahdin several times to assist park rangers. Once in the night we helped carry down a boy who had been killed in a fall near Cathedral Trail. On another occasion, we went with rangers to help bring down a boy who was dazed by lightning on the Knife Edge. A storm had struck, and lightning had knocked down several people in two different parties. Most were only stunned, but the boy was knocked unconscious and was not breathing. His father had revived him with mouth-to-mouth resuscitation, but he'd been blinded. His vision eventually returned. Several people spent the night in tents on the mountain and were escorted down the following day.

I do not suppose there remains any doubt in anyone's mind at this point as to what Katahdin is capable of dealing out to those who tempt the gods. This following episode is offered not so much because wardens were involved as it is to illustrate the unbelievable courage and will to live that men are capable of exhibiting in the face of death. Mountain climbers around the world are unique in many respects. They accept the risks of their sport. Death is a constant companion to mountain climbers. The risks taken are worth the exhilaration and sense of accomplishment felt when a summit is gained. Most of the time you win; sometimes you lose. They accept this fact unquestionably, and most do not feel at all compelled to explain to a non-climber why they do what they do.

Late in the evening of January 31, 1974, Warden Carter Smith, I, and our wives drove northward on Interstate 95 from Augusta, where we had been to a retirement party. It had gotten terribly cold, and the wind was blowing wildly. Several times, Christmas-tree-sized tops of large firs blew across the road in front of us, some seeming never to touch the ground. We remarked several times that it would be a damned poor night for a man to be caught out. Little did we know that, in fact, six climbers were caught out in the worst place of all—Mount Katahdin.

The following morning dawned crystal clear, with below-zero temperatures and a tremendous, never-ceasing wind. At one p.m., rescue team member Daniel Watson called and advised that Baxter Park supervisor Buzz Caverly had called for help. Something had gone afoul, and a six-man climbing group was in serious trouble on the mountain.

As quickly as possible, Supervisor Leonard Ritchie, Specialist Watson, Warden Davis, and I headed for the Millinocket Airport to meet Buzz and a 112th Medevac helicopter from Bangor. When we arrived, details of the incident were still vague. We went quickly to Park Headquarters to await further radioed information from the Chimney Pond ranger. Shortly, we learned that one of the climbers had reached Roaring Brook Campsite; two rangers would transport him to Avalanche Field if the helicopter could pick him up. The helicopter left immediately, and we went to the hospital to help upon their return. Within a few minutes, it returned, and we carried the severely hypothermic victim to the emergency room. He appeared to be in very rough shape and did not speak. We were still uncertain as to where other members of the party were, or their condition. Before long, more news arrived. The leader of the group, Robert Proudman, had reached Chimney Pond. Two more also had been picked up, and all were being transported to the hospital, all in very serious condition from frostbite.

At this point, all we knew for sure about the situation was that there were still two climbers on the mountain in serious condition. It was quickly decided that Dan Watson and I would be flown to Chimney Pond to assist, if possible, in locating the missing two. We loaded our gear and took off.

Upon our nearing the mountain, the strong winds became even more powerful. The pilot made several attempts, and each time we were turned away short of Chimney Pond. "It's no use," he stated. "Too dangerous." We agreed wholeheartedly and told him if he could land again at Avalanche Field, we would walk. He tried his damnedest to land the plane, and it was impossible—the wind was just too strong. Finally, he got down to about four feet. The crew chief opened the door, and with an "out" jerk of his thumb, we were suddenly on foot in the blowing snow. By the time we dragged our gear clear, he was gone from hearing.

The pilot told me later that this trip was the worst he had ever had, including Vietnam. "I did everything I know how to do to land a helicopter, and it just wouldn't land. I was registering fifty knots while we were hovering." I am glad I did not know about all that until later.

It was now 4:30 p.m. as we began the long walk up to Chimney Pond. The wind was unbelievable. It shrieked and moaned in the hardwood trees like a never-ending procession of overhead jet planes. Normally, when you climb, you can shed some clothing; not this time. Crossing Basin Pond was nearly impossible. We had to hang onto each other and walk backwards. Dan had stopped several times, complaining of severe cold and discomfort around a certain area of his anatomy. I finally got my light and checked him out. By hollering in his ear, I suggested that perhaps if he zipped up his fly, it might help. He did, and it did.

We reached Chimney Pond at seven p.m. Several seconds before we arrived, rangers had answered a thumping at the door. They had assumed it was us, since they knew we were on our way up. When they opened the door, however, a badly frozen climber toppled in. Dan and I arrived moments later. Paul DiBello's face, hands, and feet were quickly tended to. His eyes were frostbitten and quickly became very painful as the warmth returned. After bandaging his eyes, we began to remove his boots. His feet were frozen rock-solid to the top of his boots. Due to the seriousness of his condition, we decided that despite outside conditions, we would evacuate him immediately. Park Headquarters was notified by radio, and we asked that a rescue sled and personnel meet us at Roaring Brook to continue taking the victim to Togue Pond, where an ambulance could transport.

Paul was coherent and, as we prepared him for the evacuation, answered questions for us. The six climbers had spent the night trapped by a sudden temperature drop and howling winds on a small shelf. In the morning, he and another climber, Tom Keddy, were unable to attempt to continue upwards on the remaining pitch toward Pamola Peak. The other four had left to get help for him and Tom. By three p.m., no help had returned, and Paul felt that he was surely freezing to death. At this point, Tom was incoherent and unable to stand. Paul had tried to haul Tom up, but just could not do it. In what had to be the greatest display of sheer guts and the will to live, Paul had gotten himself to the ridge and stumbled down the mountain in the dark with frozen eyes and on two frozen feet. Later, it was found that he had fallen considerable distances on several occasions in his effort. Either by instinct or miracle, he reached Chimney Pond. He went to several lean-tos, unable to tell which building was which. By luck, he eventually saw the light in the ranger's camp, and stumbled to it.

After packaging Paul in warm down sleeping bags and parka, we quickly began the trip down. Frequently we stopped to check his condition, then continued on. The sliding rescue litter worked fine, and we made the descent with no trouble. Before reaching Roaring Brook, we met the party that had started up to meet us. They took the litter and headed back down to the waiting rescue sled.

It was not yet over. Rangers Arthur York, Barry McArthur, Charles Kenney, Lon Pingree, Dan, and I began the long hike back to Chimney Pond. I thought I had a pretty good idea of what tired was, but I really did not. Heavy clothing and cold air greatly reduce one's efficiency. We arrived back at 11:30 p.m. and learned that Paul had arrived at the Millinocket Hospital. We also learned that the remainder of our Warden Service team would arrive at daylight, and that two more teams were on their way up to Chimney Pond that night.

Within a short time, the Eastern Mountain Sports rescue team from North Conway, New Hampshire, and a team from Augusta headed by George Smith arrived. It was now after midnight. There was some discussion of making an attempt to reach Keddy that night; however, after evaluating all the information we had, we decided that the risks to the rescuers were too high. The temperature was -20 degrees. A handheld wind-velocity device showed wind speeds of 40 to 50 mph. Just before daylight, the wind let up for a while, and soon the familiar *whop–whop–whop* and roar of the big Huey was heard over the camp. It made a quick landing on the pond with part of the Warden Service team. In a second, it was gone, returning shortly with the remaining members. The teams quickly made ready for the attempt to reach Keddy.

The wind quickly regained its velocity as the sun came up.

Unfortunately, neither Dan nor I was able to be of much assistance following our eleven-mile hike up and down the mountain. We wished them well and watched them go, carrying a litter and all their gear.

At approximately ten a.m. we received word that the Eastern Mountain Sports team had reached Keddy's position and that he was dead. Due to the high winds and cold, it was impossible to make the recovery that day. The body was secured, and the teams began the descent.

Team member Charlie Merrill recalls how treacherous the conditions were. The litter was often held in a horizontal position by the wind while someone was holding on to one end. The possibility of being blown off your feet and rolled by the wind was very real. The thought of losing a mitten in such conditions was nightmarish. Luckily, all returned without injury.

Several days later, when the weather broke, Tom Keddy's body was brought up to the ridge below Pamola Peak and evacuated by helicopter.

The circumstances leading to the ill-fated climb were soon related by the five survivors. Again, the villain was the weather that sometimes changes so suddenly on mountains. All six climbers were members of the Appalachian Mountain Club and had excellent qualifications and the expertise to be involved in winter climbing. Katahdin offers probably the best winter climbing, especially ice, in the eastern United States. It is these conditions that draw climbers from all over to Katahdin in winter.

Like many mountain climbers before him, Tom Keddy lost his life doing what he loved. He knew and accepted the risks. Climbers Page Densmore, Robert Proudman, Doug George, and Mike Cohen recovered from their ordeal. Paul DiBello lost both feet due to frostbite. He continues his life with style, in the manner you might expect from someone who displayed so much courage and the will to live against such horrendous conditions.

In recent years, it has become rare for Pamola *not* to make his presence known. On one occasion, a camper was killed by lightning in his tent at Chimney Pond. An ice climber was strangled by his own equipment in a fall while climbing the treacherous icy Chimney itself. In 1984, two climbers perished when engulfed in an avalanche.

Game wardens joined the Baxter State Park rangers several times on Mount Katahdin in the past. The rangers now handle these occurrences, usually unassisted, and have established an excellent record in doing so. To say the least, Mount Katahdin is one hell of a pile of rocks, and—to quote former rescue team member Charlie Merrill—"One hell of a place to find out if your ice ax really will stop you when you begin to slide."

Twelve

The Mount St. Helens Eruption

Rob McNair-Huff and Natalie McNair-Huff

"Vancouver! Vancouver! This is it!"

Those frantic words crackling over a radio were the last words ever heard from thirty-year-old geologist David Johnston. He was stationed at an observation post just 5 miles from Mount St. Helens at 8:32 a.m. on the Sunday morning of May 18, 1980, when the volcano that had rumbled to life just a few months earlier exploded in front of him. Johnston was on Coldwater Ridge when he made his radio call to the headquarters office in Vancouver. A scientist until the very end, Johnston was witness to one of the largest landslides in history, followed by a violent volcanic eruption that hurled rocks and debris at speeds estimated at up to 300 miles per hour. Under the onslaught of the blast, there was nothing else to do than to send the radio transmission.

The world-famous eruption of May 18 started with a 5.1 magnitude earthquake centered a mile underneath the mountain. The quake caused the north side of the volcano, which had been growing like a bulging balloon over the days leading up to the eruption, to collapse toward the northwest, sending 3.7 billion yards of rock, ice, and debris into once-pristine Spirit Lake at the base of the mountain and down the Toutle River Valley. At the same time the pressure that had been building inside the volcano was unleashed like a cork being removed from a shaken bottle of champagne. The explosion released energy equivalent to seven megatons, sending a lateral blast out across the old growth forests and mountainous terrain to the north and northwest of the volcano. The blast caught David

Johnston a very short time after the eruption started. Anyone within 5 miles of the northwest part of the volcano—squarely in the path of the landslide and blast—died instantly, and in many cases their bodies, like Johnston's, were never found.

The blast rushed across the landscape, ripping down trees and everything in its path, first with a shock wave and then with a superheated rain of rocks. Anything directly targeted by the blast had no chance to escape. The lateral blast covered 230 square miles as it rampaged over the rugged terrain, reaching up to 17 miles northwest of the crater.

The third element of the eruption sent a towering plume of ash and pumice high into the Sunday morning sky. Within fifteen minutes the plume reached an elevation of 80,000 feet—about twice as high as commercial airplanes fly—and started its spread to the east. The fallout from the plume covered the areas up to 10 miles from the crater with a combination of ash and pumice, coating the same landscape that had just been decimated by the landslide and lateral blast, as well as areas to the east of the volcano.

Meanwhile, the upper reaches of the plume carried ash across eastern Washington and Idaho, where it turned day into night with a thick ashfall that coated the ground with inches of dark powder. Widely viewed video showed cars driving in the middle of the day with their lights on to navigate darkened streets. The ash cloud made its way across the United States within three days, eventually making its way around the world.

Fifty-seven people fell victim to the eruption. Many died within the first moments of the landslide and lateral blast, including media star and owner of the Mount St. Helens Lodge, eighty-three-year-old Harry Truman, who in the weeks leading up to the eruption had refused to leave his lodge along the shores of Spirit Lake. Truman fit the definition of crotchety old codger. He was a well-known mountain resident, but he wasn't known for his hospitality and kindly manner. Instead, he gained his fame from yelling at children who dawdled too long over their selection of ice cream treats and from throwing folks out of his lodge. Truman, however, loved his mountain, and when the call came to evacuate the Red Zone, the area around the volcano that state emergency officials had marked as a high danger area, he refused. When the mountain blew, Truman, his pink Cadillac, and sixteen cats and semi-tame, hand-fed raccoon friends, found themselves right in the path of the landslide.

During the initial moments of the eruption, geologists estimate that the landslide pushed the water from Spirit Lake out of its lakebed, burying the lake and Harry Truman's lodge in deposits that were up to 600 feet deep in places. If Truman was outside when the eruption began, he may have felt a cold mist descending from the mountain for a moment before the rush of debris and the heat of the lateral blast incinerated everything. The water in the lake sloshed up the steep sides of the surrounding ridges and then rushed down near its former location, dragging the shattered skeletons of thousands of trees back into the new Spirit Lake. Many of those trees continue to drift across Spirit Lake more than twenty-five years later, pushed from one end of the lake to the other by the prevailing winds.

Keith and Dorothy Stoffel had front row seats for the eruption. They were circling Mount St. Helens in their private plane early in the morning, and, after making one pass around the mountain, they made one last pass and witnessed the start of the landslide from the air. "The whole thing started to slide," Keith Stoffel said in a talk at the Mount St. Helens Visitor Center at Silver Lake, as reported by the *Oregonian*. "The whole north side of the mountain fell off, basically."

There were many heroes on May 18 and May 19, and helicopter pilot Jess Hagerman was one of them. Hagerman, a National Guard helicopter pilot stationed at Puyallup, was called to fly rescue missions around Mount St. Helens shortly after the eruption began. On the day of the eruption, he rescued the two survivors found closest to the volcano. Jim Scymanky and Leonty Skorohodoff were badly burned by the intense heat of the blast. They had been members of a four-person logging team working near Elk Rock, about 10 miles from the summit of the mountain. In a strange quirk of physics, the sound wave of the blast passed over them, and the ridge they were working near blocked the mountain from their view. They didn't see or hear the eruption, but one of their workmates, Jose Dias, ran around the ridge and yelled in Spanish that the mountain was exploding. No sooner had the words escaped his mouth than the team was blasted by superheated air, ash, and pumice. Scymanky and Skorohodoff stumbled over the ash and pumice to the Toutle River. Hagerman saw footprints in the ash from the air and followed them until he found the men. His crew chief, Randy Famtz, leaped out of the helicopter and into the cement-gray rushing waters of the river to help the two men to a place where Hagerman could land. Both men were badly injured with burns over more than 50 percent of their bodies; Skorohodoff died of his burns ten days after his rescue. Dias was later rescued by someone else, but he died at the hospital, and the fourth member of their crew, Evlanty Sharipoff, climbed a tree and died. His body was not found until fifty-two days after the explosion.

Nobody predicted how extreme the destruction would be if the mountain erupted. Nobody expected it to erupt the way it did, which is one of the reasons that more of the region was not in the Red Zone. Much of southwestern Washington used the mountain and the forests, streams, and lakes around it as their playground—fishing, camping, skiing, and hiking. In fact, just weeks before the blast, Natalie and her parents were skiing across a frozen Spirit Lake. The day before the eruption, the young Moore family—Lu, Mike, and their children, four-year-old Bonnie and three-month-old Terra—headed to the Green River's Valley of the Giants to camp. They felt safe in an area outside the Red Zone, 13 miles, and two peaks away from the mountain. The night of May 17 was quiet and uneventful, and May 18 dawned equally calm and peaceful. But then, as Lu was preparing the family's morning meal, they heard a low rumbling and felt the earth shake and the air grow suddenly heavy around them. Then they saw the roiling clouds of black ash rising over the nearby ridge. Lu began throwing their gear into their backpacks, and the family then sought shelter in an old hunter's cabin near their campsite. When the sky lightened again, they began hiking out of the Valley of the Giants, where most of the trees remained standing, but soon they came to an insurmountable obstacle course of fallen mammoth trees up to 8 feet thick and slick with ash. They headed back toward the valley and, out of water and with their hopes of finding their way out fading, they set up camp, found fresh water, and spent a desolate night in the woods.

The next morning, May 19, the Moore family again tried to hike to safety. A passing helicopter saw them but was unable to land, so a paramedic jumped out to assist the family. Hagerman was back in his helicopter, flying sorties along the Green River in search of survivors and went to help the Moores. With nowhere to set the helicopter down, he lowered it and set part of the landing gear on a fallen tree, then yelled for the Moores to board. As the family loaded into the helicopter, Hagerman and the paramedic yelled at Lu Moore and told her to leave her backpack behind. Lu refused, much to the confusion of the pilot. Hagerman quickly relented when he realized that the Moore's three-month-old baby was inside the pack. Once that was sorted out, the family was lifted to safety.

In the days following the rescue of the Moore family, it grew clear that Hagerman's mission was switching from rescue to the gruesome task of recovering the bodies of those who died in the eruption.

The survival of the Moore family illustrated the random luck that was an important factor in determining who lived and who died in the eruption. It took more than twenty years for many to face the fact that the majority of those who died on May 18, 1980, were killed outside the Red Zone that the state had established around the volcano. Although original news reports and statements from the governor, Dixie Lee Ray, portrayed those who died as reckless thrill seekers who snuck around ROAD CLOSED signs to catch a closer view of the volcano, the truth was that only three of the fifty-seven people killed in the eruption died inside the Red Zone. The majority of those who died were in areas similar to where the Moore family camped—close to the mountain but well outside the boundaries that state officials believed were most at risk for destruction.

The family of Ron and Barbara Seibold was among those who were unlucky and unable to escape the wrath of Mount St. Helens. The whole family, including two children ages seven and nine, were found inside their beat-up car. All four of the Seibolds died when their lungs filled with choking ash.

Trixie Anders was another of those lucky enough to escape the eruption alive. Anders was traveling with a group of geology students, and she made a quick stop for breakfast with her husband while the rest of the group continued toward Mount St. Helens from Randle. According to a story in the *News Tribune*, a friend of Anders, Jim Fitzgerald, continued ahead and was on Spud Mountain, inside the blast zone, where he was able to take fourteen pictures before the blast took his life. Although she never caught up to her original group, Anders was close enough to the volcano to feel jealous at first with the thought that Fitzgerald was getting better pictures from being closer to the eruption, but she soon realized that the group of people traveling in her Jeep was in trouble as well. As she described it to the *News Tribune*:

> *We're in a Jeep and driving it so fast, I'm sure we're going to flip it because we went into two corners on two tires. I'm hanging out the back taking pictures, and I said, "OK, if we don't flip the Jeep, the mud's going to get us or the surge is going to get us." I truly did not believe we were going to live.*

They survived because the blast ricocheted overhead, deflected by a ridge between their fleeing Jeep and the raging volcano. The story of Anders's escape echoed many others heard in the weeks and years after the eruption. There are many stories of cars flying down Forest Service roads at unspeakable speeds in a race to get away from the eruption, sometimes passing slower vehicles whose occupants did not survive.

Massive amounts of debris, combined with snowmelt and downed trees flooded the Toutle River and all of its tributaries. The river immediately overflowed its banks and swept everything downstream, taking out houses, cars, logging camps, and bridges. The debris rushed to the Cowlitz River and then to the Columbia and eventually the Pacific Ocean. Some who survived the initial blast and sped down the twisting roads were swept away by the river. Summer residents who had cabins along the river watched television broadcasts in horror as they saw their cabins and houses bobbing in the cement-thick deluge that hours before had been a clear-flowing river.

The Mount St. Helens National Volcanic Monument stands in remembrance of those who died and of the destruction that came so quickly. An unnamed ridge near the place where Johnston watched the mountain destroy itself before it took his life was renamed Johnston Ridge. More than a quarter-century later, the eruption of Mount St. Helens remains one of the most universal memories in the Pacific Northwest.

Sources

"Bringing Out the Donner Party" from *The Expedition of the Donner Party and Its Tragic Fate*. Eliza P. Donner Houghton. Los Angeles. 1911.

"Zero Dark Storm" from *Search and Rescue: A Wilderness Doctor's Life-and-Death Tales of Risk and Reward*. Christopher Van Tilburg. Guilford, CT: Globe Pequot Press. 2017.

"Faint of Heart at Yosemite Falls" from *Living, Working, Dying in the National Parks*. Andrea Lankford. Guilford, CT: Globe Pequot Press. 2010.

"Escape from Death Valley" from *Death Valley In '49*. William Lewis Manly. San Jose, CA: The Pacific Tree and Vine, Co. 1894.

"Trapped in an Instant: Death in Zion" from *Death in Zion National Park: Stories of Accidents and Foolhardiness in Utah's Grand Circle*. Randi Minetor. Guilford, CT: Globe Pequot Press. 2017.

"Downed Pilot in the Jungles of Burma: A War Rescue" from *Hell Is So Green*. Lt. William Diebold. Guilford, CT: Globe Pequot Press. 2012.

"The Mysterious Disappearance of Dennis Martin" from *Death in the Great Smoky Mountains: Stories of Accidents and Foolhardiness in the Most Popular Park*. Michael Bradley. Guilford, CT: Globe Pequot Press. 2016.

"Experience Is No Guarantee" from *Death in Mount Rainier National Park: Stories of Accidents and Foolhardiness on the Northwest's Most Iconic Peak*. Tracy Salcedo. Guilford, CT: Globe Pequot Press. 2018.

"A Decade of Heroism: Rescues in the 1970s" from *Death, Daring, and Disaster: Search and Rescue in the National Parks*. Charles R. "Butch" Farabee, Jr. Lanham, MD: Taylor Trade Publishing. 2005.

"Arctic Rescue" from *True Tales of Arctic Heroism in the New World*. A. W. Greely. New York: Charles Scribner's Sons. 1912.

"Katahdin" from *Life and Death in the North Woods: The Story of the Maine Game Warden Service*. Eric Wight. Rockport, ME: Down East Books. 1985.

"The Mount St. Helens Eruption" from *Washington Disasters: True Stories of Tragedy and Survival*. Rob McNair-Huff and Natalie McNair-Huff. Guilford, CT: Globe Pequot Press. 2016.